Role Theory and Foreign Policy Analysis

Role Theory

and Foreign Policy Analysis

Edited by *Stephen G. Walker*

Duke Press Policy Studies   **Duke University Press**

Durham 1987

© 1987 Duke University Press
All rights reserved
Printed in the United States of America on acid-free paper ∞
Library of Congress Cataloging-in-Publication Data
Role theory and foreign policy analysis.
(Duke Press policy studies)
Bibliography: p.
Includes index.
1. International relations—Research. I. Walker,
Stephen G., 1942–   II. Series.
JX1291.R58   1987   327'.072   86-29162
ISBN 0-8223-0714-6

Contents

Tables and Figures

Tables

Figures

Foreword

Readers who chance upon this brief commentary may wish to be alerted to several features of *Role Theory and Foreign Policy Analysis* that are not necessarily self-evident from a quick glance at the table of contents or browsing through selected chapters. These features will also serve as reasons why the overall significance of the volume cannot be appreciated fully solely by reading Stephen Walker's necessary and informative introductory and concluding chapters.

One reason is the relatively high degree of coherence among the eleven chapters. Unlike many social science symposia, this one does not employ a commodious umbrella concept that houses disparate and largely autonomous intellectual exercises. The three chapters of part II provide clear conceptual maps and explicit justifications for an investigative strategy focused on role theory. The eight chapters of parts III and IV represent a series of "applications" that use, as appropriate, the conceptual guidelines set forth earlier. Usage throughout is consistent and compatible.

Not all of the complex terrain mapped in the conceptual chapters is covered by the applications. But it is necessary to grasp all eight cases in order to sense how each contributes to the substantiation of the empirical viability of role theory as an effective vehicle for informing foreign policy analysis. Each application, while illuminating the process of utilizing theoretical formulations to guide systematic data collection or re-analysis, the establishment of new or different connections among variables, the preliminary testing of hypotheses, or the design of next research steps, also leads to important refinements and extensions of the overall framework. Each case is a "close-up" of a particular subset of foreign policymaking or international relations realities.

The coherence and viability noted above reflect the underwritten effects of cumulative accomplishments by a community of scholars working over a sustained period of time. K. J. Holsti's seminal paper (chapter 2) was first presented in 1970. Constructive responses to that paper are dated twelve to fourteen years later. The intervening decade was a period of intensive and fruitful activity that produced a critical mass of relevant intellectual resources including the following kinds of components: conceptual refinement (for example, how are policy and action outcomes to be conceived and measured? what are the key factors that influence decision-making processes?), new multimethod research strategies geared to special challenges (for example, studying political leaders from a distance without benefit of clinical evidence or personal contact), and the formation of extensive and theoretically relevant cross-cultural and historical data pools to serve the purposes of re-analysis (for example, the CREON Project of the Mershon Center). These developments were aided by a burgeoning cognitive science and the emergence of a revitalized transdiscipline of political psychology.

What is clearly manifest in these pages is the capacity to borrow a forty-year-old social science concept (role theory) and to demonstrate that it can be adapted and creatively applied to a domain of social action and inquiry quite far removed from the concerns which led to the concept's invention in the first place. This has been done without engaging in a superficial labeling exercise and without uncritical absorption of the concept's historical ambiguities.

It is especially noteworthy that role theory (as formulated here) fits comfortably into all three of the major traditions identified by Stephen Walker in his introductory chapter as dominating the field of foreign policy analysis: *decision making* (focus on behavior of individual decision makers); *comparative foreign policy* (focus on the nation as the acting unit); and *political realism* (focus on the basic structure of the international system). Role theory has a marked potential for bridging these three perspectives because the methodologies exhibited here demonstrate it is entirely possible, for example, to establish systematic relationships between the characteristics of official decision makers and various types of policy and action outcomes, or between national attributes and patterns of international behavior, such as cooperation and conflict.

What is set forth in this volume is preliminary evidence of an analytic infrastructure that facilitates movement across, or the establishment of equivalencies between, different levels and units. This consists of a judicious mix of three elements: first, a richly multidimensional delineation of *role* (conceptions, expectations, orientations, performance, enactment, conflict, location or selection, and sets) that allows permeation into all three of the major traditions; second, self-conscious flexibility in assigning alternating functions to independent, dependent, and intervening variables, thus facilitating sequences of variable interaction when subtlety and complexity so require; and third, key determinants of decision making (leaders' characteristics, group structures and processes, and regime variables) that are so defined as to generate linkages between familiar abstract categories of factors—for example, personal, organizational, social, and cultural traits; the size of a country, its economic development, or the nature of its political system; and the external environment.

Coherence and bridging point toward intimations of a unified theory of foreign policy that are clearly discernible in these chapters. This possibility constitutes a very significant next step in the evolution of research and theory concerning how and why nations act as they do and with what consequences. Though obviously at an early stage, this development already provides a way to clarify or mediate the either-or choices offered in recurring debates over certain theoretical and practical issues, for example, rationalist versus nonrationalist assumptions, Great Leader versus Historical Forces explanations, the latest manifestation of the contention between "realists" and their critics, and the opposing arguments over the impact of the external environment on the foreign policies of African nations—the "dependency school" versus the "decolonization" school. What the role theory developed here offers is neither a facile resolution of these divisions of opinion nor a judge's decision as to which side is right. Rather, the applied exercises suggest how the terms of these disputes might be fruitfully redefined or how the grains of partial truth embodied in each position might be combined into a larger truth.

A final reason for reading this book in its entirety is that it contains substantial nourishment for knowledgeable, though not necessarily expert, readers—policymakers, educators, and attentive citizens. The unfortunate consequences of the communications gaps separating academic research from current teaching materials and from the everyday world inhabited by policymakers are well known. Non-experts are often impatient with the laborious and cautious folkways of scholars and researchers. Scattered throughout these pages are significant insights, interpretations, and observations pertinent to public and educational interests. Experts are inclined to treat such items as incomplete or as less than well-substantiated ingredients for theory building —in short, as by-products of the real objective: validated theory. Nonexperts generally do not have access to these nuggets when they are deposited in technical monographs.

We tend to forget that much public discussion and much classroom teaching are heavily dependent on just such materials—insights, interpretations, and observations, usually from a variety of sources: journalists, media commentators, news stories, political leaders, social critics, and a myriad of self-styled experts. Generally speaking, the assumptions and "methods" that underlie these statements are hidden from view. As things now stand, we have no overt, public, formalized, and cybernetic process for the evaluation of foreign policymaking that might capitalize on the kind of research presented in this volume.

For example, what might role theory reveal regarding persistent sources of error and distortion that can seep into the decision making that produces foreign policies and external actions? We have little or no technically competent public discourse focused on what role(s) in the world would be most desirable or appropriate for the United States in the waning years of the twentieth century. What might a "role map" of the present global political system contribute to such a needed discourse? The slow, tedious road to systematization of knowledge about any complex domain of human social behavior is traveled in part in order to arrive at legitimate and reasonably well-founded *simplifications*. Today's public "simplicities" in the realm of foreign policy and international relations are dangerous precisely because they circulate without known and trustworthy underpinnings.

The insights, interpretations, and observations struck off by the main line of investigation presented in this collection deserve explicit comparison with those already in public circulation. Where there is congruence, confidence should be enhanced. Where there is discrepancy, there are ample grounds for criticism and revision of prevailing views.

Richard C. Snyder
Scottsdale, Arizona

Preface

This book is the culmination of an effort over the past five years to collect and evaluate recent research dealing with role theory and foreign policy analysis. Only three of the selections have been published elsewhere. First is the seminal article, "National Role Conceptions in the Study of Foreign Policy," by K. J. Holsti in *International Studies Quarterly*, which appears here in an abridged version. Another is "A Pre-Theory Revisited: World Politics in an Era of Global Interdependence," James N. Rosenau's Presidential Address at the 1984 Annual Meeting of the International Studies Association. Excerpts from this address in *International Studies Quarterly* appear as part of his contribution to this volume. The third previously published essay is my "The Correspondence Between Foreign Policy Rhetoric and Behavior: Insights From Role Theory and Exchange Theory," which is reprinted intact from *Behavioral Science* except for some minor editorial changes. Permission to reprint these contributions is gratefully acknowledged.

The remaining chapters include unpublished convention papers presented at recent meetings of the American Political Science Association and the International Studies Association. Some are reports drawn from research programs supported by the National Science Foundation and the Mershon Center at Ohio State University. Others are the products of doctoral dissertations based partly upon data generated by the Comparative Research on the Events of Nations (CREON) project at Ohio State University, all of which have been edited for inclusion in this book. The introduction and conclusion are entirely original to this work.

I would like to thank the authors of this volume for the patience and the assistance which they have exerted on behalf of this project throughout the editing of their contributions and during negotiations with potential publishers. In addition I would like to acknowledge the institutional support and the efforts of several members of the political science department at the University of Minnesota. Department Chair Virginia Gray accorded me all of the privileges of a faculty member as a Visiting Professor, including expenses for xeroxing and for phone calls associated with this project. Administrative Assistant Cathy See Duvall allotted departmental secretarial support for retyping parts of the manuscript. Faculty members William Flanigan and Edwin Fogelman provided a research assistant from the graduate program to aid in the swift completion of the editing tasks. Miriam Cardozo researched and compiled the references for typing. Mary Ellen Otis retyped promptly several parts of the volume with great accuracy on short notice. All of the faculty and staff in the political science department at Minnesota provided the intangibles necessary for a productive and congenial work environment. I deeply appreciate their hospitality.

Finally, I would like to recognize the enthusiasm and efficiency that Duke University Press has invested in this addition to its Duke Press Policy Studies in the political psychology area. Thanks on behalf of the authors to Richard C. Rowson, the Director, and his colleagues at the press. Each of us appreciates as well the constructive advice rendered by the anonymous referees solicited by the press, plus the suggestions and criticisms from numerous colleagues who read these chapters as papers presented at professional meetings. However, responsibility for the contents of this volume remains with the editor and the contributors.

Stephen G. Walker
Arizona State University

I Introduction

1

The Relevance of Role Theory
to Foreign Policy Analysis

Stephen G. Walker

In recent years there has developed an interest in exploring the utility of role analysis for understanding foreign policy. The initial impetus for undertaking this task was provided by Holsti's (1970) exploration of the relationships between national role conceptions and patterns of participation in international politics. His efforts stimulated subsequent research by Walker (1979, 1981), who related the patterns of conflictual and cooperative behavior directed toward the two superpowers by third nations to their own national role conceptions and to the role expectations of the superpowers regarding the behavior of these nations. Wish (1980, 532–35) also acknowledged Holsti's influence in her analysis of the relationships between national role conceptions and several dimensions of foreign policy behavior, including international participation, hostile behavior, independence of action, and the commitment of resources. More recently, the sources of national roles have been the focus of a series of ongoing investigations by associates of the CREON (Comparative Research on the Events of Nations) project at Ohio State University (M. Hermann et al. 1982b; C. Hermann with Hudson 1983; Hudson et al. 1982).

While it is still premature to reach any firm conclusions, the potential utility of role analysis for understanding foreign policy appears to be threefold: it has *descriptive, organizational,* and *explanatory* value. Descriptively, the concepts associated with role analysis provide a vocabulary of images which can focus upon foreign policy behavior at the national level of analysis, shift down to the individual level of analysis, and also move up to the systemic level of analysis (Walker 1979, 1982b). The concepts of role analysis not only have multilevel descriptive power; they also take on multidimensional scope in their application to foreign policy behavior. The types of foreign policy roles identified by Holsti (1970), Wish (1980), and M. Hermann et al. (1982b), for example, transcend the narrow conceptualization of foreign policy behavior as a continuum of cooperative and conflictual behavior.

Organizationally, in addition to multilevel and multidimensional capabilities, the concepts associated with role analysis permit the analyst to adopt either a structure-oriented or a process-oriented perspective. It is possible, for example, to concentrate upon the structure of a repertoire of roles at the national level of analysis or upon the structure of a set of roles which define the relations among a group of nations (Walker 1979). Within these structural parameters one can focus upon the processes of role location, the transmission of cues, the resolution of role conflict, the generation of new roles, and the extinction of old ones (Walker 1982a, 1982b).

One criticism of role "theory" has been that it tends to be conceptually rich but methodologically poor (Walker 1979, 176), which makes its explanatory value questionable. Scholars have conducted research with role concepts using a variety of methodologies and propositions associated with other theories. Cognitive balance theory has been employed to explain the process of role location and the resolution of role conflict when a nation must enact a role in the presence of conflicting expectations transmitted as cues from other countries (Walker 1979). Exchange theory has also been applied to explain the same phenomena (Walker 1981).

However, recent work by C. Hermann with Hudson (1983), M. Hermann et al. (1982b) and Hudson et al. (1982), has generated a theory of role location that consists only of role concepts and a set of auxiliary propositions that specify the limiting conditions for predicting the role to be enacted. Their approach resembles the one taken much earlier in another discipline by Gross et al. (1958, 281–318) to construct a theory of role-conflict resolution based upon the specification of a typology of role-conflict situations and a set of rules to resolve the conflicts. The testing procedures employed by Gross et al. (1958, 298–304) also parallel the methodology used by Hudson et al. (1982) to test their theory of role location.

Consequently the explanatory value of role analysis appears to depend upon whether its concepts are theoretically informed (a) by an appropriate set of self-contained propositions and methods, or (b) by the specification of an appropriate set of auxiliary limiting conditions and rules linking these conditions with role concepts. Propriety, in turn, would appear to be a function of context defined as a particular domain of behavior.

In the last analysis the burden is on the reader to decide whether role analysis is useful for the study of behavior in the foreign policy domain. The contents of this volume provide a sample of research for this purpose. The authors of the essays in part II articulate the case for role analysis from the context of three different perspectives: the comparative study of foreign policy, the decision-making approach, and political realism. These research traditions emphasize different levels of analysis in their respective attempts to understand foreign policy and international politics (Singer 1961; Waltz 1959; Berkowitz 1986). The comparative study of foreign policy favors the national level of analysis (Rosenau 1966), while the decision-making approach tends to emphasize the individual (Snyder, Bruck, and Sapin 1962). Political realism has gravitated toward the systemic level (Waltz 1979).

The implantation of the concepts associated with role analysis appears to enhance each research tradition's ability to incorporate other levels of analysis into its attempt to explain foreign policy. The introduction of role analysis into the comparative foreign policy and political realism literatures facilitates the analysis of psychological variables which intervene between foreign policy and their respective emphases upon ecological variables located in the domestic and international environments. Role concepts perform a similar function for the decision-making approach by defining the environmental features of the decision-making situation in a parsimonious and systematic way.

The validity of this interpretation rests upon the arguments presented by the authors of the essays in part II and the evidence supporting their arguments in the empirical research by the contributors to the remainder of the volume. The selections in part III represent the different types of foreign policy research that have employed role analysis within the research traditions represented by the essays in part II. In addition several authors engage in a role analysis of the dynamics of African foreign policies in part IV. Collectively the latter group provides an intensive view of foreign policy within a particular region and from the combined perspectives of the decision-making approach and the comparative study of foreign policy.

The conclusion of the volume is an evaluation of the theoretical contribution of role analysis to each of the three traditions in the analysis of foreign policy. The organizational strategy for this task is to evaluate the claims of each author in part II with the evidence provided by the attempts to validate their claims in parts III and IV. Consequently readers who may be interested primarily in just one or two of these traditions may want to read the chapters in a different order than they appear in the volume and then read the corresponding section of the conclusion. Chapters 2, 5, 6, and 7 focus upon the comparative study of foreign policy, while chapters 3, 8, and 10 operate within the decision-making tradition. Chapters 4 and 9 are located within the tradition of political realism, although the influence of the decision-making approach is also present in the latter chapter. Aspects of political realism, comparative foreign policy, and the decision-making tradition are combined in chapters 11 and 12. Finally, there is an attempt in the conclusion to illustrate how role theory links the three research traditions in foreign policy analysis.

II   Toward a Theory
of Foreign Policy: Making the Case
for Role Analysis

2

National Role Conceptions in the Study

of Foreign Policy

K. J. Holsti

Historians, officials, and theorists of international relations often characterize foreign policy behavior by terms which suggest patterned or
recurring decisions and actions by governments. Typical classifications
would include "nonaligned," "bloc leaders," "balancers," and "satellites."
When we classify a state as "nonaligned," we imply that in a variety of
international contexts and situations, its diplomatic-military actions
and decisions will be consistent with the "rules" subsumed under the
general category or class of states called "nonaligned." The term sum-
marizes a broad but typical range of diplomatic behaviors and attitudes.
These include anticolonial predispositions and policies, unwilling-
ness to enter into bloc-sponsored military alliances, receipt of foreign
aid from a variety of sources, prohibition against maintenance of other

This is an abridged version of "National Role Conceptions in the Study of Foreign Policy,"
International Studies Quarterly 14 (1970): 233–309. Reprinted with permission.

countries' forces on the state's territory, and practicing independent judgment on most world issues.

Theorists of international politics have for some time made references to national roles as possible causal variables in the operation of international systems, or in explaining the foreign policies of individual nations. Most versions of the balance of power theory posit three kinds of states in the system, each of which is to make certain types of commitments—enact roles—if the system is to remain stable: an aggressor state or group of states, a defending group of states, and a "balancer." If the states do not play the roles postulated in the theory (for example, if the balancer does not intervene on behalf of the defensive coalition), imbalance, war, and system transformation result.

Representing the world in terms of blocs and neutrals is only a rough categorization of reality, and perhaps increasingly obsolete. Just as designating persons as judge, professor, or politician does not indicate adequately all the tasks these individuals fulfill within their formal positions and casual relationships, so the terms bloc leader, satellites, allies, and nonaligned do not reveal all the behavioral variations observable in the different sets of relationships into which states enter.

If it is agreed that our descriptive and explanatory studies of foreign policy and international systems need more precision, a number of questions, focusing on the concept of national roles, come to mind. From the observer's vantage, what are the major national role types in the contemporary system? Can we construct a typology of national roles that is richer in detail and more sensitive to distinctions in actual diplomatic behavior than the ones currently fashionable? Or, using an approach based on perceptions, we can inquire: how do policymakers view the roles their nations should play in international affairs? Does the term nonaligned adequately summarize the roles and functions that the leaders of Egypt, Burma, or Sierra Leone perceive their states fulfilling in different sets of relationships? Or does it hide important differences of perceptions? Should we continue to assume that governments organize their diplomatic and military actions to fulfill only a single role conception?

Other interesting questions are also suggested by the notion of national role conception: what are the sources of role conceptions held by policymakers? Are there gradations in the specificity and structure of policymakers' national role conceptions? If so, what are the likely consequences for foreign policy decisions and actions? Under what conditions will knowledge of national role conceptions permit us to explain or predict typical forms of diplomatic behavior?

Moving from descriptive questions of this type to more theoretical concerns, we may inquire into the relevance of national role conceptions, both as independent and dependent variables, in foreign policy analysis. In the first instance the problem is whether, or to what extent, knowledge of national role conceptions held by policymakers would allow us to explain or predict individual decisions and actions. In the second it will be argued that in any general approach to the study of foreign policy it may be more fruitful to explain national role conceptions than to attempt to explain individual, and often unique, diplomatic decisions.

What can we predict about the structure and processes of an international system if we have detailed knowledge of the number, types, and distribution of national role conceptions among the policymakers of that system? Can we usefully compare international systems using the distribution of national role conceptions as a distinguishing criterion?

The term *role* (or role performance) refers to behavior (decisions and actions) and can be kept analytically distinct from *role prescriptions*, which are the norms and expectations cultures, societies, institutions, or groups attach to particular *positions*. The foundations of human behavior, according to role theory, are both the position and the norms and expectations the alter projects on the position. Role theory thus emphasizes the interaction between the *role prescription* of the alter and the *role performance* of the occupant of a position (ego).

Some aspects of behavior are best examined on the personal rather than organizational, social, or cultural levels. Role prescriptions of the alter may become parameters while attention is shifted to the ego's own conception of his position and functions, and the behavior appropriate to them—what we shall call a *role conception*. The perceptions, values, and attitudes of the actor occupying a position thus become the crucial independent variables in explaining role performance. In real life, of course, behavior results from a combination of self-defined goals and norms of conduct, a variety of situational variables, and social norms and expectations. If the position "makes the man," the reverse of the coin is that man interprets and defines for himself the rights, duties, privileges, and appropriate forms of behavior associated with his positions and relationships in society. Ideally, any study should combine these approaches, which respectively emphasize the states of the alter and ego as independent variables. It may be legitimate, however, to emphasize one course of behavior while neglecting the

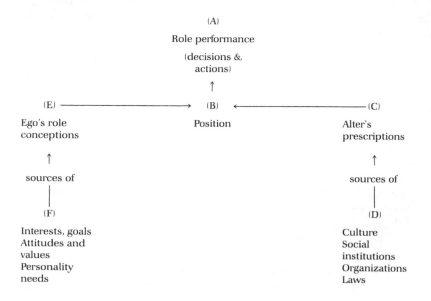

Figure 2.1   Role theory and the sources of human behavior

other. In the study of international politics and foreign policy, in particular, there are reasons—to be noted below—for assuming that the role performance (decisions and actions) of governments may be explained primarily by reference to the policymakers' *own* conceptions of their nation's role in a region or in the international system as a whole.

Thus far we have four concepts that will help us analyze foreign policy: (1) *role performance,* which encompasses the attitudes, decisions, and actions governments take to implement (2) their self-defined *national role conceptions* or (3) the *role prescriptions* emanating, under varying circumstances, from the alter or external environment. Action always takes place within (4) a *position,* that is, a system of role prescriptions.

Approaches to the study of behavior using the notion of role are illustrated in figure 2.1. This characterization, while not allowing for the complexity of role theory (where it is assumed that behavior occurs in multiple role situations and that actors' orientations to different roles will vary), suggests the distinction between studies emphasizing states of the alter and sources of the alters' norms and expectations as an explanation for behavior, and those focusing on the actors' own perceptions of role.

Most social science studies employing the concept of role explain behavior—usually modal behavior patterns (A)—by examining the relationships among (B), (C), and various components of (D). Some have inquired into the connections between role conceptions and role prescriptions, that is, among (E), (C), and (B). Phenomenological studies have explained (A) in terms of relationships among (B), (E), and (F), or more frequently between (E) and (F). Foreign policy analysis, in particular, emphasizes the self-conceptions of policymakers as determinants of behavior and generally neglects the role prescriptions of the alter—that is, of the other states in the system. This is, however, only part of a larger problem. A major question is whether the concept of role can be applied fruitfully to the analysis of foreign policy and international politics, to a milieu that is different from the integrated society or formal organization.

The Extension of Role Theory to Foreign Policy Analysis

One problem becomes apparent immediately. The concept of *position* connotes a behavioral setting with more or less well-defined functions, duties, rights, and privileges. It may also indicate a regularized set of activities associated with formal organizations. Within an integrated society or organization, the alter's role prescriptions, directed toward the position, are critical in establishing and maintaining conformity by the position's incumbent. Behavior associated with such positions as legislator, banker, union leader, or military chief is usually clearly defined by reference groups or formal enactments, leaving incumbents relatively little latitude of choice in organizing their actions. People are, in a sense, representatives of these positions.

Within some international organizations such as the United Nations or NATO, states do appear to occupy positions. Rights, duties, and special responsibilities for particular states are established both in charters (the role of the major powers in the Security Council), and through traditional practices. Traditional multinational expectations directed toward American behavior within NATO, for example, must be extensive. In such examples it would be quite feasible to apply formal role theory to analyze national behavior. Most foreign policy behavior does not occur, however, in a setting that is strictly analogous to a social position. Since nation-states are multifunctional collectivities, operating within innumerable sets of bilateral and multilateral relationships in a comparatively unorganized milieu, it is difficult to apply the concept of position (systems of role expectations) as it has been developed in social inquiry.

Another major problem is the differing impact of the alter's role prescriptions in the social and international context. Can we suggest that policymakers' national role conceptions and their foreign policy decisions and actions are similarly influenced or restrained by the international counterpart of the social alter, that is, by international legal norms, the expectations of other governments, or world opinion?

In international politics the fact of sovereignty implies that foreign policy decisions and actions (role performances) derive *primarily* from policymakers' role conceptions, domestic needs and demands, and critical events or trends in the external environment. Generally the expectations of other governments, legal norms expressed through custom, general usage, or treaties, and available sanctions to enforce these are ill-defined, flexible, or weak compared to those that exist in an integrated society and particularly within formal organizations. When incompatibility exists between highly valued national interests and the norms of behavior established through treaties and the like, the latter normally give way to the former. It is precisely in the acute international conflict that self-defined national role conceptions ("bastion of revolution" or "arsenal of democracy") seemingly take precedence over externally derived role prescriptions.

What we see, however, is primarily a difference of degree of influence. To argue that in the international context role prescriptions of the alter are relatively primitive does not mean that they are nonexistent or that their impact is necessarily negligible, even in crisis situations. Any legal norm, for instance, is an active or potential restraint on the behavior of some decision-making system, whether individual, group, or governmental. It delimits in one way or another complete freedom of choice, it specifies what individuals or more complex decision-making bodies, when enacting various roles, must do, must not do, may do, or may not do in certain situations. International laws, though primarily interpreted by the governments whose behavior they are intended to control, are no different in their restraining function. The difference between the integrated social context and the international milieu is that in the former a large portion of human action is effectively governed by legal enactments, while in the latter primarily routine mat-

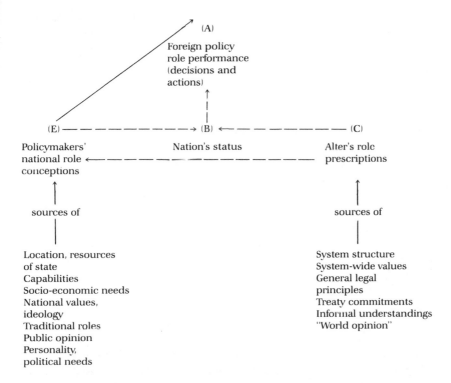

Figure 2.2   Role theory and foreign policy: national role conceptions and prescriptions as independent variables

ters such as shipping and communications are effectively governed by international legal machinery.

Considering the differences between the social and international contexts—the lack of positions and relatively less effective norms and sanctions of the alter—the framework in figure 2.1 would have to be modified before it can be employed in the analysis of foreign policy (see figure 2.2). The concept of *position* may be replaced by the term *status*, which denotes only a rough estimate of a state's ranking in the international system and which may or may not have appreciable consequences on the ways that policymakers define what they believe to be the appropriate international orientations or tasks for their nation. The position of the alter will be denoted by broken lines indicating that role prescriptions and sanctions from this source are potential and intermittent. While we must acknowledge that the alter or external environment is relevant to foreign policy analysis, this study will consider it a constant. Emphasis will be on the definition of national role conceptions and the domestic sources of those conceptions. We will assume that role performance results from, or is consistent with, policymakers' conceptions of their nation's orientations and tasks in the international system or in subordinate regional systems. Status and externally derived role prescriptions are relevant to role performance, but will not be explored further.

We may now define *national role performance* as the general foreign policy behavior of governments. It includes patterns of attitudes, decisions, responses, functions, and commitments toward other states. From the observer's point of view, these patterns or typical decisions can be called *national roles*. A *national role conception* includes the policymakers' own definitions of the general kinds of decisions, commitments, rules, and actions suitable to their state, and of the functions, if any, their state should perform on a continuing basis in the international system or in subordinate regional systems. It is their image of the appropriate orientations or functions of their state toward, or in, the external environment.

To explain different national role conceptions in different states (for example, Sweden as a *mediator*, Burma as an *isolate*), we might look to such varied sources as: location and major topographical features of the state; natural, economic, and technical resources; available capabilities; traditional policies; socio-economic demands and needs as expressed through political parties, mass movements, or interest groups; national values, doctrines, or ideologies; public opinion "mood"; and the personality or political needs of key policymakers. It remains a research problem to find out what sorts of connections exist among national role conceptions and these variables in different states.

National role conceptions are also related to, or buttressed by, the role prescriptions coming from the external environment. The sources of these role prescriptions would include the structure of the international system; system-wide values, general legal principles which ostensibly command universal support (such as the doctrine of the sovereign equality of states); the rules, traditions, and expectations of states as expressed in the charters of international and regional organizations, "world opinion," multilateral and bilateral treaties; and less formal or implicit commitments and "understandings." The extent to which these external role prescriptions become significant in developing national role conceptions varies considerably from state to state and in different situations.

National Role Conceptions of Policymakers: Research Procedures and Examples

To arrive at a typology of contemporary national role conceptions, I reviewed a large number of speeches, parliamentary debates, radio broadcasts, official communiqués, and press conferences. The list of national roles found in table 2.1 is based on statements by the leaders of seventy-one governments, found in 972 different sources.

Several rules to guide the research were formulated in order to make the data as reliable and comparable as possible. First, only statements from the highest-level policymakers were used. They reflect the foreign policy thoughts and role conceptions of presidents, prime ministers, or foreign ministers. Exceptions were made only when an ambassador or other official made a speech or statement that obviously reflected the views of the top leadership.

The second rule was that to obtain a representative sample of national role conceptions for each state, a minimum of ten sources would have to be available. This number is not arbitrary; it was determined midway through the research. If it had been higher, the number of states in the sample would have been smaller, since general statements on foreign policy are rare for many governments. If it were lower, say only five, some references to different types of national role conceptions might have been left out and the final distribution of national role conceptions for each state would have been considerably less reliable. Ten sources were only a minimum. For governments which made many statements or speeches, all the major sources were included.

Third, the sources were derived primarily from the period January 1965 to December 1967. Exceptions were made in order to obtain a reasonable minimum number of sources for each country. For instance, ten speeches or general foreign policy statements were not available from the Laotian government for this period; hence it was necessary to include several statements from 1964 to bring the total to the minimum. In other cases fundamental changes in government personnel necessitated restricting the period for which sources could be found. In the instances of minor personnel changes which did not appear to affect the major lines of a nation's foreign policy (for example, Belgium) the period 1965 to 1967 was used.

Fourth, all sources from which evidence of role conceptions was

Table 2.1   National role conceptions for 71 states

State	Years	No. of sources	No. of conceptions	Sources with no conceptions	Bastion of revolution-liberator	Regional leader	Regional protector	Active independent	Liberator supporter	Anti-imperialist agent
Afghanistan	65–67	10	15	1					3	
Albania	66–67	10	25						2	7
Algeria	65–68	13	13	4					3	3
Australia	65–67	15	32	1			7			
Belgium	63–68	12	16	2						
Brazil	67–68	10	9	1						
Bulgaria	65–67	10	9	2					2	1
Burma	64–68	10	10	2						
Cambodia	64, 65–67	10	5							
Canada	65, 67–68	11	23	1						
Ceylon	65–67	11	10	2						
China (People's R.)	67–68	37	72	3	14				2	9
China (R.)	65–66	11	28	2	20					
Congo (Braz.)	65–68	15	6	9					3	1
Congo (Kins.)	65–68	20	5	15					2	
Cuba	63–67	11	20		1				7	2
Czechoslovakia	64–67	10	10	3					2	
Ethiopia	64–68	21	13	11		1			5	
Finland	61, 64–67	11	12	1						
France	64–67	21	28	2		1		5		
Germany (Dem. R.)	66–67	16	9	8				1		
Germany (Fed. R.)	66–68	19	16	2						
Ghana	66–68	10	8	2						
Guyana	66–68	10	14	2						
Guinea	65–68	15	18	6	2				5	5
Hungary	66–67	16	42				1		4	7
India	66–68	15	20	2		1		7	5	
Indonesia	66–67	10	27	2	3			8	2	6
Iran	65–68	12	12	1				1		
Iraq	66–68	14	27	1			2		3	5

Defender of faith	Mediator/ integrator	Regional-subsystem collaborator	Developer	Bridge	Faithful ally	Independent	Example	Internal development	Isolate	Protectee	Other	No. of roles perceived	Weighted total
						10		2				3	6
					5		1				10	5	14
		3				3		1				5	13
1		12	2		6							5	13
	2	7	2	2	3							5	12
		1				2		6				3	2
		1			4					1		5	6
						2		2	6			3	2
						3			2			2	2
	8	1	7		6	1						5	8
		1				8		1				3	2
		6			16		20				5	7	23
3							1				4	4	12
		1				1						4	4
		1		2								3	5
1		1				1	5					7	9
		2			3					3		4	9
	1	3				3						5	9
	3		1	1		1	1	1	4			7	3
	9	1	3		2	4					3	8	18
2	1	1			4							5	5
	4	4	2	3	3							5	12
		2				5		1				3	5
		5		1		6		2				4	5
		6										4	16
	2	9	2		17							7	19
	4					2		1				6	13
		1				1		6				7	17
						10		1				3	2
		6			3	7		1				7	20

Table 2.1 (continued)

State	Years	No. of sources	No. of conceptions	Sources with no conceptions	Bastion of revolution-liberator	Regional leader	Regional protector	Active independent	Liberator supporter	Anti-imperialist agent
Israel	64–67	10	8	4				1	1	
Italy	65–67	10	13	1						
Ivory Coast	65–67	11	4	8					1	
Japan	64, 66–67	14	20	1		2		3		
Kenya	65–67	14	10	4	1					1
Korea (Dem. R.)	66–67	10	9	3	1				3	5
Kuwait	65–67	11	15	1					3	
Laos	64–68	10	8	3						
Lebanon	65–67	10	12	4						
Liberia	57–59, 65–68	15	11	8					3	
Malaysia	65–67	16	28	3			1	4		
Mali	65–68	11	11	1					1	2
Mongolia	63–67	10	8	2					2	
Morocco	65–68	10	9	2					1	
Nepal	64–67	10	8	2					2	
Netherlands	65–67	10	11	2						
New Zealand	64–68	10	15	3			5			
Niger	64–66, 68	10	4	6						
Pakistan	65–67	13	12	2						
Poland	66–67	13	9	6						
Portugal	61–67	19	6	15						
Rumania	66–68	24	61					7	8	15
Senegal	65–68	10	9	3						
Singapore	66–67	15	10	8						
Sudan	65–67	10	13	3		1			3	
Sweden	61, 65–66	14	15	4						
Switzerland	65–67	12	10	4						
Syrian Arab R.	66–67	16	15	6					2	5
Tanzania	65–67	11	11	5					3	
Thailand	64–66	17	10	9						
Tunisia	65–67	14	9	7				1		
Turkey	65–67	17	15	3				7		
Uganda	65–68	10	7	4						

Defender of faith	Mediator/integrator	Regional-subsystem collaborator	Developer	Bridge	Faithful ally	Independent	Example	Internal development	Isolate	Protectee	Other	No. of roles perceived	Weighted total
		3				1	2					5	4
	3	3	1		6							4	8
		1		1							1	4	0
		4	9		2							5	17
		3				4	1					5	5
												3	8
	2	2	3		1	4						6	15
						3			3	2		3	2
	4	3				5						3	8
	1				1			6				4	4
		12					2	9				5	8
	1	5				2						5	9
		3			3							3	9
		7				1						3	3
						5			1			3	6
		6	2		3							3	8
2		5	3									4	14
		4										1	3
		2		1			1	7	1			5	3
		1			5			1		2		4	2
1						4	1					3	2
	12	16					3					6	19
	1	5				2	1					4	5
		1				2		4	3			4	2
		4		2	1	2						6	10
	3	5	2			4					1	5	15
		2	2			5			1			4	8
		4			1	3						5	13
		3				4		1				4	9
		3			4			3				3	5
		4				2		2				4	5
		5			3							3	9
		1				3		3				3	2

Table 2.1   (continued)

State	Years	No. of sources	No. of conceptions	Sources with no conceptions	Bastion of revolution-liberator	Regional leader	Regional protector	Active independent	Liberator supporter	Anti-imperialist agent
Union of South Africa	65–68	10	10	3						
U.S.S.R.	62, 64, 66, 67	12	54				9		8	11
United Arab R.	63, 65–67	36	64	6	10	13	2	4	20	9
United Kingdom	66–68	20	32	1			7			
United States	65–67	25	44			2	4			
Vietnam (Dem. R.)	60, 62, 66–67	10	30		6				5	8
Yugoslavia	65–67	19	31	3				12	5	
Zambia	64–67	10	12	3				2	2	

obtained were general foreign policy statements or review. The sources do not include statements referring to specific issues.

With one important exception, the sample for which at least ten sources were available is reasonably representative of the variety of states in the international system. The large gap comes from Latin America and the Caribbean. Published reports of foreign policy speeches, whether in the world's major newspapers or government reports, are rare, and those that do appear are extreme in their generality or specificity. They tend either toward meaningless generalizations such as "supporting peace," or concentrate on specific problems, usually of a commercial nature.

Following these rules, the research procedure involved reading a large number of sources which included partial or full texts of statements or speeches by high-level foreign policy personnel, and noting themes which gave evidence of the presence of national role conceptions. Despite the varied and colorful vocabulary in the sources, there was no great problem in identifying most themes. If a theme or statement was considered ambiguous after several readings, it was discarded.

Defender of faith	Mediator/ integrator	Regional-subsystem collaborator	Developer	Bridge	Faithful ally	Independent	Example	Internal development	Isolate	Protectee	Other	No. of roles perceived	Weighted total
2		4				1			1		2	5	10
1		10	3					9			3	8	25
		4						2				8	31
	2	8	2		6						6	6	16
9	8	9	7		2						3	8	29
6					3			2				6	19
	10		4									4	14
		2				5	1					5	13

The project started inductively with a survey of seventy-five different sources for eighteen countries; this sample provided a list of twelve kinds of national role conceptions as well as clues to the ways themes might appear in other sources. The remaining five major national role conceptions were defined from subsequent sources.

Many of the sources, though general foreign policy reviews, contained no evidence of national role conceptions. We can draw no firm conclusions from the absence of certain evidence; it does not prove that policymakers in some states hold no national role conceptions. However, where a large number of a country's official foreign policy statements are confined to specific issues, such as trade, and reveal no particular orientation toward the external environment, it does suggest that policymakers have little notion of a global or regional role, or of specific international tasks. As an example, contrast these two statements from communist Chinese and Argentine sources:

> The world belongs to the people. We are convinced that, provided we follow the teachings of our great leader Chairman Mao, we will certainly build a new world without imperialism. . . . That is, pro-

vided we hold aloft the banner of opposing imperialism, unite with all those who oppose imperialism and colonialism, firmly support the armed struggles of the Vietnamese people and of Asian, African, and Latin American peoples and the revolutionary movements of the people of all countries, carry the struggle against United States-led imperialism and its lackeys through to the end, hold aloft the banner of Marxism-Leninism, unite with all the revolutionary Marxist-Leninists, and carry on the struggle against modern revisionism. . . .

The objectives of Argentina's foreign policy are to firmly uphold sovereignty . . . [and] to develop a foreign policy inspired by the country's highest historical precedent . . . ; in short, a foreign policy which will affirm its faith in the greatness of national destiny.

The first statement, a paraphrase of a statement by Zhou En Lai published in *Peking Review,* clearly implies an orientation toward the external environment and suggests types of actions appropriate to fill the two national role conceptions—anti-imperialist agent and antirevisionist agent—that appear in it. The second statement is vague and unstructured and in no way indicates orientations toward, or functions in, the external environment.

The Variety of National Role Conceptions: Some Examples

The 972 sources for this study provided evidence of seventeen role conceptions. A few role conceptions, mostly unique to a single state, were also identified and are noted under the "other" column in table 2.1. The list of national role conceptions below is arranged along a continuum reflecting the degree of passivity or activity in foreign policy that the role conceptions seem to imply.

1. *Bastion of revolution-liberator.* Some governments hold that they have a duty to organize or lead various types of revolutionary movements abroad. One task of their state, as they see it, is to liberate others or to act as the "bastion" of revolutionary movements, that is to provide an area which foreign revolutionary leaders can regard as a source of physical and moral support, as well as an ideological inspirer.

> The victory of China's great proletarian cultural revolution has not only opened a broad path for consolidating the dictatorship of the proletariat and carrying the socialist revolution to the end, but has made it possible for China to be a more powerful base for supporting world revolution. (*Peking Review,* December 25, 1967)

La Tanzanie n'est pas loin des parties du sud de l'Afrique qui ne sont pas encore libres. Nous sommes conscients de notre rôle, et notre devoir est d'aider par example le Mozambique, L'Angola, la Rhodesie du Sud à se libérer. C'est pourquoi nous avons chez nous le siège de la plupart des mouvements de libération. Nous devons libérer toute l'Afrique. . . . (Julius Nyerere, quoted in *Le Monde*, April 16, 1965)

2. *Regional leader.* The themes for this national role conception refer to duties or special responsibilities that a government perceives for itself in its relation to states in a particular region with which it identifies, or to cross-cutting subsystems such as international communist movements.

Egypt has a special role in the issue . . . of joint Arab action. It is up to Egypt more than the other Arab states to come forward with a suitable formula [for Arab unity and against Israel]. Egypt, perhaps alone, is required to make an accurate assessment [of conditions in the region]. . . . This special role assigned to Egypt is indeed a special responsibility which Egypt must accept. ("Voice of Arabs" radio broadcast, January 22, 1968)

3. *Regional protector.* This role conception, though it perhaps implies special leadership responsibilities on a regional or issue-area basis, places emphasis on the function of providing protection for adjacent regions.

Great Britain must not commit ground troops in Southeast Asia, but our responsibility is to provide sophisticated support from the sea and air with all the expert equipment that they [Malaysia and Singapore] cannot afford, necessary to deter a potential aggressor from launching a sophisticated attack. . . . To provide a deterrent . . . is our role that we should take up with Malaysia and Singapore. Our commitment is not to police the world. We have made it clear that we do not believe that to be the role of this country. (Harold Wilson statement in House of Commons, 1967)

4. *Active independent.* Most government statements supporting the concept of nonalignment are little more than affirmations of an "independent" foreign policy, free of military commitments to any of the major powers. There are differences in these affirmations of national independence, however. Most merely suggest that foreign policy decisions will be made to serve national interests rather than the interests

of others (see below under "independent"). Others imply much more diplomatic activity. In addition to shunning permanent military or ideological commitments, the themes suggest active efforts to cultivate relations with as many states as possible and occasional interposition into bloc conflicts. The role conception emphasizes at once independence, self-determination, possible mediation functions, and active programs to extend diplomatic and commercial relations to diverse areas of the world.

> [Nikezic] emphasized that the government of Yugoslavia, which has never believed in the usefulness of military blocs . . . had for many years been pursuing a policy aimed at the extension of bilateral cooperation, while at the same time actively participating in efforts . . . in seeking solutions and the peaceful settlement of controversial problems. . . . This is precisely the aim of the policy of nonalignment which, while developing cooperation among independent nations, remains opposed to all hegemony and to any sort of monopoly in international affairs. (Paraphrase of speech by Secretary of State for Foreign Affairs, Marko Nikezic, 1967)

5. *Liberation supporter.* Unlike the *bastion of the revolution-liberator* national role conception, the *liberation supporter* does not indicate formal responsibilities for organizing, leading, or physically supporting liberation movements abroad. Most statements supporting liberation movements appear routine and formal; they suggest rather unstructured and vague attitudes about actions required to enact the role conception.

> The Bulgarian people have always been and will always be with the peoples struggling for freedom and independence. They have many times responded to campaigns in support of the struggling peoples of the colonial and dependent countries. . . . Bulgaria warmly supports the struggle of all nations . . . which are marching along the road to a free life. (Editorial in *Bulgaria Today*, February 1966)

6. *Anti-imperialist agent.* Where imperialism is perceived as a serious threat, many governments—by no means limited to communist party states—see themselves as agents of "struggle" against this evil.

> Our people are living in an extremely glorious period of history. Our country has the great honor of being an outpost of the socialist camp and one of the world's peoples who are struggling against

imperialism, colonialism, and neo-colonialism. . . . We have the responsibility and great honor to stand in the front line of the world people's struggle against United States imperialist aggression. For the independence and unification of our country, for the security of the socialist camp, for the revolutionary cause and defense of peace of the world peoples, our entire people, united as one man, are resolved to fulfill their heavy but extremely glorious duty. (Statement by Ho Chi Minh, 1960)

7. *Defender of the faith*. Some governments view their foreign policy objectives and commitments in terms of defending value systems (rather than specified territories) from attack. Those who espouse the defender of the faith national role conception presumably undertake special responsibilities to guarantee ideological purity for a group of other states.

We have a common interest in defending the humanitarian traditions of the Europeans against Americanism and ruthless West German militarism. That is our common purpose. (Walther Ulbricht speech, 1967)

8. *Mediator-integrator*. In the sample of seventy-one states, a considerable number of governments perceived themselves as capable of, or responsible for, fulfilling or undertaking special tasks to reconcile conflicts between other states or groups of states. (Statements which referred to a mediatory role in only one specific crisis were not counted.) The themes for this national role conception indicate perceptions of a continuing task to help adversaries reconcile their differences.

It is obvious that our foreign policy should support realistic attempts to obtain a continued détente. Our position as a neutral state makes this particularly natural while at the same time giving us special responsibilities for fruitful contacts with different groups of states. (From speech by Torsten Nilsson, Swedish Foreign Minister, 1966)

9. *Regional-subsystem collaborator*. The themes in this national role conception differ from those in the mediator-integrator category in that they do not merely envisage occasional interposition into areas or issues of conflict; they indicate, rather, far-reaching commitments to cooperative efforts with other states to build wider communities, or to cross-cutting subsystems such as the communist movement.

The impressive universal exposition of 1958 has proven that Belgium considers itself as having a natural mission to facilitate contacts between peoples. The open door policy . . . our receptivity to foreign cultures, and the cohabitation on our territory of Latin and Germanic elements . . . predestines [us] to the role of the catalyst of European unification. (Statement by governor of Province of Anvers, quoted by Belgian government, 1964)

10. *Developer.* The themes in this national role conception indicate a special duty or obligation to assist underdeveloped countries. References to special skills or advantages for undertaking such continuing tasks also appear frequently.

I think a small country should have a vocation outside itself. If it wants to be saved from provincialism it should play some part in the broader human arena. . . . I find in all these [underdeveloped] nations a great preoccupation with development. Quite unexpectedly, Israel, despite being small, is able to play this role. . . . The variety of our efforts, the trial and error, the diversity of social experience, all of these make Israel apparently a very convenient arena in which other nations can learn the developing process. (Statements by Abba Eban on U.S. television interview, 1965)

11. *Bridge.* This national role conception often appears in vague form, and the policies deriving from it, if any, do not seem apparent. Whereas the mediator-integrator role implies various forms of diplomatic interposition into areas or issues of conflict, the bridge concept is much more ephemeral. The themes usually imply a communication function, that is, acting as a "translator" or conveyor of messages and information between peoples of different cultures.

History and tradition, civilization and customs place Cyprus in the Western world. However, we want friendship with all states. . . . We do not overestimate the role that Cyprus could play in the international arena. Nevertheless, I believe that its geographic location, as a bridge uniting three continents, and other factors give Cyprus the opportunity to play an international role greater than the size of its population and territory. (Statement by President Makarios to Cyprus House of Representatives, 1968)

12. *Faithful ally.* If one were to count up all contemporary alliance commitments made through mutual assistance and other types of treaties, almost one-half of the states in the system would have to be classified as "faithful alliance partners." A review of foreign policy

speeches and statements indicates quite different conclusions. For many states alliances are potentially useful for protective purposes, but the state which receives an external guarantee does not reciprocate by supporting the guarantor. The role conception of *faithful ally* is used in this study only where a government makes a specific commitment to support the policies of *another* government. Looked at in this way, many alliance partners today are neither faithful nor allies. The examples below indicate continuing support for another state's actions and policies.

> Too small to defend itself by its own means, Luxembourg has integrated itself with a larger collectivity. Our fidelity to the Atlantic alliance and our European convictions constitute the base of our foreign policy. (Statement in speech by Premier Pierre Werner, 1967)
>
> We Bulgarian Communists are united for life and death with the Soviet Union and the C.P.S.U. (Statement by Todor Zhivkov, 1965)

13. *Independent*. Most statements affirming commitment to the policy of nonalignment indicate that the government will make policy decisions according to the state's own interests rather than in support of the objectives of other states. The themes in the role conception of the *independent* all emphasize this element of policy self-determination; otherwise they do not imply any particular continuing task or function in the system.

> What is non-alignment? It is a determination to preserve independence, sovereignty, to respect such independence and sovereignty in other states and to decline to take sides in the major ideological struggles which rend the world. . . . We will not hitch our carriage to any nation's engine and be drawn along their railway line. (Statements by President Kaunda, shortly after Zambia's independence was established, October 1964)

14. *Example*. This national role conception emphasizes the importance of promoting prestige and gaining influence in the international system by pursuing certain domestic policies. The role conception is placed at a low position on the passivity-activity dimension because it does not require formal diplomatic programs or special tasks outside of the boundaries of the state in question.

> Our role, we feel, is not only to dispel unwarranted pessimism [about China], but to reaffirm by our own example and policy that

democracy is a better answer to the social and economic prob-
lems of this vital region than Communism ever can be. . . . We in
Malaysia see our role as one of contributing to the stability of
Southeast Asia through social and economic progress [at home].
(Quotations from article by Tunku Abdul Rahman in *Foreign Affairs*
43 [July 1965]: 620)

15. *Internal development.* This concept has little reference to any
particular task or function within the international system. The
emphasis, on the contrary, is that most efforts of the government should
be directed toward problems of internal development. There is a suggestion of wishing to remain uninvolved in international political
matters, but the statements do not preclude various forms of international cooperation, particularly in economic and technical matters.

"When the Finnish people has in the international sense . . . joined
the ranks of the independent nations, it must naturally try to
overcome to the best of its ability the difficulties it will encounter
there, but a people our size and character must, in my belief, seek
its principal tasks in the sphere of internal, cultural, social, and
economic development." I quote these words of our first president
because, in my opinion, they still set the lines of our national
activity. We must participate to the best of our strength and possibilities also in international cooperation. . . . But our main task lies
all the same within our own frontiers. We must seek with all the
determination of which the achievements of our years of independence are proof, to work for the improvement of our cultural,
economic, and social conditions. (Statement by President Kekkonen
in New Year's Speech, 1967)

16. *Isolate.* The *internal development* role conception often includes
references to external cooperation, particularly in the economic and
cultural fields. The national role of the *isolate* demands, on the contrary,
a minimum of external contacts of whatever variety. Statements such
as those below reveal fears of external involvements of any kind and
emphasize self-reliance.

We have got to rely on our own strength in everything. We cannot
depend on anybody. We should not try to find fault with anyone.
We do not want to quarrel with anyone. . . . Unless we Burmese
can learn to run our own country, we will lose it. This kind of aid
[bilateral aid to nations in the region] does not help. It cripples. It
paralyzes. The recipients never learn to do for themselves. They

rely more and more on foreign experts and foreign money. In the end they lose control of their country. (Statements by General Ne Win, 1966)

> Like a virgin, Cambodia does not wish to be approached by anyone. With China, there is only esteem, but Cambodia does not allow herself to be seduced. Therefore, Cambodia does not allow herself to be seduced by you [Americans] either, because you are too stupid. . . . Cambodia loves only her independence. (Statement by Prince Sihanouk, 1967)

17. *Protectee*. Some governments allude to the responsibility of other states to defend them, but otherwise do not indicate any particular orientation, tasks, or functions toward the external environment. The comments refer more, perhaps, to the position of the state than to a role. An example is the position of Czechoslovakia revealed in this statement by former President Novotny from a speech at a military parade during Czechoslovakia's National Day celebration in 1966:

> Our defense is backed by the Soviet army, the Soviet Union, and the Soviet people. Together with the Soviet Union we are protecting our freedom jointly with the armies and peoples of the fraternal socialist countries. Our freedom, our security, our prospects for the future, our ability to develop . . . depend upon our being backed by the Soviet Union. For this reason our alliance with the Soviet Union is the foundation of our free life.

Other roles. Several other national role conceptions appeared in the sources, but their frequency was not great enough to include them in the taxonomy. The only references to the role of a *balancer* came from the speeches of former President de Gaulle who often alluded to France's special responsibilities for creating some kind of new force between the "two hegemonies." For example, "France must be independent so that she can play her own role in the world. Toward what goal? Toward the goal of balance, of progress, of peace." On other occasions, de Gaulle stated that France was moving to the forefront of the world with the task of bringing "balance to a divided globe. France's vocation and task are the world's balance, so that each people has the place it wants to have."

Complementing the self-image of being *anti-imperialist agents*, communist Chinese and Albanian government or party statements frequently mentioned special responsibilities and tasks for fighting against "revisionism." We can classify these national role conceptions under the term *antirevisionist agent*. The Arab counterpart is the *anti-Zionist agent* role, and for some Western nations it is the *anticommunist agent* role conception.

In some of the Soviet and American sources, references were made to a *defender of the peace* national role. These statements are not qualified by reference to any particular region (*regional protector*); they seem to indicate a universal commitment to defend against any aggression or threat to peace, no matter what the locale. Others might point out that this is evidence of the world policeman role conception that has raised so much discussion recently. It should be pointed out, however, that there were few references to this latter conception and, in the case of the United States and Great Britain, some firm disavowals against playing any world policeman role.

The concept of the *balancer*, often discussed prominently in the literature, appears only in the few references made by President de Gaulle. Whatever policymakers may think about balances and power distributions, whether global or regional, they do not articulate their self-conceptions in terms of the concept of balance. Balances of power or balancing roles are not an important part of the vocabulary of contemporary international politics.

Analysis

The traditional view that states fulfill essentially a single function or play a single role in international politics is not borne out by the statements of policymakers. Whatever may be the utility of single-role assumptions in the study of international politics, from the average policymaker's point of view, his state has different sets of established relationships in the world or within a region (probably both), and hence normally several different roles in the system and its subsystems.

In the sample the average number of different role conceptions per country is 4.6. Portrayals of the international system which do not acknowledge multiple roles and the importance to most states of roles relating to regional issues will be empirically deficient and except for limited purposes (for example, analysis of the distribution of military capabilities among the major powers) theoretically inadequate.

Similar conclusions can be drawn regarding the descriptions of roles in much of the traditional and contemporary literature of international politics. There are considerable differences, for example, between allies, bloc leaders, and nonaligned states as described in the literature, and the self-conceptions of the governments which are commonly classified under these terms. Iran and Australia, for instance, are both allies of the United States. Yet twelve foreign policy speeches or statements made by the highest Iranian officials did not reveal a single reference to Iran's commitments to the CENTO alliance, or to support for American foreign policy goals; on the contrary, of the twelve role conceptions that appeared in the sources, ten emphasized Iran's independence in foreign policy, its determination to conduct its foreign policy according to its own internal needs and not to the interests, defense or otherwise, of other states (see table 2.1). It is difficult, therefore, to describe Iran as an ally, whatever its formal commitments.

Australia, on the other hand, fits the term "alliance partner" more adequately. Six of the thirty-two themes in the sources indicate a definite commitment to support American foreign policy objectives, particularly as they relate to the Southeast Asian region. The statements are usually couched in unmistakably clear language. Unlike Iran, the sources include no themes emphasizing Australia's complete freedom of action in foreign policy.

Differences between states which are commonly lumped together as nonaligned are even more apparent. Two extreme examples would be Burma and Egypt. Both have avoided references to military commitments to major powers (in the formal alliance sense), but that is about the only similarity in their foreign policy statements. Eight of the ten themes appearing in Burmese sources indicated a strong desire to remain uninvolved in the major issue areas of either the system or the Southeast Asian subordinate system. The term *isolate* is a much more appropriate summary of Burma's role—or lack of role—in the world. In contrast Egyptian foreign policy statements are rich in themes indicating continuing tasks and responsibilities in regional affairs.

India, which is often listed along with Egypt as one of the leaders of the nonaligned states, shows a third pattern of national role conceptions. Though India and Egypt hold three national role conceptions in common (*subsystem leader, active independent*, and *liberator-supporter*), there are eight national role conceptions to which one subscribes but not the other. In particular, Indian authorities give substantial emphasis to the international *mediator* role, the functions of which are not duplicated in the case of Egypt. Aside from their avoidance of formal alliance commitments to the major powers and their support for anticolonial movements, little unites the nonaligned in foreign policy outlook or interests. Their regional interests and positions are too varied to lump them under one role type.

If one were to read all 972 sources, one would be struck by the variations in specificity and number of national role conceptions and themes. Sources for some states include not only a large number of themes, but statements are succinct and indicate definite types of commitments, functions, and orientations toward the outside world. There was little problem in classifying the themes of Egypt, communist China, France, the United States, North Vietnam, Sweden, Guinea, and many others. In other statements, however, themes were few in number, vague, and in some cases difficult to classify, suggesting that national role conceptions were not significant aspects of foreign policy (for example, it would be difficult to predict diplomatic attitudes and behavior on the basis of knowledge of vague role conceptions).

If we construct a scale measuring the number of national role conceptions per source, differences between states become apparent. The scale ranges from an average of 4.5 role conceptions per source in Soviet foreign policy statements and speeches down to Portugal, in whose nineteen sources, only six themes appeared, a rounded average of 0.3. The average number of themes per source for the seventy-one nation sample is 1.3. States cluster heavily around the 0.8 to 1.0 region.

One impression is that some sort of relationship exists between ratios of role conceptions per source and degrees of activity-passivity among states in world or regional affairs. Let us assume that we had some measure of differences in levels of involvement among most contemporary states. Such figures would no doubt reveal that France, Japan, and the United States are more involved and active in regional and international issues than are Ivory Coast and Portugal. If we were required to illustrate how much more or less each of these states was involved or active, then it would be necessary to show through trade figures, exchange of diplomatic missions, communications, and the like, what the differences were. Our concern here is only to see whether there is some relationship between the number of national role conceptions mentioned by each country and a generally high or low level of involvement and activity. The listing of states in table 2.2 would roughly support the hypothesis that the more active or involved a state is in international or regional affairs, the more national role conceptions its leaders will perceive. The only major discrepancies between the number of role conceptions and levels of involvement would be Hungary, Iraq, Kuwait, Albania and Sudan, all of whose governments enunciated four or more national role conceptions. In the three-role category, one might have expected Italy to rank higher and Laos, Mongolia, and Singapore lower.

A relationship between types of national role conceptions and

Table 2.2   Number of national roles perceived by national governments

Number of roles mentioned	Governments
8	United Arab Republic, United States
7	Soviet Union, Chinese People's Republic
6	France, Hungary, Iraq, Rumania, North Vietnam
5	Belgium, Federal Republic of Germany, Indonesia, Japan, Kuwait, United Kingdom
4	Albania, Algeria, Australia, Czechoslovakia, Guinea, India, Malaysia, New Zealand, Sudan, Sweden, Syria, Yugoslavia, Zambia
3	Afghanistan, Burma, Canada, Republic of China, Cuba, Ethiopia, Guyana, Italy, Laos, Lebanon, Mali, Mongolia, Netherlands, Singapore, Switzerland, Tanzania, Thailand, Tunisia, Turkey, South Africa
2	Brazil, Bulgaria, Cambodia, Congo (Kins.), Finland, German Democratic Republic, Ghana, Israel, Kenya, North Korea, Liberia, Nepal, Pakistan, Poland, Senegal, Uganda
1	Ceylon, Congo (Braz.), Iran, Morocco, Niger, Portugal
0	Ivory Coast

degrees of international activity-passivity is revealed also by arbitrarily weighting each of the role types and then applying the values to the national role conceptions held by the different governments. For instance, let us assign values of 2 to the *independent* role, 1 to the *example*, and zero to the *isolate* role. Now assume that a government makes in its diverse statements on foreign policy six references to the role of *isolate*, two to the role of *example*, and four to the role of *independent*. Since our concern is with the types of national roles referred to, not the number of instances each role is mentioned, we add up the totals of the values assigned to each role. In this example, the total is three. If all the references by the government referred to the role of *isolate*, the total would be zero.

The following values were assigned arbitrarily to each of the role conception types:

Bastion of revolution-liberator	5
Regional leader	5
Regional protector	5

Active independent	4
Liberator supporter	4
Anti-imperialist agent	4
Defender of the faith	3
Mediator-integrator	3
Regional-subsystem collaborator	3
Developer	3
Faithful ally	2
Independent	2
Bridge	1
Example	1
Internal development	0
Isolate	0
Protectee	0

The values assigned for the infrequently appearing (listed as "other" in table 2.1) role conceptions were as follows:

Defender of the peace	5
Balancer	4
Anti-revisionist/Zionist/or Communist agent	4

Column 25 of table 2.1 is the weighted score earned by each state from adding the values assigned to each type of role conception that is mentioned two or more times in the sources. Single references to a particular role type have been eliminated. We can then devise an "activity-passivity" scale in which Egypt with a total of 31 points is at the top and Ivory Coast, with no points, is at the bottom. The scale can be reduced to four rough quartiles for easier analysis. The states within each quartile are arranged according to weighted score, not alphabetically. As shown in table 2.3, those at the top of the quartiles have the highest number of points, those at the bottom, the lowest (for example, in group I, Egypt totals 31 points, Yugoslavia 14 points).

The states in the first quartile are, in terms of the types of national role conceptions held, active. States in group IV are passive in the sense that the types of national role conceptions mentioned in the sources involve few commitments or functions in the external environment. States in this category mention primarily roles of the *independent, internal development, protectee,* and *isolate* types.

The ranking of states based on assigning values to national role conceptions and adding the scores for the types of roles referred to in

Table 2.3 Active and passive states as measured by
types of role conceptions mentioned in sources

Group I (14 to 31 points)	Group II (9 to 13 points)	Group III (5 to 8 points)	Group IV (0 to 4 points)
Egypt	Algeria	Canada	Congo (Braz.)
United States	Australia	Italy	Israel
USSR	India	North Korea	Liberia
China	Syria	Lebanon	Finland
(People's R.)	Zambia	Malaysia	Morocco
Iraq	Belgium	Netherlands	Niger
Hungary	Rep. of China	Switzerland	Pakistan
Rumania	Fed. Rep. of Germany	Afghanistan	Brazil
North Vietnam	Sudan	Nepal	Burma
France	South Africa	Congo (Kins.)	Cambodia
Indonesia	Cuba	German Dem. Rep.	Ceylon
Japan	Czechoslovakia	Ghana	Iran
Guinea	Ethiopia	Guyana	Laos
United Kingdom	Mali	Kenya	Poland
Kuwait	Mongolia	Senegal	Portugal
Sweden	Tanzania	Thailand	Singapore
Albania	Turkey	Tunisia	Uganda
New Zealand			Ivory Coast
Yugoslavia			

foreign policy statements seems to conform to our common-sense impressions. All the major powers except West Germany emerge in the upper quartile. Most of the "middle" powers, regional leaders, and active nonaligned states are found in the second group, and a few rank in the first quartile. It is more difficult to explain the presence of Iraq, Hungary, Indonesia, Kuwait, and New Zealand in the top category, however. They are active states in terms of their role conceptions, but they would not be ranked so in terms of their worldwide or even regional influence. The bottom quartile and the lower end of the third quartile are composed of states not commonly associated with an active foreign policy. Perhaps the only surprise here is Israel. Its low position is probably explained by the Israelis' strong preoccupation with the immediate conflict with the Arab states.

We can conclude, using these three types of measures, that the pattern of role conceptions for any state is a fair indicator and possible predictor of diplomatic involvements. Those governments that perceive many and active role types will tend to be much more highly involved in the affairs of the system or in subordinate systems than those states which have few and passive type role conceptions. A test of the adequacy of national role conceptions as indicators of degrees of activity and passivity would be to compare the rankings in these quartiles with hard data such as volume of trade, mutual visits of heads of state, alliance commitments, participation in international and regional organizations, size of military forces, and the like.

The Pattern of Role Conceptions in the International System

As a characterization of the conservative aspects of the eighteenth- and nineteenth-century European-centered international systems, balance-of-power images of the world may have been reasonably accurate. But balance of power, polar, and even multipolar models do not adequately alert us to some aspects of contemporary international politics, such as the great variation of diplomatic behavior covered under the term nonalignment. Most important, however, these models ignore the great importance of regional issues, regional relationships, and regional roles. The distribution of national role conceptions in this study, while in part supporting the polar view of the world, also emphasizes a rich and varied diplomatic life at the regional level. When references to the various national role conceptions are added together, a ranking occurs as shown in table 2.4.

The role conception of the *regional-subsystem collaborator* predominates distinctively in the list: fifty-four of the seventy-one governments in the sample refer to a continuing commitment to facilitate and promote economic and political cooperation within regions. Of all references to national roles, almost one out of five (18 percent) is in terms of regional collaboration. The second most popular national role conception is that of the *independent*: the government which sees itself as free to maneuver as it wishes, eschewing all permanent military commitments to bloc leaders or cold warriors. Indeed the first national role conception which reflects polarity, balance of power, or cold war, is ranked fourth: twenty-eight governments (40 percent of the sample) conceive of themselves, among other roles, as *faithful allies*. However, only 9 percent of all themes in the sources refer to alliance commitment.

Contrary to the portrayals of the balance-of-power or loose bipolar systems, the contemporary international system may well be defined as subordinate system dominant, not only in the sense that critical

Table 2.4   Government references to national roles

Role type	Governments referring to role type		Total references	
	Number	*Percent*	*Number*	*Percent*
1. Regional-subsystem collaborator	54	(76)	227	(17.8)
2. Independent	39	(55)	134	(10.6)
3. Liberator-supporter	33	(46)	123	(9.6)
4. Faithful ally	28	(40)	117	(9.2)
5. Mediator-integrator	22	(31)	87	(6.8)
6. Internal development	21	(30)	62	(4.9)
7. Developer	19	(27)	60	(4.7)
8. Anti-imperialist agent	18	(25)	102	(8.0)
9. Example	15	(21)	52	(4.1)
10. Active independent	14	(20)	63	(4.9)
11. Defender of the faith	10	(14)	29	(2.3)
12. Bastion of the revolution-liberator	9	(13)	58	(4.6)
13. Regional protector	9	(13)	38	(3.0)
14. Isolate	9	(13)	22	(1.7)
15. Regional leader	8	(11)	22	(1.7)
16. Bridge	8	(11)	13	(1.0)
17. Protectee	4	(6)	11	(0.9)
18. Other	12	(17)	49	(3.9)

decisions are made by national actors, but also because, to most states in the world, regional roles and problems are of considerably greater importance than system-wide issues. There is nothing startling in this observation; it is apparent when the world is seen through eyes other than those of political leaders in the great powers. Yet the fact is too often overlooked in the theoretical and descriptive literature of international politics.

Does the distribution of role conceptions reveal anything about conflict and collaboration in the international system? Most of the national role conceptions can be placed in one of the two categories, conflict and collaboration. Others, such as *example, protectee,* and *regional leader,* are hard to classify, so will be omitted. In the category of "conflict" type roles let us include the following, on the assumption that the diplomatic attitudes underlying them and the actions taken to fulfill them will probably cause conflict with other states: *liberator sup-*

*porter, anti-imperialist agent, defender of the faith, bastion of the revo-
lution,* and *regional protector.* Collaboration type roles would include
*regional-subsystem collaborator, mediator-integrator, developer, active
independent,* and *bridge.* Comparing the two we find that there is a
difference in total references, but probably not a significant one.
Thirty-five percent (450) of the references or themes are indicative of
collaborative type national roles; 28 percent (350) are references to
conflict type roles. When measured by the states rather than number
of references, we find that 70 governments refer to conflict-type national
roles and 117 refer to collaborative type national roles. The totals are,
of course, exaggerated since some states are counted two or more
times, if they referred to more than one collaborative or conflict type
national roles in the various sources. No particular conclusion can be
drawn from the figures, but this type of analysis could be useful in
measuring potential for conflict or stability when comparing different
types of international systems on an historical basis, or comparing
regions within the same system.

The Sources of National Role Conceptions

The preceding analysis has two major gaps: it is essentially a static
description of the distribution of national role conceptions and offers
no discussion of the sources of national role conceptions. These two
questions are of course linked. A dynamic or linear analysis on the
origin and change of national role conceptions must assess the sources
of change: what internal and external conditions prompt policymakers to reassess traditional roles and adopt new ones. In the sample
only two states—Australia and Great Britain— were undergoing reap-
praisal of their foreign policy commitments for the period under review.
For Australia, reassessment was brought about by the British decision
to withdraw extensive military commitments from Southeast Asia by
1971—that is, by a fundamental redistribution of military capabilities
in the external environment. Domestic economic pressures are cited
as the main consideration underlying the British desire to abandon
the Southeast Asian and Middle Eastern *regional protector* roles in
favor of ultimately filling a leading position within Europe. Studies of
selected countries over a period of time should enable us to learn
more about fluctuations in domestic and external variables which
prompt similar reappraisals of traditional national role conceptions.

The sources consulted in this study do not regularly reveal the origins of the various national role conceptions. Statements make occa-

sional references to commitments, traditional policies, perceptions of threat, or to specific advantages to be gained from adopting one or another orientation toward the external environment, but the linkages between such variables as location, socio-economic needs, public opinion, capabilities, and system structure and national role conceptions are not always specified. Fortunately, there were enough exceptions—statements that reveal clearly from which perceived domestic and external conditions certain role conceptions are a response—to enable us to construct at least a partial list. As one example, the speeches of former President Khan of Pakistan constantly referred to that country's geographic location (the fact that it has common frontiers with three great powers, including India), economic needs, and perception of threat as underlying the role conceptions of *bridge* and *internal development*. Perceptions of external threat and insufficient capabilities are the main conditions cited as underlying the Burmese and Cambodian isolationist role conceptions. Intensive analysis of each country would probably uncover relationships between this national role and Burmese and Cambodian traditional policies, various socio-economic characteristics, public opinion, and the personalities of their leaders. The relationship between some of the national role conceptions of communist regimes and official ideology are quite apparent. References to Marxism-Leninism as the ultimate fountain of diplomatic activity are many and varied.

Table 2.5 should not be interpreted as meaning that all governments that subscribed to each of the national role conceptions attributed them to the same sources. The problem of establishing definitive relationships remains an area for further research, probably intensive study of individual countries.

National Role Conceptions as Independent Variables: The Problem of Congruence between Role Conceptions and Diplomatic Actions

A major assumption of this analysis has been that foreign policy attitudes, decisions, and actions will be congruent with policymakers' national role conceptions. If this assumption is valid, we could predict with reasonable accuracy typical foreign policy decisions and actions on the basis of our knowledge of the pattern of role conceptions for a particular country. It has been argued that in many situations policymakers operate as "guardians" of one or more national role conceptions. As these national role conceptions become a more pervasive part of

Table 2.5 Some sources of national role conceptions

Role conception	Sources	Countries
Bastion of revolution-liberator	ideological principles; anticolonial attitudes; desire for ethnic unity	Com. China Cuba Indonesia North Korea
Regional leader	superior capabilities; traditional national role	Egypt Japan
Regional protector	perception of threat; geographic location; traditional policies; needs of threatened states	Australia New Zealand United States USSR
Active independent	antibloc attitudes; economic needs; trade expansion; geographic location	France India Yugoslavia Rumania Zambia
Liberator supporter	anticolonial attitudes; ideological principles	most African, Asian, and communist states in sample
Anti-imperialist agent	ideological principles; perception of threat; anticolonial attitudes	Iraq Syria most communist states
Defender of the faith	perceptions of threat; ideological principles; traditional national role	Rep. China United States North Vietnam
Mediator-integrator	traditional national role; cultural-ethnic composition of state; traditional noninvolvement in conflicts; geographic location	Lebanon Sweden
Regional-subsystem collaborator	economic needs; sense of "belonging" to region; common political-ideological traditions; geographic location	Belgium Ethiopia Guyana Japan Sweden Switzerland
Developer	humanitarian concern; anticipated consequences of underdevelopment; superior economic capabilities; balance	Canada France Japan

Table 2.5   (continued)

Role conception	Sources	Countries
	U.S.-USSR competition in underdeveloped areas	Kuwait United States
Bridge	geographic location; multi-ethnic composition of state	Belgium Pakistan
Faithful ally	perception of threat; insufficient capabilities; traditional policies; ideological compatibility	Albania Hungary Italy Portugal Great Britan
Independent	antibloc sentiments; anticolonial sentiments; economic needs; threat perception	many new African states; Nepal, etc.
Example	no revealed sources	
Internal development	socio-economic needs; perception of threat through foreign involvement	Brazil Finland Indonesia Pakistan
Isolate	perception of threat; insufficient capabilities	Burma Cambodia Laos
Protectee	perception of threat; insufficient capabilities	Laos Czechoslovakia

the political culture of a nation, they are more likely to set limits on perceived or politically feasible policy alternatives, and less likely to allow idiosyncratic variables to play a crucial part in decision making.

Role conceptions and prescriptions cannot dictate every aspect of foreign policy behavior. Role theory allows for the exercise of individuality; if we apply some of the concepts of this theory to the foreign policy setting, we must also expect some foreign policy decisions to be inconsistent with the expectations of public opinion and foreign governments, declared national policy, treaty obligations, and stated national roles. Moreover, the relevance of national role conceptions as an independent variable may vary from issue to issue. Normally we would be concerned with explaining those types of decisions and actions which are designed to implement or support role conceptions and expectations. On a technical issue such as delimiting fishing areas, however, most national role conceptions would be irrelevant. So role and issue must be perceived to be linked before knowledge of role conceptions can be used to predict typical responses, decisions, and actions (role performance).

The range of behaviors that role prescriptions and role conceptions cover would be expected to vary with the detail of their specification. As we have seen, some national role conceptions are more highly structured than others. Thus the first situation where a knowledge of national role conceptions might not serve adequately as a basis for predicting typical attitudes and decisions is one in which those conceptions are rapidly changing, weak, or vague. This condition might relate particularly to the leadership of new states and to states which are only weakly linked to, or involved in, the major issue areas of the international system or within regions.

A second situation which might diminish the relevance of national role conceptions as guides to policymaking or as predictors of typical decisions is one in which unprecedented or highly ambiguous circumstances arise in the external environment. The problem policymakers face is to adjust as rapidly as possible to new threats or opportunities; without adequate flexibility in public opinion or sufficient public support, the definition of new and appropriate national roles might be difficult.

It would also be difficult to predict individual foreign policy decisions and actions where the leader of the state in question is in a position—unrestrained by popular sentiments, traditional role conceptions, or externally derived role prescriptions—to act capriciously without fear of political retribution or diplomatic retaliation. The literature of political history includes many descriptions of autocrats whose policies and actions were unrelated to any set of coherent role conceptions or to the expectations of friends and allies.

Finally one could expect a higher number of atypical decisions from a government which subscribed to incompatible national role conceptions. There is probably no inherent logical incompatibility between adherence to a worldwide revolutionary role and a continuing commitment to undertaking mediating functions. In diplomatic practice, however, such a combination would be most unlikely since mediators are often chosen for their noninvolvement in international politics and crisis areas. Similarly the requirements for being a *faithful ally* and a *mediator* would seem to be incompatible, and questions would certainly arise if a government emphasized an external orientation of *active independent* while professing dependence, through an alliance, on the foreign policy objectives of another state. Where governments maintain commitments to such incompatible national roles, we could expect considerable difficulty in determining which national roles were being performed in any set of circumstances.

The most important conclusion, however, confirms a point stressed earlier. Some governments subscribe to more or less incompatible national role conceptions, yet when one looks at these governments, it is clear that they are only expressing different orientations *toward different sets of relationships*. This is another way of saying that governments perceive different actions, commitments, and functions as appropriate to different states, regional groupings, or issue areas. Formal role theory predicts precisely the same conclusion: people develop different role orientations in different sets of relationships. There are some cases of genuine role incompatibility, of course (Pakistan simultaneously as a *bridge* and *isolate*, Singapore as a *regional collaborator* and *isolate*), but many of the other role conflicts in fact reflect the looseness of the blocs or the variety of relationship "nets" for a given state. In the Middle East context, Syria and Iraq are *faithful allies* in the anti-Israel cause; in the cold war context they are *independents* in the sense of eschewing permanent military commitments toward the major powers.

Seemingly incompatible or conflicting national role conceptions must therefore be qualified by relating each role conception to a particular set of relationships. Predicting typical foreign policy decisions and actions thus becomes difficult only where incompatible national role conceptions are enunciated within the context of a single set of relationships.

National Role Conceptions as Dependent Variables in Foreign Policy Analysis

If we continue using the decision as the major dependent variable in foreign policy analysis, explanation of outputs, though not of processes, will probably remain reconstructed history with emphasis on the actions of unique individuals operating within unique organizations in a unique set of historical circumstances. The notion of national role conceptions may well enable us to use broader independent variables in foreign policy analysis. Such factors as public opinion "mood," socio-economic needs, geographic location, traditional policies, as well as idiosyncratic variables (policymakers' "definitions of the situation") could be related to national role conceptions without too much difficulty.

There is another reason why national role conceptions rather than individual decisions might aid the development of foreign policy analysis as well as the study of international politics. Presently it is difficult to relate case studies of decision making to the broader concerns of those working on the structure and functioning of past and contemporary international systems. International systems analysis is concerned with the typical behavior of all states over a considerable period of time, changes in critical variables, and the totality of foreign policy decisions and actions conceived as resulting in identifiable interaction patterns. The analyst of international systems can have little interest in work which inquires into decision-making processes of a single government in one brief atypical scene, usually a crisis situation.

One possible way around this problem would be to specify broader units of behavior as the outputs of decision-making studies. Because the notion of national role suggests general orientations and continuing types of commitments, actions, and functions, it has a level of generality appropriate for both foreign policy theories or frameworks, and systems studies. Carefully refined and combined with studies of patterns of action, it can serve as a *dependent variable* in foreign policy analysis and as one *independent variable* in systems analysis. Role and action patterns rather than individual decisions or actions can be seen as *the* output of foreign policy and as *one* input into the international system. Indeed it is possible to conceive of an international system as a particular distribution of national roles or role conceptions at any given time. Beyond this, examination of role distributions and patterns in a variety of historical and contemporary international and regional systems should provide the field with a time perspective, offer a basis for cross-cultural comparison, and provide data with which to test abstract system types.

Foreign policy decisions are one of the inputs into a "system," but because of the generality of the systems approach, it is difficult to connect individual actions (decisions to start major wars are exceptions, of course) with any particular change in the major characteristics of the system. Modification in the distribution of national role conceptions, however, can be seen as one type of change in the major properties of the system. Significant growth or decline in the number of *active independent, faithful ally,* or *bastion of the revolution-liberator* national role conceptions, for example, could signify transformation of one system type into another. The notion of national role conception, then, offers one avenue for describing types of, and explaining changes in, international systems. It lends itself to empirical analysis, and therefore can supplement interaction and transaction flow studies based on hard data. Studies focusing on national role conceptions can help build bridges between those who work at the personal and national levels of analysis, and those who adopt the broader perspective of international systems studies.

3

Roles and Role Scenarios in Foreign Policy

James N. Rosenau

Recent years have witnessed more than a few pleas that the individual be made more central to the study of world politics. Some of the pleas stem mainly from value considerations (for example, Burton 1983), and others derive largely from a conceptual conviction that macroanalysis must have some roots in microphenomena (for example, North and Choucri 1983). Whatever their source, however, none of the pleas have been accompanied by puzzlement as to what is meant by the "individual." Somehow it is a concept with specifications that are taken for granted, as if everyone, being an individual, knows what the concept signifies.

Such a lapse in our conceptual impulses strikes me as regrettable. If micro-units are to be central to macrotheories, as I am convinced they should be, then we must be as vigorous in our formulations of what we

This chapter was originally presented at the Annual Meeting of the International Studies Association, Atlanta, Georgia, March 28, 1984. Parts of it have also been drawn from James N. Rosenau, "A Pre-Theory Revisited: World Politics in an Era of Global Interdependence," *International Studies Quarterly* 28 (September 1984): 267–76. Reprinted with permission.

mean by the "person" as we are in our models of the "state," the "regime," or any other macro-units. It is not enough to note that people are differentiated by culture, circumstances, and prior experience. More precise understanding of what underlies individual actions is needed if our efforts at micro-macro theorizing are to avoid being thrown off course by our sentimental attachments to the worth and dignity of the individual.

This conclusion, along with an ever-growing belief that theoretical progress cannot occur without viable micro-macro syntheses, has led me to reconsider the concept of role as a possible micro-unit of analysis. More specifically, I have been led to explore the utility of treating individuals not as concrete, identifiable persons, but as complexes of roles and statuses, as members of a variety of systems that so fully account for the expectations to which they respond that nothing meaningful is left over as the quintessentially unique person. Stated even more bluntly so as to arrest attention on the need for more precise conceptualizing, there is no individual apart from the network of systems in which he or she is embedded.

This is not to argue for a mechanistic view of people or otherwise to dismiss the values associated with the human spirit. Nor is it to say that people do not experience themselves and the feeling of being unique. Rather, conceiving of them as role composites provides an analytic context in which theorizing about world politics can systematically and meaningfully build in micro-units expressive of needs, wants, orientations, and actions at the individual level. If it is important to argue that some undefinable variance reflective of the human spirit is left over after the expectations attached to a person's role networks are taken into account, then such an argument can readily be made without undermining a role-composite formulation.

Roles as Analytic Units

This line of reasoning became especially salient in the course of revisiting my "Pre-Theories and Theories of Foreign Policy" (Farrell 1966). Viewed with the hindsight of twenty years, that original paper seems flawed in many ways, one of them being the absence of any effort to specify microanalytic units. The role concept was a central feature of the formulation, but its scope was confined to the attitudes, behaviors, and expectations that attach to top positions in the foreign policymaking process. The various role variables were, in turn, posited as competing with individual, governmental, societal, and systemic variables for influence in shaping how the occupants of the top positions made their decisions. This formulation of the sources of international action now seems too vague as a means of achieving a theoretical link between micro- and macrophenomena. Most notably it suffers from the absence of common dimensions across the five types of source variables that could serve as a basis for comparing among them. As it stands, the Pre-Theory suggests that societal and systemic variables consist of *forces* operating on top officials, that governmental variables involve institutional *practices* to which they must accommodate, that individual variables are comprised of previously acquired *values* which predispose them in certain directions, and that the various forces, practices, and values are in endless tension among themselves and with the *expectations* attached to the top roles.

But how to assess the relative strength of forces, practices, values, and expectations? Clearly, it is like comparing apples and oranges. The different variables have to be conceptualized as different types of fruit if the competition among them is to be fully discerned and cogently assessed. The concept of role readily lends itself to this need for a unifying dimension across the variables, and it is in this context of revisiting the Pre-Theory that the ensuing analysis seeks to pursue the move to make the individual more central to the study of world politics.

The concept of role looms as a unifying dimension when one conceives of all the other types of variables as consisting of role expectations, the differences among them being the differences among the systems in which each role is located. That is, the individuals who make foreign policy occupy a number of roles in a number of systems and, accordingly, they are simultaneously subjected to a number of conflicting role expectations—those that derive from the private systems in which they are or previously were members, from the governmental institutions in which their policymaking position is located, from the society for which they make policy, and from the international systems in which their society is a subsystem *as well as* the expectations to which they are exposed in their top-level, face-to-face decision-making unit. The interaction among the source variables, in other words, culminates in the individual policymaker, creating role conflicts that, in turn, reflect the different values, capabilities, and histories that differentiate the various systems in which the policymaking position is situated.

Some examples are in order. Consider President Reagan's retreat from campaign pledges not to make concessions in arms control negotiations prior to a substantial defense buildup. Instead of attributing the shift in his attitudes and behavior to vague forces at work on a global level, it can usefully be treated as the outcome of a competition between the expectations attached to his longtime party role as a conservative "hawk" and those embedded in his role as the top leader of a superpower in a system marked by cross-pressures from economic exigencies, peace movements in Europe, and an aroused public at home. Likewise, Richard Nixon's 1972 trip to China can be viewed as resulting not from an idiosyncratic trait or skill, but from the requirements of a superpower leader whose country needed more leverage in the increasingly significant Chinese-Soviet-U.S. triad. Or consider the interpretation that John Foster Dulles's alleged religious fervor underlay his conduct as secretary of state. Whatever the degree to which this was the case, his secretaryship can be assessed in terms of the relative potency of his roles in the policymaking process on the one hand and the Presbyterian church on the other.

Lest these examples suggest that the role concept is useful only with respect to the policymaking activities of officials, it must quickly be noted that its utility is no less where internationally relevant activities of those private citizens who act on behalf of nongovernmental organizations and mass publics are concerned. The expectations attached to unofficial roles may be more ambiguous and less demanding than those to which officials are exposed, but analytic rigor does not have to be stretched to treat the attitudes and actions of private individuals in the public arena as responses to diverse system requirements. An enraged peace movement, an apathetic citizenry, an aroused peasantry, a quiescent ethnic minority, an informed elite, and an aggressive multinational corporation can pose role conflicts no less intense for their members and leaders than those experienced by public officials.

A number of advantages flow from reconceptualizing roles as the common denominator for all the source variables that may underlie the behavior of international actors. First, it is responsive to the plea of those who argue that the individual, as distinguished from the institution, the process, or the collectivity, should be the prime unit of analysis. To treat individuals as complexes of identifiable and competing roles and thus as a prime site of the world's conflicts does not, admittedly, fully meet the plea. Such a conception divides people up into analytical parts rather than treating each one as a "real individual, that awful and inconvenient person who does not fit into any convenient analytical model" (Burton 1983, 1). Nevertheless, not only does positing the individual as a complex of roles provide a convenient model, it also serves to focus inquiry on that level of analysis wherein the aggregative processes that produce and differentiate collectivities and global structures originate.

As the Dulles example suggests, moreover, according a central place to role expectations facilitates clarification of a research issue that for many analysts, myself included (Rosenau 1968), has loomed large and troublesome: namely, the issue of where individuals and their idiosyncrasies fit in the dynamics of world politics. At stake here are value questions pertaining to how much discretion individuals can exercise as policymakers and empirical questions as to the extent to which the policymaking process can be randomly distorted, improved, or otherwise affected by the unique talents and beliefs that particular policymakers might bring to their responsibilities. Although good, systematic inquiries into the vagaries of individual variables are now available (Hermann 1974, 1978, 1980; Stassen 1972; Steiner 1983; Walker 1983a), the predominant tendency has been to view them as encompassing such extensive variability as to be beyond the competence of the analyst to observe and thus as constituting a realm of global life where unknowable and unpredictable events originate.

If the idiosyncratic tendencies and belief systems of policymakers are seen as reflective of role phenomena, however, the task of accounting for the impact of individuals on world politics is eased considerably. Under this conceptualization their inexplicable actions do not have to be consigned to the unknowable. Their prior experiences and commitments are transformed from a residual category into a readily identifiable series of roles occupied in private life. Not all of the variance would be picked up this way, of course. Values derived from childhood socialization and personality traits stemming from early family experience would probably remain inaccessible. But the variance left over after treating inexplicable actions as the products of role conflicts seems likely to be much less than is presently the case.

As previously implied, another virtue of transforming individual, governmental, societal, and systemic variables into role phenomena is that a means is provided for systematically probing and comparing the many transnational structures, from the nongovernmental organization to the international regime, now relevant to global politics. Unlike governments, the roles comprising regimes and other transnational structures are identified not so much by formal, authoritative, and legal instruments that accord their occupants the legitimacy necessary to perform their tasks as by informal "principles, norms, rules, and decision-making procedures" that regularize and shape behavior "in a given area of international relations" (Krasner 1982, 186). The presence and relevance of any regime or transnational entity is thus not readily apparent. By definition informal sources of behavior are rooted in predispositions that are both undocumented and habitual. Hence the presence of such entities and their structures must be inferred from patterned activities that cannot be traced back to formal sources.

Once such entities are identified in this manner, further inferences are necessary to clarify the principles, norms, rules, and procedures that govern their behavior. And it is here that the role concept becomes valuable. For a major component of the expectations that comprise any role are the informal principles, norms, rules, and procedures that others require of its occupants and that the occupants require of themselves (Rosenau 1968). Accordingly, viewing the leaders of regimes and other transnational entities as role occupants in systems whose goals may be in conflict with the demands of international, societal, governmental, and private systems puts them on the same analytic plane with foreign policy officials and provides a common dimension along which to observe their actions and interactions.

The role concept also gives meaning to the "given area of international relations" that defines the boundaries of a regime. What is such an area? If it has any empirical expression at all, it consists of the expectations that derive from the values at stake in a particular realm of endeavor. These values may be associated with such diverse issues as trade, security, or balance-of-payments financing—to cite the three "cases" explored in a recent volume devoted exclusively to regimes (Krasner 1982)—but they have in common that they are the basis for the role expectations through which the principles, norms, rules, and procedures of regimes are sustained. Conceiving the values encompassed by regime boundaries in terms of unique role expectations, moreover, makes it easier to break down and analyze the conduct of those actors, such as chiefs of state and foreign secretaries, who are active in a multiplicity of regimes. For such officials, regimes take the form of role conflicts, the analysis of which seems likely to be as revealing of the nature of regimes as of the conduct of officials. To a large extent, in other words, regimes are comparable to what were identified as "issue areas" in the Pre-Theory. Like regimes, issue areas were posited as informal structures derived from, founded on, and delineated by a specifiable set of unique values contested in different ways by the individuals and groups for whom the values are especially salient.

Still another advantage of giving analytic prominence to the role concept is that it serves well those who treat the state as the prime international actor. Viewed as a complex of role expectations, the state is transformed from an abstract, vague, and undefined entity into a precise and observable set of phenomena. Stated simply, the state becomes the actions of those who are expected—and who expect of themselves—to act on behalf of the polity rather than any other societal system or subsystem. That is, if the state has interests beyond government and party, as those who assert the relevance of the concept contend, surely the interests will be manifest in the activities of those in bureaucratic and military organizations who are expected to articulate and serve them. And, obviously, their servicing of these interests is not likely to be easily accomplished.

Those who occupy state roles are not free of role conflicts. These can range widely across all the contradictory expectations that derive from the domestic disputes and international situations in which states become embroiled. Indeed, such a formulation also offers Marxists and non-Marxists alike a means of building their perspectives into the analysis of states: the former can presume that the occupants of state roles avoid conflicts with their class positions by treating the two roles as identical, while the latter can posit them as subject to conflict between the expectations of the state on the one hand and of their occupational, party, or organizational memberships on the other.

Finally, and perhaps most importantly, the role concept is well suited to discerning the microdynamics of global change and interdependence. To the extent that individuals occupy multiple roles in some systems dominated by integrating processes and in others marked by fragmenting processes—such as citizens in Poland and Lebanon, labor leaders in Detroit and Great Britain, or political leaders in El Salvador and France—then to that extent their role conflicts are precisely those that impel change across systems. In such conflicts individuals have to choose which role has the greater legitimacy and which is linked to the highest authority, and the aggregate consequences of these choices then shape the flow of change throughout the global system.

The confluence and simultaneity of conflicting role demands in the cognitive and emotional space of people, in other words, has transformed them into an arena in which world politics unfold. Individuals have become a major battleground on which the state, its subgroups, and transnational organizations compete for their loyalties, thereby posing for them choices that cannot be easily ignored and that, for us as analysts, can serve as both a measure of global change and a challenge to global stability.

Role Scenarios as Action Schema

But the foregoing understates the potential of the role concept. Even as a common denominator across system levels, the Pre-Theory's formulation of roles as sets of formal and informal expectations experienced and held by their occupants now seems insufficient. It limits roles to static phenomena. Expectations highlight the constant constraints and opportunities attached to any role, but the concept so defined does not allow for the flexibility in role expectations that its occupant must employ as situations unfold through time. More specifically, conceived merely as a set of expectations, the concept specifies the attitudes and actions an occupant is expected to maintain in order to perform effectively in the role, but it does not anticipate what the occupants do once they confront their role conflicts and undertake action in response to one or another set of expectations.

To fill this conceptual gap and infuse dynamism into role expectations, roles can be viewed as embedded in more encompassing schemata, what I shall refer to as *role scenarios* or *action scripts.* These embed the expectations of any role in those more elaborate and precise premises upon which any of its occupants is likely to draw in order to depict where he or she fits in relation to other role occupants in the system as they collectively conflict, collaborate, or otherwise cope with the chores and challenges that make up the daily life of the system. In any role, in other words, we not only have an understanding of what is expected of us, but we also carry around a multitude of assumptions about how others in the relevant systems conduct themselves in relation both to us and to the problem at hand, and from these we derive scenarios as to how events are likely to develop as we and the others, each of us conforming to the expectations of or exercising the flexibilities in our role, might react to each other as the problem unfolds.

To recur to the foregoing example of Reagan's role conflict in the field of arms control, the concept of action scripts enables us to understand his behavior as much more than simply a choice to favor his role as a superpower leader over his longtime party role as a conservative hawk. Presumably his decision to retreat from campaign pledges and to make negotiating concessions also sprang from a choice among conflicting scenarios in which the responses of the Soviets, the peace movement in Western Europe, and publics in the United States varied as each reacted differently, depending on whether he acted out of his hawk or superpower role.

Or consider how Prime Minister Thatcher moved in a short span of fifteen months from a tough to a weak stand in negotiations with the Chinese over Hong Kong, from insisting in late 1982 on Britain's retaining administrative control over the territory for an indefinite period after 1997 to pressing in early 1984 for the best guarantees available from the Chinese. Her earlier position was asserted in the context of being flushed with victory in the Falklands and the domestic and international prestige that flowed from having asserted the inviolability of sovereignty in that situation. Subsequently, however, she discovered that the expectations built into the East Asian system are not those of the South Atlantic system, that the strategic and legal circumstances surrounding Hong Kong, not to mention the differences between the Argentine and Chinese armed forces, were such that the original scenario derived from a tough stand was not viable when she later occupied the British head-of-government role in the Pacific (Apple 1984).

Or consider the twice-postponed summit meeting of the Organization of African Unity at Addis Ababa in June 1983. All the chiefs of state brought with them not only expectations of how they had to tailor their conduct to their own society's goals and demands, but each also had scenarios of how the others would react if their collective votes led to a seating of the delegation from the Polesario guerrilla movement. Each anticipated that a vote to seat the delegation would lead to another Moroccan-led boycott that would prevent a quorum from convening and thus give rise to a third postponement which, in turn, could have resulted in the collapse of the OAU. The aggregation of these role scenarios resulted in enough pressure on the Polesario delegation for them to "voluntarily and temporarily" relinquish their seat, a decision which permitted the nineteenth summit meeting to get under way. To conclude that the Polesario delegation bowed to pressure, however, is to overlook the full richness provided by action scripts as analytic tools. Presumably members of the Polesario delegation also made a choice among their own role scenarios, in the end preferring not to risk evoking the scenario in which they would lose the support of their African allies and be perceived as having brought about the OAU's demise.

Much the same kind of reasoning could be employed to dissect and explain the 1983 summit meeting at Williamsburg of the leaders of the Western alliance. Although in this case the continued existence of that structure did not seem to be at stake, the accounts of the deliberations made clear that all seven of the chiefs of state were anxious to prevent the discord that had marked their previous summit meeting, and, accordingly, all of them were keenly aware of how the others would react if the deliberations failed to take into account the difficult domestic circumstances confronting each of them. Thus, for instance, although he preferred not to acknowledge the international consequences of U.S. budget deficits, Reagan knew that to press for avoiding the issue would be to evoke a set of role-derived responses from the other six leaders that, in turn, would run counter to the goals embedded in his role as a possible candidate for reelection in 1984. The six leaders, on the other hand, apparently had action scripts in which Reagan would revert to the issue that had marred the 1982 summit, the Siberian gas pipeline, if they pushed the budget deficit issue too hard. And so the somewhat platitudinous outcome at Williamsburg resulted from each leader responding to the requirements of his or her head-of-government role as those fit into a role scenario which they shared.

The centrality of role scenarios is also evident in the interaction dynamics that occur within as well as between governments. In the United States, for example, all of the key role occupants in the policymaking process are familiar with the goals, calculations, constraints, and conflicts that the others experience in their multiple roles. Thus all of them can envision a variety of outcomes from their interaction over any salient foreign policy issue. More specifically, they can envision the various stages through which different interaction sequences will unfold and culminate as, at each stage, each of them chooses to resolve their other role conflicts in one or another way. The Democratic Speaker of the House of Representatives knows that if he is responsive to the partisan requirements of his party role rather than the bipartisan expectations of his governmental role on, say, the question of El Salvador, the Republican President's reactions are likely to vary accordingly, as will those of the secretary of state, the Senate minority leader, the pro- and antimilitary aid factions in the House, and any other role occupants whose responsibilities may be evoked by the issue.

In one important respect the foregoing examples are misleading. They imply that the relevance of role scenarios is confined to the analysis of decision making. Certainly they are central to the ways in which individuals and bureaucracies frame and make their choices (see below), but the reasoning and reactions of officials is not the only level at which action scripts are core phenomena. As suggested earlier, they are also the basis on which publics participate in global life, with choices among various scenarios underlying the degree to which they are active and the direction which their collective actions take. Stated more emphatically, role scenarios are among the basic understandings and values that are transmitted through political socialization and that sustain collectivities across generations. As such, as culturally derived premises for relating to the political arena, they are also among the prime phenomena that get aggregated when the energies of a collectivity are mobilized and concerted around goals. Put in still another way, the task of leadership is that of selling action scripts, of getting publics to regard one set of scripts as more viable and valid than any other they may find compelling.

Whether applied to micro-decision-making activities or macro-collective actions, role scenarios are at once issue-specific and generalized in their scope. That is, while they are framed in the context of particular issues, they are not transitory in the way issues are. Issues come and go, but the scenarios anticipating their course are based on the more enduring understandings that the occupants of any role are likely to have of the opportunities, constraints, and conflicts built into the other roles comprising the system. In effect the scenarios reflect the comprehension attached to any role of how the system functions —its goals, procedures, cultural premises, capabilities, and historical patterns—both in general and in relation to particular issues.

Note that *the scenarios are inherent in the role and not in its occupants*. Different occupants may resolve a role's conflicts differently, but such resolutions are likely to be founded on similar conceptions of the alternative scenarios that are in conflict. Why? Because the scenarios are the action side of a role's expectations: in experiencing and learning the expectations, the role's occupants also become knowledgeable about the dynamics of the other roles in the system and the contingencies that thus underlie the interactions among them. That is, they cannot learn about the opportunities and limitations built into their own roles without at least a minimal grasp of the requirements faced by the occupants of other roles with whom they must interact. Thus there are no role expectations divorced from the systems in which the roles are lodged, and thus there can be no system without role-derived scenarios among which its members choose as they sustain or change its patterns through time.

This is in no way to imply that role scenarios are clear-cut, orderly, logical, or in any other way standardized. They may well be akin, rather, to what has been called "working knowledge"—that "organized body of knowledge that administrators and policy-makers use spontaneously and routinely in the context of their work," including "the entire array of beliefs, assumptions, interests, and experiences that influence the behavior of individuals at work" (Kennedy 1983, 193–94). Role scenarios can be thought of as translating these arrays of understanding into diverse paths that stretch into and anticipate the future, with each path consisting of segments that are linked by and fan out from choice points and with movement along any segment being a consequence of the interactive expectations held and choices made by all the participants whose paths cross in a situation.

At each choice point in a scenario, moreover, new segments may be introduced as the prior interactions create new circumstances that tap working knowledge in different ways and divert the path onto a new course. Thus, beyond the framework of segmented paths to and from the decision points in a situation, action scripts are anything but standardized. Founded on a composite of beliefs, assumptions, interests, and experiences as well as observation and information, their segments may form paths that are long or short, straight or circuitous, clear or obscure, continuous or broken—to mention only a few of the dimensions along which variation can occur. And the more change is at work in a situation, of course, the greater is the likelihood of extensive and rapid fluctuations along these dimensions. Role scenarios are as operative under chaotic conditions as under orderly ones, but their length, direction, clarity, and continuity are likely to be highly volatile the more changes cascade upon each other.

Yet some generalizations about the nature of role scenarios can be recorded. Most importantly perhaps, they are likely to be marked by a tension between their tendency toward complexity and the limits to which their complexity can be comprehended. The complexity derives from the fact that an action script can potentially embrace a great number and variety of segments, as many permutations and combinations as a role occupant is able to manage in anticipating how the choices he or she makes among competing role expectations will interact sequentially with the alternative choices others in the system may make.

One can begin to appreciate the complexity of interactive scenarios by thinking of their paths metaphorically as maps of the system with decision routes for each of the relevant actors marked by lights that blink at every choice point when one scenario is selected rather than another, thereby sending the unfolding chain of blinking lights off in a new direction. Viewed from the perspective of an observer outside the system, the sequence of lights either moves forward to the conclusion of an issue or it is marked by circularity and back-and-forth vacillation as the choices made by the role occupants offset, negate, or otherwise fall short of the collaboration necessary to a resolution of the situation. Viewed from the perspective of any of the role occupants, the issue maps and their trails of light lie at the core of their activities and either (for the pragmatist) serve to guide the pursuit of their goals in the context of what is feasible or (for the idealist) highlight the obstacles that hinder the realization of their values.

Of course, viewed from the perspective of policymakers who may occupy a number of roles in private systems as well as the many built into their official positions, the scenarios are even more elaborate and complex. They approach mammoth proportions as the crisscrossing, blinking light patterns also trace the personal conflicts and consequences that may follow from immersion in the action schema of their public roles, as in the stimulating discussion of the tensions between private and public role scenarios by Sennett (1976). But as scenarios tend toward increasing complexity, so do the constraints against playing out in the imagination all the segments they might encompass. There is, it seems reasonable to hypothesize, a high correlation between the length and clarity of a scenario: other things being equal, the longer and more diffuse it is—that is, the greater the number of choice points through which it fans out from time 1—the more obscure will be its segments at the distant ends (time n) and the more clear-cut will be those in the near future (say, times 2 and 3). Why? Because anticipating the path beyond a few segments involves managing a great deal of complex information and confronting a great number of hypothetical situations for which prior experience provides no guide, and this combination of complexity and uncertainty tends to curb the inclination to be precise as scenarios stretch further into the future.

With so many segments having fanned out by time n, anticipating likelihoods begins to appear impossible. Thus citizens and officials alike tend to fall back on the early segments and to settle for the obscurity that appears to envelop the later ones. Consider, for example, acting at time 1 in a conflict with two other participants, each of which might move in three new directions at each new stage of the unfolding situation. By the time the fourth choice point arrives the situation might well require information about and demand imaginative forecasting of dozens of possible scenario segments along which the conflict might evolve, a challenge that even the more skilled role occupants would probably want to simplify by treating some segments at time 4 as "unrealistic" or otherwise streamlining the path to manageable proportions. Given the potential of the microelectronic revolution for storing, proliferating, and analyzing interactive files of information, however, other things may not remain equal for very long so far as the construction of role scenarios is concerned.

The expectations attached to roles also operate as constraints that keep scenarios both streamlined and stretched toward time n. A number of the possible segments that can fan out from future choice points are likely to require action that exceeds the maximum leeway that a role permits its occupants to exercise. At time 3, for example, a scenario might require a foreign secretary to undertake initiatives that he could not pursue without prior cabinet or legislative approval. Or consider the informal role expectations involved in the deployment of new weaponry in Europe. Doubtless leaders of the peace movement excluded from their scenarios those segments that might have flowed from choices that allowed for missile deployment in exchange for future compromises in arms control negotiations. Similarly, surely the key NATO governments managed to simplify their action scripts by dismissing a choice point in which they agreed to postpone deployment. Hence, on the grounds that the course must be stayed and that the commitment to goals is unwavering, the tendency toward complexity is often limited and the anticipated paths into the future kept straighter, longer, and more continuous than might otherwise be the case.

Whatever the basis for keeping role scenarios streamlined, it seems reasonable to hypothesize that the longer people occupy a role, the more elaborate their scenarios will be. Indeed, the more elaborate a person's scripts become, the more that person is thought to have political wisdom. For, if the term means anything as it is normally used, political wisdom refers to an astute knowledge of a system and an ability to anticipate how its key actors are likely to conduct themselves under varying circumstances—which is another way of saying that those who are politically wise are able to juggle a more extensive set of scenarios than most people. On the contrary, the less elaborate a person's scenarios, the more that person is likely to be viewed as "lacking in political experience."

Such a characterization, for example, was widely used in 1981 when William P. Clark was first appointed under secretary of state and, later, as national security adviser to the president. Although Clark's unfamiliarity with the names of foreign officials and places captured the headlines at the time, a close examination of the criticism of the appointment reveals that it was faulted less because Clark's prior experience as a judge in California left him uninformed about the details of foreign affairs and more because he lacked knowledge of how international systems function and what events abroad trigger what global trends —that is, he lacked a feel for the premises that allow one to frame sound scenarios that are likely to follow various foreign policy initiatives.

The more elaborate a role scenario is, of course, the more it encompasses all the varied sources out of which action flows. Virtually by definition, for example, wise politicians develop their scenarios out of their general perceptions and knowledge of the other relevant roles and their specific information about the goals the others may seek, the means they may consider, the capabilities they may have available, the cost-benefit calculations they may make, and the support they may mobilize—all of this in the context of how their own choices might variously affect the choices and scenarios of the others.

While role scenarios also embrace game-theoretical calculations as to how the various role occupants may bluff, threaten, or otherwise seek to enhance desired outcomes through strategic posturing in their interactions with each other, it would be erroneous to conclude that the concept of action scripts requires us to depend on game theory for our analyses. The concept posits role scenarios as empirical phenomena, as action-oriented premises held by role occupants, and not as hypothetical constructs employed by rational actors in which stress is placed on scenarios as a means of processing information rather than as a source of action (for example, Abelson 1973 and Axelrod 1973).

Being inherent in the dynamics of any system, in other words, role scenarios are observable. They can be discerned in the position papers prepared for decision makers, in the public accountings of their actions and what they hope to achieve, in the problems they encounter, and in the choices they make. And scenarios can also be empirically traced in the claims and actions of citizens, in the enduring collaborative and conflictful patterns of collectivities, and in the stalemates and transformations of international systems. Game-theoretical analysis would be useful in assessing the options open to a role occupant, but it is quite secondary if the analyst's task is defined as one of estimating how and why the occupant did or might behave in a particular way or of comprehending how diverse role scenarios aggregate to one system outcome rather than another.

Furthermore, as noted, action scripts derive from deeply ingrained subconscious predispositions as well as explicit analytic assessments. The blinking lights along the decision routes of scenarios are linked as much by unstated cultural premises (such as challenges should be met, friends should be rewarded, or alternatives should be considered) and historical memories (such as dictators cannot be trusted, organizations can be paralyzed by inertia, and unruly mobs can foment change) as by current role requirements and situational imperatives. From early in childhood we acquire the givens of social interaction, the inclinations, perceptions, and values through which role expectations are filtered and structured, and as these implicit orientations cumulate into working knowledge across time they increasingly serve as guides to the behavior of others as well as sources of our own conduct. Thus, for example, the scenarios that Western officials and publics developed after a Soviet fighter shot down a Korean airliner consisted not only of decision points shaped by the ongoing arms control negotiations, but also by the cultural premises that killing innocent civilians is unacceptable and the historical memory that the Russians are obsessed with territorial security.

Given the extent to which role scenarios are compounded out of unspoken, tacit assumptions, therefore, they can hardly be the basis for game-theoretical calculations. Moreover, as previously noted, the subconscious components of action scripts are the basis of a more important function: through socialization and the transmission of culture they serve as the underlying foundations from which aggregative processes derive and thereby sustain collectivities across generations. That action scripts are compounded out of tacit and deeply ingrained premises as well as explicit and current role expectations also accounts for the capacity of individuals, officials, and citizens alike to draw on a multitude of scripts as they respond to the vast array of issues that may evoke their interest.

Every culture has its own logic, its own self-contained values and symbols for interpreting and adapting to any challenge, and thus those who are socialized into it never want for the ability to concoct scenarios to cope with the many ongoing situations and the few unexpected developments that claim their attention at any one time. The individuals need not be well informed, and they may even be uninformed, about a situation in order to respond to it. Nor do they need to have clear and elaborate pictures of future choice points and the scripts that connect them. The rich and all-encompassing values and presumptions of their culture will always enable them to develop competing scenarios in which they can fit themselves as well as the others involved in the problem.

It follows that integrated and consensual role scenarios are the glue that holds collectivities together, just as discrepant and competitive scenarios are the acid that paralyze or tear them apart. Depending on whether or not they are widely shared, therefore, action schemata can also underlie system stability or they can foment system collapse.

In a general sense, in other words, a collectivity is no more coherent than the degree to which its members share an appreciation of the different scenarios that may ensue when they do or do not support the processes whereby policies are framed and implemented. In a specific policy sense the degree of agreement among scenarios relevant to how an issue will unfold anticipates the degree to which the policies pursued will be supported and, accordingly, effective. Thus some of Solidarity's calls to rally were successful because enough members perceived that the greater the number who marched under threatening circumstances, the greater would be the effect on the Polish government and the union's friends and adversaries abroad. Thus, too, can those rallies that failed be attributed to the pervasiveness of alternative scenarios among the union's membership in which the consequences of arrest or violence were seen as too great vis-à-vis the perceived impact of a large turnout on governmental and other actors. Likewise, the effectiveness of U.S. foreign policy in, say, Central America will correspond closely to the degree to which legislative and executive officials frame policies on the basis of shared scenarios of what will happen in the region as a consequence of one or another level of U.S. military and economic aid.

In the same manner widespread and rapid shifts in the shared action schemata of a system's members can be said to underlie the momentum and success of revolutionary movements and any other changes that profoundly alter the system's structures. For example, at some point in Iran, perhaps upon Khomeini's return from France, the scenario of a successful overthrow of the Shah became viable as well as desirable for millions of Iranians and their collective actions that followed proved this assessment to be sound. Indeed, the convergence of a society around new role scenarios quintessentially reveals the aggregative dynamics that underlie system transformations. It also points up why revolutions occur so rarely: given the complexity of social processes, the chances of simultaneous convergence occurring around new scenarios are extremely small and yet, as Crozier and Friedberg (1980, 223–24) have noted, profound collective changes only unfold when all the actors learn the new scenario together.

Scenarios in Foreign Policy

Of course, role scenarios derive from intellectual as well as cultural sources. While they are not conceived as game-theoretical products of rational actors, neither are they simple resultants of a culture's logic. They do have intellectual structure and content relevant to the conduct of foreign policy. Subject to the constraints of their cultures, bureaucracies, and personalities, officials do construct their role scenarios on the basis of calculations and reasoning in which the available information is sorted and evaluated. Consider, for example, how the prime targets of foreign policy are likely to derive from role scenarios. Presumably the most compelling targets are those links in role scenarios perceived to be both most vulnerable to influence and, if altered, most susceptible to turning a scenario in a more favorable direction. The makers of foreign policy may speak abstractly of the goals they hope to realize in the global system, but when they move beyond aspirations to concrete actions their focus narrows to the specific links in the interaction patterns abroad that are conceived to be manipulable and capable of leading to outcomes they want to either preserve or promote.

Thus it is, for example, that the Reagan administration developed a scenario in which the sale of gas to Western Europe by the Soviets would enable the Russians to aggregate both needed hard currencies and a dependence on them by their European buyers, outcomes that would then enhance their military capabilities and weaken the cohesion of NATO. To prevent such developments the United States deemed the completion of the gas pipeline from Siberia to be a far weaker segment in the scenario than, say, the Soviet commitment to alleviate its currency shortages or the West European concern to avoid excessive dependence on the Middle East for energy. Hence its policies were directed at curbing the importation into the Soviet Union of the equipment needed to complete the pipeline that American companies had contracted to supply. In the same manner, to cite another recent example, American policy in El Salvador focuses on strengthening the military capabilities of that country's government, apparently on the grounds that none of the other links in the complex scenarios descriptive of Salvadorian futures is as amenable to influence.

Foreign policies, in other words, are addressed not so much to immediate situations as to what they might, preferably or regrettably, become, and what they might become is, as noted, a sequence of future interactions that are vitally alive in the reality world of the minds of both the policymakers and those comprising the collectivity toward which the foreign policies are directed. Foreign policy officials thus think and act in terms of scenarios that stretch into the future, that are envisioned as comprising aggregated segments which vary in their vulnerability to external influence, and that are seen as susceptible to evolving in new, more desirable directions if the most vulnerable segments can be reaggregated through policies specific to them rather than addressed to all the links in the complex scenarios.

It follows that the kinds of segments in foreign policy scenarios to which officials ascribe the greatest vulnerability are likely to be those that are of recent origin and thus not founded on the deeply ingrained and habitual attitudinal and behavioral patterns of publics and their officials. The ties that bind societies, such as shared cultural definitions and nationalistic feelings, and the long-standing interaction patterns that sustain their structures, such as modes of production and forms of governance, are so far beyond modification that foreign policy officials have long since learned that it is fruitless, even counterproductive, to devote their energies to altering them. More accurately, such ties and structures tend to be perceived as given, as not subject to modification over the short term, and therefore as constraints that form the context within which viable scenarios are framed and policy goals selected.

Stated differently, the ties and structures that sustain societies are resolved (or at least quiescent) issues. Whether they delineate relationships between church and state, officials and publics, producers and consumers, or geographic and functional jurisdictions, the ties and structures consist of values pertaining to legitimacy and authority that have been settled for so long as to be widely shared contextual assumptions. But current issues, those value conflicts out of which ties and structures may or may not emerge, are pervaded with unfamiliar circumstances and unknown outcomes, with uncertainties as to who will do what to whom, for how long, and with what degree of intensity before being ready to accommodate; and it is on these current situations abroad marked by fluidity and open-ended scenarios that foreign policy officials are likely to focus as prime targets for their actions.

Occasionally, of course, the essential structures of societies that are normally contextual givens do get caught up in the fluidities and uncertainties of current scenarios. And the greater the extent to which this overlap occurs, it can be hypothesized, the more momentous and memorable will be the events that follow. The Cuban missile crisis, for example, stands out precisely because a long-standing given, U.S. predominance in the Caribbean, was challenged by the Soviets and fostered scenarios in Washington that envisioned potential fluctuations in the country's essential structures pertaining to physical security which were so untenable as to warrant stern responses.

The notion of foreign policy choices as deriving partly from action scripts depicting aggregative processes abroad also facilitates analysis of the blunders that mark world affairs. Two kinds of blunders are especially noteworthy. One involves a failure to stretch the segments in the paths that constitute scenarios far enough into the future or to allow the most distant segments to become progressively ambiguous and obscure. If the segments are too few or too fuzzy, the course of events subsequent to those anticipated by the original scenario can all too quickly move in counterproductive directions. The early U.S. decisions to commit military forces in Vietnam, for example, amounted to a monumental blunder precisely because they were founded on scenarios composed of segments that did not stretch beyond immediate circumstances and specify how events might develop once the battle was joined.

A second, and related, type of blunder ensues when any link in a scenario's path is based on erroneous information and poor judgment. One faulty segment may be sufficient to get a policy into deep trouble and necessitate a reversal of course. The Soviets had to dismantle their missiles in Cuba because the U.S. segment in their scenarios proved to be inaccurate, just as the United States had to rescind the Siberian pipeline policy because the European segment was based on incorrect estimates of how the aggregative processes among its allies would unfold. The premises of the early postwar foreign aid programs, which explicitly acknowledged that the economic and political institutions they sought to promote could require decade-long segments, are another example of this point. Whether such programs can be fairly described as blunders is a moot question, but in retrospect it seems clear that they foundered because a number of segments in their underlying scenarios were obtuse or otherwise defective.

The potential for blunders inherent in role scenarios helps explain the caution that normally marks policymaking organizations. Those who make foreign policy are aware that their scenarios are likely to become increasingly fuzzy and that, accordingly, they need to be sure not to stretch their scripts across too much time and to include in them segments that allow for a retreat in the event the scenario goes off course.

The problems associated with elaborating role scenarios also serve to explain why makers of foreign policy in democratic politics are so readily subject to criticism. If they are cautious and confine their scenarios to only a few segments, they may be charged with being unimaginative and victims of bureaucratic inertia. If they offer clear-cut scenarios that elaborate many segments across long stretches of time, they may be seen as ideologues with tunnel vision. That both kinds of criticism point to the utility of including, so to speak, mid-term computerized models in the day-to-day policymaking process — models that extend the interaction of diplomatic actors and foreign publics beyond immediate circumstances and yet do not stretch so far into the future as to risk overlooking crucial turning points or being too elaborate for comprehension—would probably be even more disturbing to those who voice them.

Given the enormous multiplicity of role scenarios that may be operative in the foreign policy situations of interest to analysts, the question arises as to how the concept can be rendered manageable. How, that is, might the number and variety of scenarios be reduced so that the concept can be incorporated into parsimonious theoretical formulations? Or could it be that the multiplicity of segments and choice points beyond time 2 demonstrates the utter futility of decision-making analysis? For those who posit only macrosources of action, a positive answer to this last question is easily offered: the sheer complexity of role-derived scenarios and their obscure existence as emotional-intellectual phenomena make it impossible to analyze them empirically, but this impossibility need be of no concern since it is the action of states in the context of the global system that sustains and shapes world politics. Such an answer is not acceptable, however, for those like myself who see a need to view action as originating at micro as well as macro levels. For us the multiplicity, complexity, and evanescence of role scenarios cannot be denied, but neither can their cruciality as analytic units. Difficult as they may be to trace and assess, role scenarios seem too central to the continuities and transformations through which action occurs on the global stage to ignore. The scenarios to which officials and collectivities become wedded can and do lead to crises and upheaval, and turning points in international history can and do stem from blunders in structuring and streamlining them. Viewed in this way, action scripts loom as a methodological challenge and not as an obstacle to theory building.

One possible avenue for meeting the challenge comes quickly to mind, namely, the microelectronic revolution and the advent of a fifth generation of computers. As I understand the potential of the upcoming generation, it should prove possible to extend scenario analysis well into time n, and to do so without excessive concern for streamlining the scripts in the interest of manageability. Now it may be plausible, in other words, to include in programmed scenarios seemingly unlikely segments derived from seemingly unimaginable future choices and then to trace the interplay to which they might give rise at new choice points and in new segments. Just as the computer can now play full and imaginative games of chess, taking into account a multiplicity of possible moves and situations that might sustain the game to time n, so might the potentials of complex international situations be played out across time. To be sure, chess is played by a much simpler set of rules than is world politics, and to this extent the analogy breaks down. But we are not lacking in knowledge of the foreign policy rules and surely the utility of this knowledge can be enhanced by the technology now available. One suspects that even now many foreign offices are engaged in scenario construction with fourth generation equipment, and there is no reason why observers of the international scene cannot do the same. What has been said about how "the newer information technologies" may affect inter-nation conflict is just as applicable to those who analyze role conflict; as a consequence of these technologies, "each party may reveal more about its planned surprise moves as more of its behavior is available for sampling. It may also reveal more about its images and unplanned or unconsciously steered behavior patterns, as another party may be better able to analyze it" (Kochen 1981, 396).

Stated differently, like everything else associated with the dynamics of technological change, research methodologies need not be viewed as constants. We may be reaching that happy moment when the most stringent criteria of parsimony in the theory-building enterprise can be relaxed, allowing us to acknowledge and cope more fully with the complexity that we know pervades the world we want to comprehend.

4

Role Theory and the International System:
A Postscript to Waltz's Theory
of International Politics?

Stephen G. Walker

Since its appearance in 1979, Kenneth Waltz's book, *Theory of International Politics*, has provoked considerable controversy and received careful scrutiny by other scholars (Hoffmann 1978, 146–47; Kaplan 1979; Rosecrance 1981; Keohane 1986). His work has generated this attention for a variety of reasons. The book includes an indictment of the notion of "theory" which has guided the efforts of other analysts in their attempts to theorize about international politics (Waltz 1979, 1–17, 68–78). He is also critical of theories that focus upon the individual or national levels of analysis for their explanations of international politics (Waltz 1979, 19–37). Other systems theorists do not escape his reductionist critique, even though Waltz himself favors a systemic level of analysis for thinking theoretically about international politics (Waltz 1979, 38–67). The purpose in this paper, however, is not to add to the debate over Waltz's theory. Instead, after a brief explication of its core ideas, the goal is to explore its implications for thinking theoretically about foreign policy. This task is both more and less than a simple refinement and extension of Waltz's work.

It is less in the sense that the approach here is the study of foreign policy from a domestic perspective rather than the systemic perspective taken by Waltz. The ideas advanced in this paper can stand by themselves and actually began to germinate prior to reading Waltz. Furthermore these concepts are not novel in themselves, since they have appeared previously in bits and pieces in the writings of other scholars prior to the publication of Waltz's book. However, the logic of Waltz's analysis does reinforce the theoretical argument to be presented here. In this sense the theory of foreign policy under consideration is an extension of some elements of Waltz's analysis.

At the same time there is a focus in this paper upon the explanation of *foreign policy* rather than *international politics*, which is the primary focal point of the Waltzian theory. Implicit in this shift is a critique of the scope of Waltz's explanation. It is limited to international outcomes (war, peace, domination, interdependence) as dependent variables, bandwagoning, balancing, competition, and socialization processes as intervening variables, and structural features (the distribution of capabilities, unit differentiation and functional specification, the ordering principle of organization) as independent variables. All of these variables are located at the systemic level of analysis.

Although Waltz makes a few relatively inchoate allusions to the impact of systemic structure upon the actions of states, he is primarily concerned with the constraining effect of systemic structure upon interaction processes among states and the range of international outcomes that emerge from these interactions (Waltz 1979, 71–73, 99–101). Consequently, Waltz does not explain the actions of states but only their consequences. Even with this limited focus he does not attempt to explain by specifying particular outcomes. Instead, he is content to delimit the range of international outcomes permitted by the structure of the international system. He defends this mode of explanation on two grounds.

First, he argues that a desirable property of theory is elegance, which "means that explanations and predictions will be general" (Waltz 1979, 69). The inference here is that there is a trade-off between a theory's degree of elegance and its predictive or explanatory specificity. "A theory of international politics will, for example, explain why war recurs, and it will indicate some of the conditions that will make war more or less likely; but it will not predict the outbreak of particular wars" (Waltz 1979, 69). Second, Waltz asserts that a structural theory explains continuities and not variations. "Structural concepts, although they lack detailed content, help to explain some big, important, and enduring patterns." The implication is that significant change occurs only when structures change (Waltz 1979, 70).

Instead of acknowledging a vulnerability to the criticism that, by indiscriminately accounting for a broad range of outcomes he is really accounting for none of them, Waltz dismisses this variety as insignificant. From the perspective of a foreign policy analyst, however, this variety is significant as the primary puzzle to be understood in theoretical terms along with the variety of actions by states which contribute to these outcomes.

Therefore, a theory of foreign policy is more than an extension and a refinement of Waltzian theory. It has a different focus and is perhaps a more difficult puzzle to solve. Whether a theory of foreign policy is a postscript to a theory of international politics, or vice versa, appears to depend upon the interests of the analyst. In any event, by limiting his explanation to the circumscription of the range of international outcomes at the systemic level of analysis, Waltz has left an equally challenging theoretical puzzle to be solved by foreign policy analysts.

Toward a Theory of Foreign Policy

The remainder of this paper contains some notions and propositions that are a first cut at the formulation of a theory of foreign policy. These theoretical arguments appear at the same level of generalization and in the same form as Waltz's theory of international politics. There is no attempt to test the theory in a rigorously empirical manner, but it shall be illustrated by exploring the implications of its application to some questions which are common in the foreign policy literature. Since this analysis uses the same notion of "theory" that Waltz does, let us begin by clarifying what he means by "theory." By the end of the presentation, it should become clear how and why Waltz's theory of international politics at the systemic level of analysis reinforces the theory of foreign policy at the national level of analysis. To make this connection clear, however, it will be necessary to articulate Waltz's theory of international politics in more detail before presenting the theory of foreign policy.

According to Waltz (1979, 8–10):

A theory is a picture, mentally formed, of a bounded realm or domain of activity.... A theory indicates that some factors are more important than others and specifies relations among them.... A theory is *not* (italics added) the occurrences seen and the associations recorded, but is instead the explanation of them.... Theories are combinations of descriptive and theoretical statements. The theoretical statements are nonfactual elements of a theory.

Waltz distinguishes here between statements which describe invariant or highly probable relationships (laws) that are established by rigorous observation and the concepts and assumptions which explain them. Whereas laws are intimately tied to reality, a theory is invented by the intellectual processes of speculation and the exercise of the imagination (Waltz 1979, 5–7).

Theorizing inevitably involves simplification in order to organize data so that one can "try to find the central tendency among a confusion of tendencies, to single out the propelling principle even though other principles operate, to seek the essential factors where innumerable factors are present.... Both induction and deduction are indispensable in the construction of a theory, but using them in combination gives rise to a theory only if a creative idea emerges" (Waltz 1979, 10–11). He identifies four strategies of simplification which facilitate the emergence of theory (Waltz 1979, 10):

1. *isolation*, which requires viewing the actions and interactions of a small number of factors and forces as though in the meantime other things remain equal

2. *abstraction*, which requires leaving some things aside in order to concentrate on others

3. *aggregation*, which requires lumping disparate elements together according to criteria derived from a theoretical purpose

4. *idealization*, which requires proceeding as though perfection were attained or a limit reached even though neither can be

Waltz employs these strategies in the formulation of his theory of international politics. First he simplifies the realities of domestic and international politics by distinguishing between two ideal types of structures according to their respective ordering principles of hierarchy and anarchy. Then he aggregates every political order into one type or the other (Waltz 1979, 114). This typology is obviously an abstraction which concentrates upon one feature of politics and leaves others aside. However, the creation of a typology based upon this ordering principle permits Waltz to isolate the actions and interactions of a small number of forces and factors, which he postulates as theoretical assumptions about international politics, that is, politics in an anarchical political order. They include the following:

1. Self-help is necessarily the principle of action in an anarchical order since, by definition, units in a condition of anarchy must rely on the means they can generate and the arrangements they can make for themselves to achieve their objectives and maintain their security (Waltz 1979, 111).

2. A self-help system is one in which those who do not help themselves, or who do so less effectively than others, will fail to prosper, will lay themselves open to dangers, will suffer; fear of such unwanted consequences stimulates states to behave in ways that tend toward the creation of balances of power (Waltz 1979, 118).

3. Balance-of-power politics prevail wherever two, and only two, requirements are met: that the order be anarchic and that it be populated by units wishing to survive (Waltz 1979, 121).

4. A balance-of-power theory assumes that in an anarchic order states (or those who act for them) at a minimum seek their own preservation and, at a maximum, drive for universal domination by seeking to maintain or increase their power *vis-à-vis* other states either by internal efforts (increasing economic or military capability, developing clever strategies) or by external efforts (strengthening one's own alliances and weakening opposing ones) (Waltz 1979, 118).

5. In the context of balance-of-power theory, the condition of its operation (and also the operational definition of an anarchical political order) is as follows: that two or more states coexist in a self-help system, one with no superior agent to come to the aid of states that may be weakening or to deny to any of them the use of whatever instruments they think will serve their purposes (Waltz 1979, 118).

6. In an anarchical order where the victory of one coalition over another leaves the weaker members of the winning coalition at the mercy of the stronger ones, the first concern of states is not to maximize power but to maintain their positions in the system; hence, balancing (the joining of weaker coalitions) and not band-

wagoning (the joining of potentially hegemonic coalitions) is the characteristic behavior of international politics (Waltz 1979, 126).

7. Since balance-of-power theory depicts international politics as a competitive system, states will display characteristics common to competitors, namely, that they will imitate each other and become socialized to their system (Waltz 1979, 128).

8. Behavior and outcomes vary in international systems whose ordering principle endures but whose structures differ in other ways through changes in the distribution of capabilities among states, defined as changes in the number of great powers (and not in terms of the number of power blocs) (Waltz 1979, 129).

9. Among the great powers in an international system, military and economic interdependence among them is lower in a bipolar system than in a multipolar system (Waltz 1979, 143–46, 163–70).

10. The smaller the number of great powers, and the wider the disparities between the few most powerful states and the many others, the more likely the former are to act for the sake of the system and to participate in the managerial tasks of transforming or maintaining the international system, preserving the peace, promoting economic development and ecological stability (Waltz 1979, 198–99).

These ten propositions summarize a systemic theory of international politics in which the structure of the system operates in two ways. First, its structural features act as antecedent variables that shape the actions of states in both cooperative situations and conflict situations by limiting the degree to which any one state will tolerate either an increase in dependence upon another state or an increase in the capabilities of another state. Second, the structure intervenes to limit the range of outcomes that occur when states interact. In both cases, the "self-help" feature of the system's structure is at the core of the explanation.

Foreign Policy in a Self-Help System

The following theory of foreign policy is ultimately compatible with the ten propositions that summarize Waltz's theory of international politics. The central proposition in the theory of foreign policy appears as a corollary of the central proposition in the Waltzian theory of international politics. However, it is possible to formulate the foreign policy theory's initial premise without including an introductory clause referring to systemic variables.

1. *Self-help/domestic primacy proposition*. Because of the self-help imperative imposed by the structure of the international system, a state's foreign policy is an instrument for the pursuit or maintenance of domestic policy goals.

An alternative rationale to the internationally based self-help imperative is the domestically based one that, after all, the state does exist to govern the society and only acquires the foreign policy function as a consequence of the existence of other states. Domestically, the state functions to focus the political process within the society, defined in Eastonian terms as the process of authoritative allocation of values for the society (Easton 1953). Four more propositions in the theory define four aspects, or subprocesses, within the political process.

2. *The exchange process*. The allocation of values can take four forms, distributive, regulatory, redistributive, and collective (Lowi 1964; Zimmerman 1973; McGowan and Walker 1981), which refer to the terms of the allocation of values among the members of the society.

3. *The role-location process*. The establishment of a shared set of expectations among the participants is part of the allocation process.

4. *The conflict process*. The creation of adversary relations among participants in the political process occurs when (a) the terms of allocation have not been established among the participants in the allocation process, or (b) the existing set of shared expectations among the participants in the allocation process breaks down.

5. *The institution-building process*. As the terms of allocation and the set of shared expectations regarding the terms of allocation persist over a long enough time, they become formalized into institutions as a consequence.

Each of these subprocesses has been the subject of theorizing in the domains of both domestic politics and international politics. Exchange theory focuses upon the exchange process (Baldwin 1978; Blau 1964; Emerson 1972a and 1972b; Walker 1981). Role analysis encompasses the role location process (Sarbin and Allen 1968; Wahlke et al., 1962;

Walker 1979, 1981, 1982b; Hudson et al. 1982). Coalition theory addresses the dynamics of the conflict process (Riker 1962; Waltz 1979). Positivist jurisprudence and the literature on international regimes deals with the institution-building process (Keohane and Nye 1977; Krasner 1982). In the context of these aspects of the political process, *policy* (domestic and foreign) becomes the behavior of the state's policymakers which articulates the terms of allocation and establishes the set of expectations associated with them. In domestic politics the participants in the political process are limited to the state's officials and different sectors of the society, whose identities are likely to vary depending upon the form of the allocation process (Lowi 1964). In international politics the participants may be limited to a set of states or may include transnational actors, again depending upon the form of the allocation process (Zimmerman 1973; McGowan and Walker 1981).

Although states and their societies exist in a multitude of sizes, levels of economic development, and cultural milieus which create a vast diversity of values to be allocated in their domestic political processes, the sixth proposition in the theory of foreign policy postulates that all states allocate three values: physical security, wealth, and social identity.

> 6. *The national security proposition*. The leaders of all states make policies to protect themselves and their subjects from armed attack, severe economic dislocation, and cultural emasculation or territorial dismemberment.

This proposition is phrased negatively, that is, in terms of avoiding undesirable conditions, but it may also be phrased positively as the assumption that all states seek to survive and flourish. In this form it is virtually identical to one element of Waltz's third proposition: "Balance-of-power politics prevail wherever . . . the order [is] anarchic *and . . . it [is] populated by units wishing to survive*" (italics added).

The crucial theoretical relationship between domestic policy and foreign policy is that a state's foreign policy is either (a) a request addressed to another state for assistance in the protection or achievement of national security, or (b) a response by one state to another state's request for assistance in the area of national security. In a self-help international system each state is ultimately responsible for the authoritative allocation of its own values. But at the same time the leaders of states often find it tempting and sometimes necessary to seek external assistance if their regime and perhaps their society are to survive. Consequently, the sources of national insecurity can be internal if there is a lack of sufficient resources available within the society to establish terms of allocation that will satisfy the security claims of the participants. It may also be external if the demands placed upon another state by a state with inadequate resources are not met or if an existing set of shared expectations among a set of states breaks down.

Systemic versus Domestic Theories of Foreign Policy

In order to illustrate the points of convergence and divergence between Waltz's systemic theory and the domestic theory presented here, let us consider some prominent puzzles in the study of contemporary foreign policy and international politics. This exercise should also help to flesh out the explication of the foreign policy theory.

First let us focus upon the controversy over the origins of the cold war. Systemically oriented theorists, such as Morgenthau (1970a) and Waltz, regard the occurrence of the cold war as a function of the impact of a bipolar distribution of capabilities in a system of anarchy. Morgenthau (1970a) argues that competition and the development of a balance of power between the two superpowers was almost inevitable, while the existence of the balance kept a cold war from escalating into a hot war. Orthodox historians such as Schlesinger (1970) assert that the domestic dynamics of the Soviet political system disrupted Soviet-American postwar relations and led to the cold war. The regime's totalitarian structure and expansionist ideology created incentives among Soviet leaders to create international tensions in order to justify their political organization and ideology. Revisionist historians such as Gardner (1970) claim that domestic economic pressures and an anti-communist, democratic ideology drove U.S. leaders to place demands upon the Soviet Union which threatened their national security concerns in Central and Eastern Europe.

All three historical interpretations contain bits and pieces of the answer to the puzzle. A domestic theory of foreign policy would arrange the pieces this way. An analysis of Soviet domestic policy at the end of World War II would reveal that the first major domestic problem facing the regime was economic recovery from the ravages of the German invasion. Soviet foreign policy toward Eastern Europe, Germany, and even Turkey, Iran, and China, was directed toward the acquisition of resources from these nations to assist in Soviet economic recovery. The second major problem for the Stalinist government was to insure against an armed attack from Germany in the future along with any potential German allies among the East European states. The incentives for planning against such a contingency were not merely the historical experiences associated with World War I and World War II; there would also be the potential conflicts arising between Russia and the neighboring states over the terms of redistributing resources from these Soviet-occupied areas into the Soviet Union's economic recovery effort. The solution that Stalin ultimately selected as a foreign policy in response to these problems was the division of Germany and the communization of Eastern Europe.

The Soviet domestic demand for external resources to aid in economic recovery could have conceivably been managed another way. The only other available source was the United States, which would handle similar claims from the West European states through the Marshall Plan. The terms of exchange which the American government would attempt to exact from the USSR, however, would be too high a domestic price for the Soviet regime to pay. Participation in the Marshall Plan would link the Soviet socialist economy too closely to the capitalist economies and threaten the social identity dimension of Soviet national security. On the other hand, to fail in an attempt to gain outside assistance could threaten Soviet national security through severe economic dislocation. So Stalin's cold war policies represented a trade-off among the three aspects of national security: it raised slightly the threat of armed attack while it reduced the threat of severe economic dislocation and protected the social identity of the Soviet socialist society.

American policymakers probably did not appreciate Stalin's problems in the terms used here to delineate them. From their perspective the Soviets were violating the shared set of expectations which had been established earlier among the Allies at the wartime summit conferences culminating at Yalta and Potsdam. The Soviet Union's actions were in violation of the Declaration on Liberated Europe and the consensus that Germany should remain united. Moreover, the Soviet violations of these expectations had important consequences for the United States.

For example, the Soviet failure to provide agricultural goods from Germany's Eastern zone in exchange for capital and consumer goods from the Western zones created a dilemma for the occupying powers in the West. Without food, the West Germans would starve. If the occupying powers raised the production ceilings for industrial goods in the Western zones, the surplus could be exported in return for agricultural imports. However, the new production ceilings would place the Western powers in violation of the Potsdam agreements too. On the other hand, unless the Soviets also honored the Potsdam agreements and provided food, the United States would have to feed the West Germans gratis, which would create domestic economic and political problems for the Truman administration. The resolution of this American policy dilemma was in favor of U.S. domestic considerations. West German production ceilings were raised, the British, French, and American zones were unified, and Stalin responded with the Berlin blockade (Hartmann 1965; Hanrieder 1967).

Second, let us analyze the development of the Sino-Soviet conflict and the emergence of Soviet-American détente followed by Sino-American détente. When the Beijing regime came to power in 1949, Mao Zedong aligned his new government with the recently established Soviet bloc under Moscow's leadership. He made this choice after attempts to probe the possibilities for an amicable relationship with the United States failed to produce substantive results. With the outbreak of McCarthyism in the United States, the escalation of the Korean War to include Sino-American combat, and the U.S. alignment with Chiang Kai-Shek's Nationalist regime, Mao's initial choice was reinforced. Nevertheless, by 1956 the Sino-Soviet rift had begun. It flared into the open in 1963, escalated to the point of military confrontation by 1969, and was followed by Sino-American détente. What accounts for this reversal in Chinese foreign policy?

The new Chinese regime faced three problems in 1949: the restoration of traditional Chinese territorial frontiers, the recovery of an economy ravaged by civil war and Japanese occupation, and the consolidation of all of China under a single government. Mao's regime sought Soviet assistance in the resolution of all three problems, and the Soviet government ultimately refused to provide the resources necessary for managing any of them. The Chinese were unable to renegotiate Sino-Soviet territorial frontiers. Soviet economic aid proved to be inadequate for the adoption of a capital-intensive economic development plan for China. The Russians also refused to use their nuclear might in support of China's attempts at regaining Quemoy and Matsu in confrontations with Taiwan and the United States (Zagoria 1962). To honor fully any of these Chinese demands would have threatened Soviet national security. Redrawing the Soviet-Chinese frontier would have threatened the territorial integrity of the USSR. Providing economic assistance on the scale necessary to develop China would have resulted in severe economic dislocation in Russia. Backing China against the United States over Quemoy and Matsu raised the threat of nuclear war with the United States.

Sino-Soviet relations were further complicated by the process of de-Stalinization initiated for domestic reasons inside the Soviet Union after Stalin's death in 1953. The de-Stalinization process included a repudiation of Stalinist command economics and political repression within the Soviet Union plus the rejection of the Stalinist doctrines of capitalist encirclement and the inevitability of wars as an international outgrowth of the class struggle as cornerstones of Soviet foreign policy. China's adoption of self-help domestic and foreign policies which resembled Stalinism exacerbated the relations between the two communist states. These developments in Chinese foreign policy were followed by an intensification of the Sino-Soviet conflict as both the terms of their previous exchange relationships and their mutual expectations regarding those relations broke down.

Soviet-American détente and Sino-American détente subsequently emerged partly as a consequence of the balancing process identified in Waltz's systemic theory of international politics. The Soviets attempted to reduce Soviet-American tension so that they could turn more of their attention to the Sino-Soviet conflict. Sino-American détente developed as the Chinese attempted to gain an ally against the Soviet Union or at least weaken the Soviet-American link. However, these détente relationships have also depended for their existence upon the establishment of exchange relationships and shared expectations that help to solve the domestic problems of each member of the dyad. In the Soviet-American relationship, arms control and trade agreements reflected a joint concern for the economic costs of the arms race and the benefits of an increase in trade to the economies of both countries. In the Sino-American relationship, mutually beneficial trade arrangements provided domestic incentives to both countries. The Moscow Declaration and the Shanghai Communiqué attempted to establish a set of mutual expectations to guide the two détente relationships.

Foreign Policy Roles and the International System

The examples of cold war and détente relationships in the postwar world can be explained within the organizational framework provided by a domestic theory of foreign policy. The state with the most pressing domestic problems took the initiative in each case to gain assistance from abroad in the resolution of domestic problems. The targets of these initiatives could respond with aid or refuse the request. If the response was positive, it was also contingent upon the fulfillment of conditions which would benefit the domestic situation of the respondent. If the response was negative, the initiator could ask some other state or could press the original request. If the latter option was selected, then a conflict was likely to develop.

Consequently, we may identify three basic types of foreign policy roles, *consumer*, *producer*, and *belligerent*, plus two auxiliary types whose derivation will require the postulation of one more proposition. The consumer type refers to those foreign policies in which the goal is to gain or maintain assistance from another state. The assistance may take several forms, including economic resources, military aid, and diplomatic support. The policies which supply assistance to other states are manifestations of a producer type. A belligerent role is one in which the state either resists requests for assistance or else presses demands for assistance in the face of resistance by the target.

Two more foreign policy roles, *facilitator* and *provocateur*, may also be identified, if we allow for the simultaneous inclusion of more than two states in the analysis of foreign policy. The introduction of this possibility is provided in a seventh proposition.

> 7. *The linkage proposition*. In order to pursue or maintain domestic policy goals, a state may act to establish, maintain, or disrupt a shared set of expectations or the allocation of values among other states.

A facilitator role is one which attempts to establish or maintain an exchange process and a set of shared expectations among other states (see also Hudson et al. 1982). A provocateur role seeks to disrupt already-existing relationships of this kind or to prevent them from coming into existence (see also Wilkinson 1969, 12–13).

In the facilitator case, the state either requests or supplies assistance on behalf of another state. The incentive is the potential threat to the facilitator's own relationships with the state the facilitator represents. The disruption of this relationship would, in turn, disrupt the domestic policies of the facilitator. The incentive for a state to select a provocateur policy is the threat to the provocateur posed by the creation or the continuation of an exchange process among other states. The provocateur's own exchange relations with some or all of the other states would break down, causing the disruption of the provocateur's own domestic policies.

In addition to the generation of this typology of foreign policy roles, a major insight which a domestically-oriented theory of foreign policy provides is an understanding of the origins of the conflict relationships that a balance-of-power theory emphasizes. Balancing processes occur (a) when existing exchange relationships or shared sets of expectations break down and (b) when attempts to establish mutually beneficial exchange relations and shared expectations fail. The anarchic self-help structure of the international system compels each state to be primarily responsible for its own domestic welfare and also constrains the range of international outcomes in its attempts at self-help. However, the causes of failure and breakdown are to be located through an analysis of domestic conditions within the states under examination.

III   International Roles: National Sources, Behavioral Consequences, and Policy Analysis

---

5

The Correspondence between Foreign Policy Rhetoric and Behavior:

Insights from Role Theory and Exchange Theory

Stephen G. Walker

The search for an adequate description and explanation of foreign policy patterns is a task that continues to engage scholars in several of the social sciences. In this paper two individual-level models, role theory and exchange theory, are employed to analyze patterns of rhetoric and behavior at the national level. The research design incorporates some concepts from role theory, relates them to Homans's (1961, 1974) principles of classical exchange theory, and tests some derivative hypotheses about the relationships between foreign policy rhetoric and behavior. The data sources for the analysis are national policy speeches between 1965 and 1967 by the leaders of forty-five nations (Holsti 1970) and an inventory of international actions attributed to these nations between 1965 and 1969 (McGowan and O'Leary 1975).

Reprinted with permission from *Behavioral Science* 26 (1981): 272–81.

In an earlier analysis of these data sets (Walker 1979) the following four major propositions from role theory were tested regarding the description and explanation of foreign policy. First, there tends to be a congruent relationship between role conception (foreign policy rhetoric) and role enactment (foreign policy behavior) for 3rd nations and super-powers in their dyadic relationships. Second, there is a tendency among 3rd nations to avoid role conflict by adopting foreign policy behavior toward both superpowers that corresponds to the principles of bal-ance and congruence associated with triadic relationships. Third, devia-tions from these first two propositions are attributable to the effects of the expectations created by the target's role conception (rhetoric) and/or the cues provided by the target's role enactment (behavior). Fourth, nations with balanced relationships between role conception and role enactment will also tend to show congruent relationships between these foreign policy traits.

The terms "congruence" and "balance" in these propositions refer to the "degree of fit" or "match-up" between an actor's rhetoric and behavior when they are compared with respect to their valence. Valence is the overall orientation of the rhetoric or the behavior toward the target, that is, the other member of the dyad. A balanced relationship exists when the rhetorical valence and the behavioral valence have the same signs. A congruent relationship is a special case of balance in which the magnitudes of the valence scores are identical. The formu-lae for the calculation of valence scores for rhetoric and behavior are:

$$\text{RCV} = \left[\frac{\text{COOP}-\text{CONF}}{\text{COOP}+\text{CONF}} \right] \times \frac{1}{1+\text{NEU}} \times 100$$

$$\text{REV} = \left[\frac{\text{COOP}-\text{CONF}}{\text{COOP}+\text{CONF}} \right] \times \quad 100$$

where RCV = Role Conception Valence and REV = Role Enactment Val-ence. COOP = the frequency of cooperative role conceptions in the RCV formula and the frequency of cooperative behavior in the REV formula. CONF = the frequency of conflict role conceptions in the RCV formula and the frequency of conflict behavior in the REV formula. NEU = the frequency of neutral, unaligned role conceptions in the RCV formula. The range for the RCV and REV scores is −100 to +100.

"3rd nation" stands for any nation in the data set with the exception of the two superpowers, the United States and the USSR. A triad is balanced when all three relations are positive or when two relations are negative and one is positive (Zajonc 1968, 339−45; see also O. Holsti 1966, 346−48). For the cold war triads formed by the U.S., USSR, and the

Table 5.1 Congruence relationships between role-conception
and role-enactment valences for all nations

N = 45 Actor-target	Pearson's correlations zero-order r's* congruence	Partial correlations Controls for cues/ expectations		Variance	
		Target(s) behavior	Target(s) conception	Explained[a]	Revised[b]
3rd-U.S.	+ .27	+ .21	—**	.07	.04
3rd-USSR	+ .37	+ .20	+ .25	.14	.06
3rd-Super- powers***	+ .19	+ .23/+ .09	+ .22/+ .17	.04	.01

* If r ⩾ .30, then p < .05 for both zero and partial r's.
** Multicollinearity precludes use of this variable in either the analysis of the partials or the variance.
*** The correlations for this triad are between the 3rd nation's role-enactment valences toward each superpower. The partial correlation is listed first for U.S. and second for USSR when targets' cues and expectations are introduced as controls.
[a] The explained reduction in the variance measures the congruence between role-conception and role-enactment valences without taking the effects of cues (target's behavior) and expectations (target's conception) into account.
[b] The revised reduction in the variance measures the congruence between role-conception and role-enactment valences after the effects of cues (target's behavior) and expectations (target's conceptions) are removed. It is the square of the partial correlation when all eligible control variables are introduced into the analysis.

3rd nations in this study, the U.S.-USSR relationship is given as negative. Consequently, the signs of the 3rd nation-superpower relationships must be mixed in order for the triads to be balanced. For these two relationships to be congruent, there should be an inverse relationship between the magnitude of their valences.

The results of this analysis are reported fully in Walker (1979) and summarized in table 5.1. The findings in table 5.1 indicate that (1) the congruence between the role conceptions and foreign policy actions of 3rd nations in relation to the superpowers (United States and USSR) is relatively weak, (2) the simultaneous behavior of 3rd nations toward both superpowers does not covary strongly in the congruent fashion predicted by the research hypotheses from role theory, and (3) these findings continue to hold when the effects of the target's role conceptions and cues are taken into account. The only strong relationships are in support of the fourth major proposition. For nations with a balanced relationship between role conception and role enactment,

Table 5.2   Congruence relationships between role-conception
and role-enactment valences for balanced nations

Actor-target	N	Pearson's correlations zero-order r's congruence	Partial correlations Controls for cues/ expectations		Variance*	
			Target(s) behavior	Target(s) conception	Explained	Revised
3rd-U.S.	(23)	+ .78**	+ .72**	—***	.61	.52
3rd-USSR	(26)	+ .73**	+ .63**	—***	.53	.40
3rd-Super- powers*	(19)	− .66**	− .69/− .64**	—***/− .70**	.44	.53

* See notes in table 5.1 for definitions of explained and revised variance and for definitions of the correlations for the 3rd-superpowers triad.
** p < .01.
*** Multicollinearity precludes the use of this variable either in the analysis of the partials
or the variance.

there are also strongly congruent relationships in support of the first
two major propositions (see table 5.2).

In spite of the lack of correspondence between role conceptions
and role enactments for the entire group of nations, it may be possible
to construct and test an explanation that is consistent with role theory
and the data for subsets of these nations. In the earlier analysis (Walker
1979) there is the caveat that the process of "role location" is an uncertain one. The target's cues, expectations, and the actor's role conceptions all influence the selection and enactment of a role. Cues and
expectations may be ambiguous, complex, and contradictory; the actor
may have multiple role conceptions which are activated by the target's
cues. Expectations may be imperfectly understood and modified by
the actor to conform to the actor's role conceptions. Moreover, the
selection of role enactment behavior that does not correspond to role
conception rhetoric may be the result of successful "altercasting." This
process can occur because of the reciprocal nature of role relations.
Theoretically one member of a role set can select a role which is
advantageous to the former (Backman 1970, 313). By extension the
altercaster could even select behavior that does not correspond to any
elements of the actor's own publicly known repertoire of role
conceptions.

The emphases upon uncertainty and the possibility of altercasting
in the role location process appear to be consistent with the thrust of

the principles of operant psychology, which emphasize the conditioning effects of reinforcement from a stimulus in the environment. Exchange theory offers a description and explanation of behavior in precisely these terms.

The Intellectual Origins of Exchange Theory

As the literal meaning of the term implies, "exchange" theory focuses upon the *act* of giving or taking one thing in return for another. As theory qua theory, exchange theory is an *explanation* of the act of giving or taking one thing in return for another. The intellectual origins of exchange theory are somewhat complex, since today it constitutes a collection of concepts and propositions from the disciplines of economics, sociology, political science, and social psychology (see Baldwin 1978). As one moves across these disciplinary orientations, the scope of exchange theory broadens from the exchange of concrete commodities or money in a market to the exchange of behaviors that may be beneficial to one or more participants in the exchange. As it has been developed by Homans (1961, 1974), exchange theory has become abstract enough to be applied to a variety of situations. His social exchange theory consists of the following general propositions (paraphrased from Homans 1961; 1974, 15–50).

1. In choosing between alternative actions, an actor will choose that one for which (as perceived by the actor at the time) the value (V) of the result, multiplied by the probability (p) of getting the result, is the greater. (rationality proposition)

2. The more often in the recent past an actor has received a particular reward, the less valuable any further unit of that reward becomes. (deprivation-satiation proposition)

3. When an actor's action does not receive an expected reward or receives unexpected punishment, aggressive behavior becomes more likely. (aggression proposition)

4. When an actor's action receives an expected reward, especially a greater reward than expected, or does not receive an expected punishment, the actor becomes more likely to perform approving behavior. (approval proposition)

Kunkel (1977, 445–46) and Kunkel and Nagasawa (1973, 531–32) claim that Homans has based his propositions largely upon axioms from elementary economics and Skinnerian propositions from animal studies. They point out that Homans provides only one explanation of how behaviors are established, namely, "that behavior must occur before it can be re-inforced; hence a new behavior must 'exist' before it can be 'learned.'" Kunkel and Nagasawa contend that there is "much evidence ... (e.g., Bandura, 1969) ... that most human learning proceeds through modeling rather than direct experience, as Homans' model implies." They conclude (p. 540) that one important implication of learning by vicarious modeling is that changes in value depend on modeling as well as the nature of deprivations. Contrary to Homans's deprivation-satiation proposition, more recent reinforcers are not always less valuable than earlier ones once the following modeling proposition is added to Homans's set of propositions (Kunkel and Nagasawa 1973, 535).

5. If an activity is learned through modeling, then the actor is likely to repeat it in similar circumstances (provided the model's behavior was reinforced).

The Relationship Between Exchange Theory and Role Theory

With the substitution of the modeling proposition for the deprivation-satiation proposition, the principles of exchange theory may be used to extend and refine role theory. Specifically, exchange principles may account for role enactment behavior under conditions of uncertainty, when altercasting or the absence of cues in the presence of multiple role conceptions may create incongruity between role enactment and some role conceptions. In role theory the concepts of role competition and role conflict account for incongruity between role conception and role enactment. Role *competition* occurs when "actions taken to honor one expectation compete in time and resources with actions necessary to meet another expectation" (Backman 1970, 315). This phenomenon may occur even when honoring one expectation does not violate another expectation, which is the distinguishing feature of role *conflict*.

Multiple role conceptions toward one or more targets appear to be a logical precondition for either role competition or role conflict to exist. Sarbin and Allen (1968, 538) identify three patterns of simultaneous enactment of multiple roles within a given time frame:

1. the alternation of two or more roles within the period of observation

2. the merging of two or more roles so they are indistinguishable in terms of role enactment behavior within the period of observation

3. the interpenetration of roles without their merger in behavioral terms within the period of observation

However, this classification scheme does not address the most extreme conditions of role competition and role conflict under which one role is selected at the expense of another. Nor does it identify which role to select in the absence of cues from the target or when the cues constitute altercasting by the target.

Exchange principles may provide answers to some of these problems. First, in the absence of immediate reinforcement (cues) from the target, the modeling proposition would account for the initiation of behavior of a particular type through prior reinforcement in similar circumstances. Second, the application of the rationality proposition to the process of role location would predict that under conditions of role competition or role conflict, an actor will choose that role enactment for which the probable reward is the greater. Once an actor initiates role enactment on the basis of the modeling and rationality propositions, other exchange principles may account for the continuation or modification of the behavior under different circumstances. In figure 5.1 the possible combinations of role conception and cue valences are defined in terms of their signs and magnitudes. For those cases where role conceptions and cues have the same signs (quadrants I and III), the cues reinforce the tendency toward balance and congruence between role conception and role enactment. The process of role location is relatively unambiguous, since the balance/congruence and altercasting propositions from role theory do not compete with one another.

However, role location is a more uncertain process in quadrants II and IV. The different signs for role conceptions and cues indicate the existence of an ambiguous situation in which the role-enactment sign may correspond with the sign for the actor's role conception (balance proposition) or for the target's cue (altercasting proposition). Under these conditions the approval and aggression propositions from exchange theory would predict that the altercasting proposition will dominate the balance proposition in accounting for the observed sign of the actor's role enactment. By extension, the role-enactment valence will also be more congruent with the cue valence than with the role-conception valence for those cases that fall into these quadrants. In each of these uncertain situations, the assumption in the following discussion is that approval and reward behavior are equivalent with cooperative behavior, while aggressive and punishment behavior are inter-

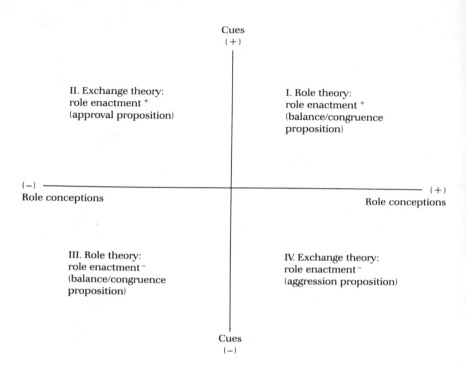

Figure 5.1   The domains of role theory and exchange theory

changeable with conflictual behavior. This auxiliary hypothesis acts as a bridge between role theory's altercasting proposition and the approval and aggression propositions of exchange theory. These exchange propositions become, in effect, corollaries of the altercasting proposition.

Specifically, if the actor's role-conception valence is conflictual (−), but the valence of the target's cue is cooperative (+), then the altercasting proposition from role theory will take the form of the approval proposition from exchange theory. The approval proposition predicts approving behavior by an actor which either does not receive an expected punishment or does receive an expected reward. For the cases in quadrant II, the inferred expectation (based upon the "−" sign of the actor's role conception) is conflictual behavior from the target. But the unexpected, actual behavior (inferred from the "+" sign of the target's cue) is cooperative. Therefore, the actor is likely to adopt approving behavior and the role enactment sign will be "+".

On the other hand, if the actor's role conception valence is cooperative (+), but the valence of the target's cue is conflictual (−), then the altercasting effect will follow the aggression principle from exchange theory. The aggression proposition predicts aggressive behavior if an actor receives unexpected punishment or does not receive an expected reward. For the cases in quadrant IV, the " + " sign of the actor's role conception implies an expectation of cooperative behavior from the target. But the "−" sign of the target's cue indicates that the actual behavior is conflictual. Therefore, the actor is likely to adopt aggressive behavior and the role enactment sign will be "−".

The Relative Potency of Role Theory versus Exchange Theory

In order to test the predictions in figure 5.1, the dyads in table 5.1 are subdivided into the four quadrants, Q-I, Q-II, Q-III, Q-IV. In the social psychology literature, the congruence principle has failed to achieve its potential for predicting the magnitude of a relationship, but the balance principle has been relatively successful in attaining its more modest goal of predicting the direction of a relationship (Zajonc 1968, 345–59). Therefore, the quadrant analysis involves two steps. First the frequency distributions of the signs for the role enactment valences within each quadrant are examined in order to determine whether the predicted sign is more frequent. Second, bivariate and multivariate Pearsonian correlation analysis is employed to test the relative potency of role conceptions and cues upon the magnitude of role enactment valences. The results of each step are in table 5.3 and table 5.4, respectively.

The findings in table 5.3 show a preponderance of role enactment valences with the predicted signs in quadrants I and III, where the role conception and cue valences reinforce one another. In quadrants II and IV, the exchange corollaries of the altercasting principle predict that the role enactment valence will have a different sign from the role conception valence. However, this hypothesis is confirmed only for the USSR dyads in these quadrants. Altercasting by the United States does not work in quadrant II, where it is almost equally likely that the sign of a 3rd nation's role enactment will correspond to the sign of its role conception or to the cues of the United States.

This pattern of mixed findings continues when the correlations among the magnitudes of these variables are examined. Quadrants I and II have a sufficient number of cases to calculate zero-order and partial coefficients, which appear in table 5.4. The low correlations between role conception and cue valences indicate that the effect of

Table 5.3   Balance relationships within the four quadrants

Cases		Role-enactment frequencies			Interpretation	
Quadrant/N	Dyad	Positive (+)	Zero (0)	Negative (−)	Prediction	Hypothesis
(N = 18)	3rd-U.S.	66.7% (12)	16.7% (3)	16.7% (3)	(+)	True
Q-I						
(N = 24)	3rd-USSR	83.3% (20)	4.2% (1)	12.5% (3)	(+)	True
(N = 22)	3rd-U.S.	50.0% (11)	4.5% (1)	45.5% (10)	(+)	False
Q-II						
(N = 17)	3rd-USSR	70.6% (12)	11.8% (2)	17.6% (3)	(+)	True
(N = 4)	3rd-U.S.	25.0% (1)	0.0% (0)	75.0% (3)	(−)	True
Q-III						
(N = 3)	3rd-USSR	33.3% (1)	0.0% (0)	66.7% (2)	(−)	True
(N = 1)	3rd-U.S.	100.0% (1)	0.0% (0)	0.0% (0)	(−)	False
Q-IV						
(N = 1)	3rd-USSR	0.0% (0)	0.0% (0)	100.0% (1)	(−)	True

these variables upon role enactment can be considered to be independent, even in quadrant I where their predicted signs are the same. For
the USSR dyads, the effects of these variables are in the predicted
direction. The degree of association between a 3rd nation's role enactment and the cues provided by the USSR is the stronger relationship
in both quadrants. In contrast, the association between a 3rd nation's
role enactment and cues from the United States is negligible. The
relationship between role conception and role enactment for U.S. dyads
is weak and erratic in quadrant I, but stronger and in the predicted
direction in quadrant II. All of these correlations are fairly "case
sensitive," that is, they are based upon such a limited number of observations that small measurement errors could easily affect their magnitudes and signs.

Discussion

With the aid of an auxiliary hypothesis to connect role theory and
exchange theory, some research hypotheses which are derived from
the synthesis of the two theories have been tested with the Holsti
(1970) and McGowan and O'Leary (1975) data sets. The small number
of cases and various methodological problems associated with merging two data sets for a secondary analysis make the results heuristic
rather than conclusive in nature. Ideally, one would want (a) a great

many observations, (b) a clear chronological separation between the observation of independent and dependent variables, (c) longitudinal as well as cross-sectional observations, and (d) observations that are capable of disaggregation by target and issue area.

Although the Holsti and McGowan/O'Leary data sets approximate these characteristics in some respects, there are too many inadequacies to consider the results of the data analysis as conclusive. For example, the McGowan/O'Leary data are from the World Events Interaction Survey (WEIS), which used the *New York Times* as its source for these data. Other scholars (Borrows 1974; see also Hoggard 1974) have demonstrated that the *New York Times* reports events unevenly within the various regions of the Third World. This bias may very well undermine the validity of the data for testing the research hypotheses.

There are also some problems associated with the aggregated form in which the data are analyzed. The coding rules for aggregating role conceptions and inferring the targets of the role conceptions are reproducible (Walker 1979), but their reliability and validity rest upon the quality of the inferences that are possible from the coding decisions in the original data set. Holsti (1970, 260–72) provides an extensive discussion of the face validity for his role-classification scheme, but he does not report reliability coefficients. The cooperation/conflict dichotomy in which the behavioral data are reported by McGowan and O'Leary (1975) may also conceivably mask important relationships, although

Table 5.4 Relationships among role-enactment,[a] role-conception,[b] and cue valences[c]

Cases		Zero-order r's			Partial r's		Variance	
Quadrant/N	Dyad	r_{RCRE}	r_{CURE}	r_{CURC}	$r_{RCRE \cdot CU}$	$r_{CURE \cdot RC}$	$r^2_{RCRE \cdot CU}$	$r^2_{CURE \cdot RC}$
(N = 18)	3rd-U.S.	− .21	+ .05	+ .32	− .24	+ .12	.06	.01
Q-I								
(N = 24)	3rd-USSR	+ .17	+ .39	+ .03	+ .18	+ .39*	.03	.15*
(N = 22)	3rd-U.S.	+ .48	+ .21	+ .13	+ .47*	+ .17	.22*	.03
Q-II								
(N = 17)	3rd-USSR	+ .44	+ .60	+ .11	+ .48*	+ .63**	.23*	.40**

[a] Role enactment is assigned the subscript "RE" in the table.
[b] Role conception is assigned the subscript "RC" in the table.
[c] Cue is assigned the subscript "CU" in the table.
* $p \leq .05$.
** $p = .01$.

reliability coefficients exceeding .80 for the WEIS data are available (Burgess and Lawton 1972, 29).

Similarly the chronological aggregation of both data sets into two partially overlapping time frames of roughly three years may confound to some extent the attempts to uncover theoretically significant relationships. However, unless these data are aggregated chronologically into a relatively small number of categories, the number of observations per actor and the number of actors for inclusion in the data analysis become too infrequent for quantitative analysis. These trade-offs unfortunately reflect the shortcomings of the currently available data and are intractable for the short run. Until more and better data are collected, the empirical payoff from this approach will remain a matter for debate rather than demonstration.

The main contributions of this paper, therefore, are theoretical and methodological. Role theory is characterized as conceptually rich but lacking a parsimonious set of propositions which can be tested rigorously (Sarbin and Allen 1968). The exchange theory of George Homans (1961, 1974), on the other hand, modestly claims to account for only "elementary" forms of human behavior with a small number of fairly rigorous propositions. Relating the concepts of role theory by means of Homans's exchange propositions creates a synthesis which combines some of the richness of role theory with the rigor of exchange theory. The quadrant analysis (figure 5.1) identifies theoretical areas of compatibility and incompatibility between the two theories and suggests a hypothetical solution in the form of the predicted values for the role-enactment variable in each quadrant.

Within the constraints imposed by the use of secondary data, the analysis also illustrates one solution to the methodological problems associated with the application of individual-level propositions to account for the actions of collectivities. Role concepts are employed most easily at the individual level of analysis to examine cognitive orientations and behavior. Singer (1968, 140–42) advocates a summative aggregation strategy as the best method of dealing with a collectivity whose individuals have heterogeneous psychological traits. He maintains that "the [summative] aggregation of individual *psychological* properties provides a quite sufficient base for describing the *cultural* properties of the larger social entity which is comprised of those individuals."

The actual construction of summative indices is a somewhat arbitrary procedure. The operational definition of a "general impression," namely, the valence for a set of cognitive elements such as an individual's multiple role conceptions, has taken several forms in the cognitive dynamics literature (Zajonc 1968, 324). However, the important point is that the aggregation of role conceptions and role enactments either within a single individual or across a collection of individuals creates a summative property. Assuming the same target for multiple roles, the formulae for the valences of an individual's or a nation's roles vis-à-vis a common target resemble one another closely enough for these aggregated descriptions to be classified as isomorphic. That is, their structures are sufficiently similar so that the concepts for describing one can be used to describe the other. In this paper a variant of the summative aggregation strategy is applied to create indices which describe the overall valence of the multiple role conceptions and role enactments for each nation toward each superpower. Methodologically the pursuit of this strategy makes it possible to employ two abstracted systems, role theory and exchange theory, in the exploration of living systems at two levels, individual and society (Miller 1978, 16–22).

6

National Attributes as Sources of National
Role Conceptions: A Capability-Motivation Model

Naomi Bailin Wish

In 1970 a pathbreaking article appeared in *International Studies Quarterly*. It was K. J. Holsti's "National Role Conceptions in the Study of Foreign Policy." Holsti defined national role conceptions as "...the policymakers' own definitions of the general kinds of decisions, commitments, rules and actions suitable to their state and the functions, if any, their state should perform on a continuing basis in the international system or in subordinate regional systems (1970, 246). Holsti suggested that foreign policy behavior (decisions and actions taken by authoritative governmental actors) is, to a great extent, role performance and can be explained by decision makers' national role conceptions.

Although the explanatory power of national role conceptions has never been thoroughly investigated, a few researchers have attempted to examine the relationship between national role conceptions and foreign policy behavior. Walker (1979) studied the congruence and balance between national role conceptions and foreign policy behavior focusing on roles concerned with the cold war and development. Wish (1980) systematically categorized a wide sample of national role conceptions and empirically investigated the relationships between these conceptions and many aspects of foreign policy behavior. The results indicated that there were strong correspondences between many characteristics of national role conceptions and foreign policy behavior. These findings demonstrated the potential for using national role conceptions to explain and possibly eventually predict patterns in foreign policy behavior.

The next logical step in examining the relationships between national role conceptions and foreign policy behavior is to focus on the sources for the variance in national role conceptions and thereby move toward a two-stage explanation of foreign policy behavior. The current study is devoted to that task, one which Holsti recognized as a major gap in his original study. His research did not "reveal the origins of various national role conceptions" (1970, 295) which might indicate when and how national roles evolve and change. He suggested that an investigation of these sources is crucial, since it may lead to development of foreign policy theory.

The National Attribute/National Role Conception Model

According to Holsti, major sources of national role conceptions are the socio-economic characteristics of the state itself. Other researchers agree. For example, Puchala writes, "resource availability may influence or even determine a state's choice of international political goals. Not only are government demands for resources adjusted to match goals, but goals too often are adjusted to match resources available to governments" (1971, 184–85). Mentioning roles specifically, Brecher et al. state "the choice among policy options derives from decision-makers' perceptions of their nation's environment and its roles in international politics" (1968, preface). Finally, East presents a detailed theoretical framework on this subject. His model is based on the concept of capacity to act, which East defines as "the amount of resources a nation has and the ability to utilize them" (1978, 123). East suggests that national attributes not only affect a nation's foreign policy decisions directly by determining the nation's capacity to act, but also influence its foreign policy behavior indirectly by affecting its decision makers' foreign policy goals and objectives.

Psychologists have long suggested that behavior is a product of both

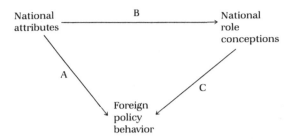

Figure 6.1   Relationships between national attributes, role conceptions, and foreign policy behavior

capability and motivation, and political scientists have found the same situation exists on the national level. As Crabb states, "reduced to its most fundamental ingredients, foreign policy consists of two elements, national objectives to be achieved and the means for achieving them" (1972, 1). Thus, the national attribute-national role conception model is similar to a capability-motivation model. It postulates that a nation's foreign policy behavior is in large measure a product of its national capabilities or attributes and that its decision makers' national motivations are expressed as national role conceptions. The latter are defined as foreign policymakers' perceptions of their nations' positions in the international system. They include perceptions of the general kinds of decisions, commitments, and associated long-term international functions which are associated with these positions.

According to this model (figure 6.1), national attributes affect foreign policy behavior both directly and indirectly. Directly, national attributes affect the "amount of resources that can be used in the execution of national actions and [function] as factors affecting the nation's ability to utilize the nation's resources" (East et al., 1978, 126). Decision makers consider their national capabilities when formulating their national role conceptions, which in turn provide guidelines and standards for their foreign policy behavior. Thus, national attributes provide a major source for the formulation of national role conceptions and in this manner are also indirectly related to foreign policy.

Beginning with Rosenau (1966), many researchers (Hopple 1979; Rosenau and Hoggard 1974; Moore 1974) have hypothesized that three national characteristics, size or capability, economic development, and political orientation or accountability, have profound effects on foreign policy behavior. East (1975) has tested these hypotheses empirically. Using factor scores for size and modernity, his results indicate that these characteristics are closely related to some aspects of foreign policy behavior. Thus, we anticipate that they may influence national role conceptions in the following manner.

Size or power indicates the amount of resources a nation may possibly have available to use for foreign policy purposes. Since decision makers from larger nations usually have more available resources than decision makers from smaller nations, in their national role conceptions they will (a) perceive larger domains of national influence, (b) more often perceive their nations in dominant or leadership positions, (c) perceive a greater proportion of national roles which involve competitive or cooperative-competitive rather than cooperative interests, (d) seek less system change, (e) express greater proportions of roles concerned with territory and security, and (f) perceive smaller proportions of individualistically (domestically) oriented roles.

What are the assumed attributes of large and small states that lead us to these expectations concerning national role conceptions? "Decision-makers from larger nations will have greater concern with influencing larger domains and demonstrating dominance since they will accurately perceive their greater potential for international influence and see their national interests as entangled in a great variety of world affairs..." (East and Hermann 1974, 274). Furthermore, decision makers from large nations, in contrast to small ones, have a greater felt need to influence international affairs on a wider range of issues. Therefore, they will more often perceive their nations in roles which involve conflict or differences with other nations. Although their roles will involve competition, however, they will express less of a desire for international system change. They will more often express territorial roles such as "policeman of the world" and want to maintain their own security as well as the international status quo. Thus, size will be positively related to the perception of status, size of the influence domain, as well as the proportion of territorial issues. Size will be negatively related to change and the proportion of domestic or individualistic role orientations.

Economic development is the second national characteristic that has been associated with the variation in foreign policy behavior. Decision makers from nations that are more economically developed (in contrast to those that are less economically developed) will (a) perceive larger domains of national influence, (b) more often perceive their nation in a dominant or leadership position, (c) perceive a greater proportion of national roles which are concerned with political or diplomatic issues and/or universal values, (d) perceive a smaller proportion of national roles which are concerned with ideology and/or territory, (e) perceive a smaller proportion of national roles which involve competitive or cooperative-competitive rather than cooperative interests, (f) perceive a smaller proportion of national roles involving individualistic interests, and (g) seek less system change.

The assumed attributes of economically developed and developing states that lead us to these expectations concerning national role conceptions are similar to the size or capability attributes. Since decision makers from economically developed nations perceive that their nations not only have greater resources but also have the ability to utilize them in the international arena, they will express greater concern with influencing larger domains and demonstrating their dominance. Furthermore, since their nations' advantageous positions are obvious to these policymakers, they will less often express a need for change in the international system. "In fact, they will be vigilant against the emergence of any revolutionary society that threatens to disrupt its domestic living standard by reordering the international political or economic system" (East and Hermann 1974, 277).

Since Morse (1970) has suggested that decision makers from more economically developed nations are more often concerned with "low politics," we have also hypothesized that they will tend to perceive more cooperative roles, that is, those concerned with political and diplomatic issues as well as universal values. Therefore, economic development should be positively correlated with the level of the influence domain, the perception of dominance, and the percentage of diplomatic and/or universal value issues. The nation's level of economic development should be negatively correlated with the percentage of ideological and territorial issues, the proportion of competitively motivated and individualistically motivated issues, and the amount of desired change.

Political orientation is the third characteristic that has been associated with foreign policy behavior. Decision makers from nations that are more open or democratic will (a) perceive a greater proportion of national roles that are concerned with political and diplomatic issues and/or universal values, and/or economic issues, (b) perceive a smaller proportion of national roles that are concerned with ideology and/or territory, and (c) perceive a smaller proportion of roles that involve competitive or cooperative-competitive rather than cooperative interests.

"An open political system is one in which the overwhelming majority of adults in the nation regularly have the opportunity to influence those who govern, and the government is vulnerable to defeat by this majority" (East and Hermann 1974, 280). Decision makers from more open political systems will realize that the private sector will be interested in various kinds of international transactions such as trade, financial investment, and tourism. Thus, these decision makers will express greater proportions of roles concerned with political and diplomatic, and/or economic issues as well as roles concerned with universal values. They will also more often express cooperatively oriented roles and less often express roles concerned with ideology and territory. The power of the private sector in the open system will decrease these kinds of conflict-laden role expressions. Therefore, political orientation should be positively correlated with the percentage of diplomatic issues, the percentage of universal value issues, and the percentage of economic issues, yet negatively correlated with the percentage of ideological and/or territorial issues and the proportion of competitively motivated role conceptions.

Methods and Results

The sample for testing these hypotheses includes twenty-nine political elites from seventeen nations who were heads of state or top foreign policy makers between 1959 and 1968. In order to obtain indicators of national role conceptions, transcripts of elite interviews and speeches, as well as articles that they had written, were collected from books and reference volumes. The contents of paragraphs indicating role conceptions were analyzed by three undergraduates trained by the author. By the end of four training sessions, the intercoder agreement was 82 percent. The coders used a multiple choice form to code each of approximately 1900 paragraphs and calculated role-conception scores for each leader on the following ten role-conception variables, which were coded and analyzed according to the protocols in appendix 1:

1. The perception of dominance
2. The size or level of the influence domain
3. Individualistic domestic motivations
4. Competitive motivations
5. The amount of change proposed
6. Territorial defense issues
7. Ideological issue
8. Political/diplomatic issue
9. Universal value orientation
10. Economic issue

Table 6.1   Relationships between national attributes
and attributes of national role conceptions

National attributes	Dominant	Influence domain	Individualistic	Competitive
Size	.81***	.52**	−.36*	.04
Economic development	.73***	.45**	−.50**	−.15
Political orientation	.13	.23	−.41**	−.68**

* p < .05
** p < .01

Since East (1975) had found that moderate associations existed between national attributes and foreign policy behavior, his factor scores for size and modernity are used in this study to operationalize these national attributes and examine their relationships with national role conceptions. For political orientation, the press freedom variable obtained from the Cross Polity Survey (Banks and Textor 1968) is used. Nations were assigned values ranging from one, indicating no press freedom, through six, which indicates a great deal of press freedom (see appendix 1).

A Pearson product-moment correlational analysis of these role-conception scores and the indicators of size, economic development, and political orientation appears in table 6.1. The results indicate that, as expected, there is a very strong positive correlation between size and the perception of dominance, larger influence domains, and involvement with territorial roles. Decision makers from larger nations or those with greater amounts of resources perceived these resource capabilities and sensed their ability to perform dominant and influential roles in the international system. They often expressed roles concerned with territorial defense, such as policeman of the world. As expected, the results also demonstrate that decision makers from larger as opposed to smaller nations were less individualistic, that is, domestically oriented. However, there is little relationship between size and the change or competitive orientation of the role conceptions.

The results in table 6.1 also demonstrate that, as hypothesized, decision makers from economically developed nations perceived larger domains of national influence (r = .45) and more often perceive their nations in dominant or leadership positions (r = .73). And, as expected,

Change	Territorial	Ideological	Pol./Dip.	Universal	Economic
−.11	.53**	.09	−.42**	.16	−.13
.11	.37*	−.14	−.29	.09	.04
−.07	−.15	−.57***	.43**	.42**	−.03

* p < .001

these decision makers were less likely to express national role conceptions concerned with individualistic motivations (r = −.50). However,
we incorrectly hypothesized the relationships between the nation's
level of modernization or economic development and the issue areas
of concern. Following Morse's proposals (1970), we had hypothesized
that leaders from more modernized nations would more often express
national role conceptions concerned with low policies such as diplomacy and universal values, as opposed to the high policies of territory
and ideology. However, we were correct in hypothesizing that the level
of economic development would *not* be related to the proportion of
economically concerned role conceptions (r = .04). Morse (1970) had
hypothesized that these two variables would be positively related.

We also reasoned that if leaders of modernized nations showed a
greater concern with low policies as opposed to high policies, they
would express a smaller proportion of competitive motivations. Our
results indicate that a nation's level of economic development is
not related to the proportion of competitive motivations which its
decision maker expresses (r = .15), and is only related to one issue
area. Furthermore, this relationship appears to be in the opposite
direction from that which was hypothesized. Contrary to Morse's
(1970) hypothesis, leaders from economically developed nations are
more concerned with territorial and security issues than are leaders
from the developing nations (r = .37).

The findings in table 6.1 show that the direction of the relationships
between the political orientation of the nation and the issue areas
expressed has been hypothesized correctly in four of the five cases.
Leaders from open nations are more likely to express role conceptions

concerned with political/diplomatic issues (r = .43) and/or universal values (r = .42), and are less likely to express roles concerned with ideological (r = −.57) or territorial issues (r = −.15), although the latter relationship is statistically insignificant. However, the political orientation of the nation is not related to the proportion of economic role conceptions that decision makers perceive (r = −.03). Finally, as hypothesized, the proportion of national role conceptions including competitive motivations is smaller for decision makers from more open nations (r = −.68).

Summary and Conclusions

In attempting to explain patterns in the foreign policy behavior of nations, comparative foreign policy specialists have usually focused on either aggregate national attributes or decision makers' perceptions and personal characteristics. We have suggested that a two-stage, national attribute-role conception model would offer a more adequate alternative explanation of foreign policy behavior. The model includes three variable clusters, national attributes, national role conceptions, and foreign policy behavior. This conceptual framework suggests that national attributes are both indirectly and directly related to foreign policy behavior. Previous studies indicate that national attributes directly affect foreign policy behavior by determining to a great extent a nation's resources and its ability to use them. We have hypothesized that they also act as one of the many sources of national role conceptions, which provide guidelines, norms, or standards for foreign policy behavior. Thus, in this chapter we have explored the direct relationship between national attributes and national role conceptions.

To summarize the relationships between national attributes and national role conceptions, our results indicate that the size and level of economic development of the nation are strongly related to role conception characteristics dealing with the perception of influence and dominance. Both size and economic development are positively related to the perception of dominance, the size or level of the domain of influence, and the concern with territorial issues. They are also both negatively related to the percentage of individualistic interests and the concern with diplomatic roles. Political orientation, on the other hand, is more closely related to motivational interests and issues of concern. Decision makers from more open rather than closed nations express a greater percentage of roles concerned with political and diplomatic issues and/or universal values and a smaller percentage of roles with ideological concerns. They are also less likely to express competitive and/or individualistic motivations.

These results indicate that variations in national attributes are in many instances related to variations in national role conceptions. They add credibility to the notion that certain national attributes serve as major sources for national role conceptions. Since the latter provide guidelines, norms, or standards for foreign policy behavior (Wish 1980), there probably is also an indirect relationship between national attributes and foreign policy behavior with national role conceptions acting as mediating variables.

7

Cultural Norms and National Roles:
A Comparison of Japan and France

Martin W. Sampson III and Stephen G. Walker

In the analysis of the relationship between culture and foreign policy, it is important to distinguish two strategies. One attempts to establish direct links between individuals' characteristics in a national population and the content of the nation's foreign policy. The other strategy tries to identify the direct impact of such characteristics upon the process of policymaking and then find linkages to the content through the process. Previously, one of us (Sampson 1987) adopted the second approach in a comparative analysis of the relationship between cultural variables and the process of foreign policymaking in Japan and France. That study eschewed "... direct jumps from individuals to policy content ... [and addressed] ... the rather different matter of whether cultures affect the decision making process in certain identifiable and analytically useful ways" (Sampson 1987). In the present paper we intend to build upon the results of those comparisons to link cultural variables indirectly but more explicitly with the content of Japanese and French foreign policies.

In order to accomplish this task, it is necessary for us to begin by reviewing the relevant findings from the earlier study and establish working definitions of "culture" and "foreign policy." Various definitions of culture share the common notion that culture is a set of norms that are operative within a particular, specified community (Nadler, Nadler, and Broome 1985, 89; Barnlund and Araki 1985, 25; Hofstede 1980, 43). The community of concern to us is the nation, and the norms are ones shared across the various communities that constitute the nation. From this working definition of national culture Sampson (1987) attempted to identify a set of socially created and learned practices or rules in Japan and France with the following properties:

1. They exist across a variety of institutions within the nation-state.
2. They are typical and common within the population but have a probabilistic rather than deterministic impact upon behavior.
3. They are familiar to the people in a population, who respond to these norms even though their own behavior may not always conform to them.
4. They can be appropriately regarded as incentives that have the effect of organizing and structuring behavior.

We shall examine the Japanese and French cases in an attempt to identify such norms and their impact upon foreign policy. A definition of foreign policy that lends itself readily to this goal is the one associated with role theory. Holsti (1970, 240) identifies four concepts from role theory as helpful in analyzing foreign policy: "(1) *role performance*, which encompasses the attitudes, decisions, and actions governments take to implement (2) their self-defined *national role conceptions* or (3) the *role prescriptions* emanating, under varying circumstances, from the alter or external environment. Action always takes place within (4) a *position*, that is, a system of role prescriptions." He argues that in the study of foreign policy, role performance may be explained primarily by referring to role conceptions and their domestic sources. The fact of national sovereignty makes the impact of role prescriptions external to the nation relatively small (Holsti 1970, 243).

According to Holsti (1970, 245–46), "A *national role conception* includes the policymakers' own definitions of the general kinds of decisions, commitments, rules, and actions suitable to their state, and of the functions, if any, their state should perform on a continuing basis in the international system or in subordinate regional systems. It is the 'image' of the appropriate orientations or functions of their state toward, or in, the external environment." These conceptions establish norms for national role performance, that is, the general behavior of governments toward other states. An example of such a role is "developer," which Holsti defines as concern for economic growth and progress in underdeveloped countries.

The central hypothesis in this paper is that there is a specific link between the organizational norms of a particular national culture and the foreign policy of that nation state. The assertion that organizational norms exist within a national culture means that decision processes are in some ways similar in various settings found within that culture, such as businesses, local government, and foreign policy decision making. The assertion that these norms relate to the content of foreign policy is less a definitional issue than a question of what that relationship might be. The argument of this paper is that norms that govern how upper-level people in a decision-making organization interact with others also establish a sort of central tendency for how that nation-state will deal with other nation-states. More bluntly, a state will tend to deal with foreign targets in much the same way that the upper levels in its own decision-making environments deal with other levels of those environments.

Why should this be—especially if people, inside and outside of government, support foreign policies according to the effectiveness of those policies? The answer is that the legitimacy and attractiveness of foreign policy endeavors to these audiences often have little to do with the actual effectiveness of the policy. This possibility may be *especially* true in the realm of foreign policy, where so much is beyond the control of a single actor, where there is chronic uncertainty as to what success and failure actually are, and where much decision making is elitist. Confronted with such circumstances, people may apply different kinds of standards to foreign policy than the standard of effectiveness, meaning that the legitimacy or support for a particular policy may be largely unrelated to its success in any objective sense.

A more meaningful test may be whether or not the policy fits a pattern that meshes with patterns that people know from other circumstances. To a Japanese, cautious, harmonious efforts toward the international system may seem intuitively plausible, appropriate, and effective because such a norm is important in the organizational behavior of Japanese society. On the other hand, abstract, elegant, and individualistic policies toward the outside world may seem appropriate to a French person for exactly the same reasons. The crux of this argument is that policies, especially in the vague realm of foreign policies, can have merit because of their congruence with norms and practices that are deeply rooted in particular societies.

If so, this argument has certain implications. First, organizational norms identifiable in a national culture would correspond to foreign policy outputs in a process sense. Second, such policies would be most likely to appear in environments where everything else is equal and there is not an alternative criterion that demands other kinds of policies. Third, sharply different national organizational cultures would be associated with different kinds of foreign policies.

The link between national culture and the content of a nation's foreign policy remains an indirect one, if by content one means the goals and actions that constitute a nation's *role performance*. These goals and behaviors are in some ways constrained by national *role conceptions*, which act as normative, procedural constraints upon the range of acceptable goals and the variety of appropriate means in the domain of foreign policy. A nation's role conceptions, in turn, possess normative properties that embody procedurally significant national cultural traits. There is either a one-to-one correspondence between the identities of these cultural norms and the norms described in the national role conceptions, or else the latter's norms include derivatives of the former. Since we have already postulated a probabilistic rather than a deterministic relationship in our working definition of culture, a nation's policymakers may adopt national role conceptions and foreign policy behaviors that possess other characteristics in addition to the ones consistent with cultural norms.

The nations of Japan and France are particularly suited for testing this argument because their national cultures differ sharply in important respects. At the same time, the two societies are similar in several other national attributes. They have relatively few ethnic minorities. They are rich, industrialized, capitalist democracies with well-developed foreign policy bureaucracies. They are alike in having over thirty years to chart their respective courses following the devastation of defeat during World War II. Their foreign policies are also similar with respect to the level of overall involvement and the variety of involvement in international politics. Holsti (1970, 281–89) reports that both nations are located in the same quartiles for the seventy-one states whom he investigated to determine their national role conceptions. Japan and France are ranked in the top quartile of states as measured by types of role conceptions mentioned in speeches by their policymakers. They are located in the second quartile of states as measured by the number of role conceptions mentioned per speech. Moreover, their scores within each of these quartiles are virtually identical (Holsti 1970, 274–75, 287).

These similarities allow us to infer with greater confidence that differences between national role conceptions may be attributed to differences in national culture. According to the logic of a "most similar systems" research design, the high degree of similarity between the two nations along other dimensions rules them out as competing sources of explanation for any differences in national role conceptions or as the source of a spurious relationship between culture and role conceptions (Przeworski and Teune 1970, 31–46). Let us turn now to an examination of differences in the national cultures of Japan and France in order to assess whether they have had an impact upon their respective national role conceptions.

Japan and France: Culture and Decision Making*

Studies of how Japanese deal with people of differing status levels draw upon vocabulary associated with concepts such as group harmony (*wa*), indebtedness (*on*), and concern for and dependency upon other people (*amae*). Cathcart and Cathcart stress that dependency upon others is viewed in Japanese society as a natural, normal circumstance. *On*, the Cathcarts note, "should be viewed as part of a group structure and not as a relationship between two persons only. Everyone in a group is at the same time an *on*-receiver and an *on*-giver.... (*On*) is based upon the natural dependency inherent in human relationships rather than upon inherent individual qualities or attributes that enable some human beings to assume superior positions to others" (Cathcart and Cathcart 1976, 61–62). Japanese psychiatrist Doi comments that a rich Japanese vocabulary surrounds the concept of *amae*, which is the idea of depending and also presuming upon another person's love. Thus unanimous agreement or consensus becomes important in Japanese culture as "a token that the mutuality of all members has been preserved" (Doi 1976, 89). Communication patterns, moreover, reinforce the sense of group identity. People avoid disclosing much about themselves and avoid open conflict (Barnlund 1975, 413).

---

*This comparison is a revised and expanded version of the discussion in Sampson (1987).

It has been suggested that in Japan there is only one basic organizational motif, the family. The implication is that organizations in Japan typically function much as families function. Accordingly the themes of mutuality and indebtedness appear also in studies by Kume (1985), Cushman and King (1985), Stewart (1985), and others that compare Japanese businesses with businesses in other parts of the world. This point is especially clear in Kume's summary of how Japanese and U.S. businesses compare. In his view the Japanese practice for reaching decisions is consensual, reflecting cultural factors such as "acceptance of a given option, conformity, tentativeness." The locus of decision making is the group, with leaders facilitating shared responsibility; the attendant cultural factors are collectivism, interdependence, and group orientation. Kume describes the criteria of decision making as "intuition, group harmony," reflecting cultural factors of "holistic, spiritual consistency" (Kume 1985, 235).

It follows that Japanese management would include techniques such as *ringesi*, described by Tsuji (1968, 457) as "literally a system of reverential inquiry about a superior's intentions . . . although seldom defined, it is a . . . word to refer to a system whereby administrative plans and decisions are made through the circulation of a document called ringisho . . ." among all relevant officials until it is approved by the top official, usually "without change or modification because of this long process of prior scrutiny." Ting-Toomey (1985), Cushman and King (1985), and Kume (1985) discuss *nemawashi* as a process in which extensive consultation occurs and "through *nemawashi* or personal interaction, one seeks to improve the empathy and cooperation necessary to attain group harmony" (Cushman and King 1985, 127). Japanese businesses are consequently prone to a kind of "radical empiricism" (Stewart 1985, 193–96) as extensive amounts of time are devoted to collection and assessment of information. Communication, moreover, is widely dispersed, so that many people are familiar with the issue. Such a process may not be rapid, but a feature of this kind of decision making is the lessened chance of difficulties in implementing the decision.

Thus in Japanese organizations efforts are made to avoid circumstances that produce clear-cut winners and losers within the organization or that force consensus to coincide with approval. Japanese organizations have a predictable deference to seniority, a practice of people attaching themselves to mentors, and patterns of employees devoting careers to one organization. This is a system that is typically dominated by the upper level, but that domination exists in a style that does not maximize speed or minimize dispersal of information. The inclusion of a wide array of people implies a relatively cumbersome process that Americans would regard as too time consuming and Japanese would regard as insulation against the apparent carelessness of rapid, high-handed decisions by Americans (Barnlund 1975).

Crozier's early study of French culture differs sharply from these generalizations about Japan. As summarized by Clark, families are also important in French society but in ways that have implications different from Japan. In France the individual is isolated, authority is centralized and impersonal, interaction patterns tend to be formal, and there are substantial status differences. According to Schofield's study of education, French people are raised in a setting that requires behavioral conformity but allows ideological diversity: "within the authority-laden mode, there is a very high level of attempted and effective control over what to do, how to do it, and how to behave in class, but a very low level of idea control" (1976, 63). He pushes this idea further with his comments that "the French secondary school students tend to have a dualistic normative structure. This permits those who desire serious modifications in the nature of the unit to remain behaviorally within the bounds of the actual system without suffering from cognitive strain. . . . Such dual guides to action seem to have a particular value in the regimented social unit, the function of which is highly valued and in which the subordinates have developed a strong critical spirit" (1976, 64).

From these general observations certain things would be expected to follow for French organizations. One, certainly, is a lack of elements or underpinnings for consensual organization in the Japanese sense of that idea. Antipathy to informal organizations, the value of analytic diversity, difficulties of developing and accepting task-based leadership, and concern for remaining within established, general, formal guidelines are a combination that would seem to thwart either trust among people or extensive, creative, and task-oriented communication within the groups. As in the case of Japan, studies of businesses offer evidence that some of these expectations are accurate. The following discussion draws upon studies by Granick (1978, 1979), Horovitz (1978, 1980), Laurent (1980), and Maurice (1979).

Horovitz (1978) finds that in France "many decisions are centralized at the top level . . . and committee management is scarce. The chief executive is often left with many final decisions when problems arise between functions. Much of the control is left to him personally" (1978, 19). In a subsequent study (1980, 188) he says, "as long as the chief

executive, through his personality, charismatic role, and sense of direction can stay on top of things . . . a company can develop without
much formal planning and control." That such success is not inevitable is suggested by Horovitz's finding that less than half the French
companies he studied do long-range planning (1978, 19).

Horovitz states that coordination in French businesses is relatively
infrequent compared to the British and German businesses that he
studied. Control tends to be personalistic and formal. "French control
practices tend towards a high degree of detail at the top management
level, high centralism in control, and heavy emphasis on production
control" (1980, 156). It may be that the emphasis on production meshes
with a tendency to control and monitor on the basis of easily quantified
information (1980, 156). Also related to these points is Horovitz's observation that ". . . many studies and observations show the overall lack of
trust of managers in their subordinates, the high level of centralization
as well as the low rate of accountability they are ready to require in
terms of performance" (1980, 157–58). The studies suggest that French
management is a blend of formal and informal. Managers at the very
highest levels have and exercise abundant opportunities for informal
control, where they personally intervene in ways that are not part of a
prescribed procedure. People at lower levels, however, "would be
required to use formal rules" (Horovitz 1980, 158).

In regard to recruitment Granick finds that many upper-level managers have been educated at the same institutions. Where someone pro-
gresses in an organization is highly predictable from the institution
from which the person received a degree (1978, 48; 1979, 88, 91). The
Horovitz studies make the same point. Education typically is technical,
which suggests that the training of French managers is not unrelated
to the kinds of challenges they encounter as industrialists. That does
not, however, mean that they are as well acquainted with details important to their own businesses as they might be. Maurice (1979, 52)
reports that authority and technical hierarchies overlap much less in
France than they do in Germany, where in some respects management
practices are similar to those in France (see Horovitz 1980, 148). The
1980 Horovitz study argues that in French businesses there are barri-
ers that "prevent people from sharing information, thereby keeping
their options open" (1980, 159). Horovitz also notes that French managers "feel guilty about business and profits—getting along with others
is more important" (1980, 158). Clearly "others" in this context refers to
people of similar status, not to people in the broader sense that would
apply in Japan.

Some other points appear in a Granick typology (1979, 88–89) that compares organizations in a variety of countries. Managerial turnover tends to be low in France. Ascriptive criteria are very important for determining who is hired in France, more so than in the United States or seven other nations examined in the study. France also is high in income differentials between managers and manual workers, and France is low in regard to the importance of managers having extensive prior practical experience. Overall the impression is that French organizations are stratified, ascriptive, formal, and quite rigid.

Are there certain procedural characteristics that one might expect would follow from this? It might be expected that such organizations would be relatively weak in their capacity to disperse information widely, to absorb extensive amounts of information at the upper levels, or to implement a significant portion of the decisions that are taken. With upper-level people whose selection and advancement is heavily related to criteria external to the organization, there is relatively little scope for spectacular advancement based upon merit. By the same token one might anticipate that the incentives for people at the top to use or creatively seek more information from people lower down are muted. One would expect substantial resentment and complaint on the part of lower-level people but very little expression of that between levels, so that this tension would rarely become a force for positive change.

The outputs of such an organization would presumably not be well tailored to the task of implementation except in straightforward, quantifiable tasks. The preference for the general, overarching, and abstract focus instead of attention to detail hardly leaves the implementation people high and dry; after all, they too can abide by the philosophic principles. The lack of incentives for focusing on detail, however, may mean that the philosophic tenets are ill suited to the issue that has just been decided.

Points of Difference: Cultural Norms and National Roles

The preceding discussion indicates that Japan and France have contrasting national cultures along the following dimensions:

group harmony
indebtedness
concern, dependence upon others
a superior's empathy for an inferior

emphasis upon collaboration and consultation
sense of responsibility owed above and below within an organization

These traits are valued highly in Japan and act as incentives for structuring behavior. They are not cultural traits shared by France. In fact the opposite trait clearly characterizes French national culture in at least one instance: individualism is valued over group harmony. A concern for others is also less important in France than in Japan, and superior-inferior relations are marked in France by less empathy, consultation, and mutual responsibility. The impact of these differences upon the process of foreign policymaking in the two countries is discussed elsewhere (Sampson 1987) in detail and summarized in table 7.1.

The logic which links these characteristics of the decision process to cultural norms is based upon the premise that their configuration in Japan represents behavior in conformity with the emphasis upon group harmony and mutual respect for superior-inferior relations. Enhanced communication, slower decision making, increased consultation, a reluctance to justify consensus with abstractions, extensive coordination without imposition by top decision makers—all are behaviors that preserve empathy and respect between superiors and inferiors in an organization and help to maintain group harmony. In contrast, the absence of these cultural norms in France together with an emphasis upon individualism accounts for the more rapid pace of French decision making, its centralization among top decision makers, and the low levels of consultation and coordination. The lack of emphasis upon group harmony also allows decisions to be justified by abstract principles rather than the criterion of group consensus (Sampson 1987). The same contrast can be applied to a comparative examination of Japanese and French national role conceptions: decision makers would treat the outside world differently if they, as argued earlier, tend to employ the same norms in dealing with other states that they use for dealing with subordinates.

Holsti (1970) has identified seventeen national role conceptions in an analysis of seventy-one states. These role conceptions and their definitions appear in table 7.2. The distribution of types of role conceptions for France and Japan are displayed in table 7.3 as frequency histograms which contrast the percentages for each type of role conception mentioned by the policymakers of at least one of the two nations. Japan's policymakers mentioned "developer" most frequently (45 percent), while the most frequently mentioned French role concep-

Table 7.1 Differences in the Japanese and French
foreign policymaking processes

Decision process characteristics	Countries	
	Japan	France
Circulation of documents	High	Low
Pace of decision making	Slow	Fast
Consultation with others	High	Low
Use of abstract principles	Low	High
Intervention by top decision makers	Low	High
Extent of coordination	High	Low

Source: Sampson (1987).

tion (36 percent) was "mediator-integrator." The source for these observations is Holsti (1970), who analyzed the contents of speeches of Japanese and French policymakers as part of a larger sample of nations for
the period 1964–67.

In order to ascertain whether these distributions of national role
conceptions reflect the influence of national cultural norms, we have
reanalyzed Holsti's descriptions of the role conceptions and scaled
them by the paired-comparison method (North et al. 1963, 79–90) to
form a continuum. This scale ranks the role conceptions according to
the degree to which they share Japanese cultural traits of group harmony and mutual empathy between superiors and inferiors versus the
opposite traits of individualism and autonomy associated with French
culture. According to our central hypothesis and its corollary, we
would expect the Japanese to adopt role conceptions located at one
end of the scale and the French to select the ones at the other end.
The actual distributions of role conceptions for each nation are shown
in table 7.4.

Two general patterns appear in table 7.4. One is a decrease in the
frequency of role conceptions for Japan and a corresponding increase
for France as one moves from the group solidarity end of the scale to
the individualism end of the continuum. The other is its corollary, a
pattern of predictable contrasts between the frequency distributions
for the pair of nations at each location on the scale. In order to estimate the strength of this support for our hypothesis and its corollary,
we have calculated three measures of association and a test of statistical inference that are appropriate ordinal-level estimates of the variation in these distributions.

Table 7.2   Definitions of national role conceptions

Type	Description
1. Bastion of revolution-liberator	Organize or lead various types of movements abroad
2. Regional leader	Lead states in a particular region or cross-cutting subsystem
3. Regional protector	Provide protection for adjacent regions
4. Active independent	Cultivate self-determination and relations with many states and occasional interposition into bloc conflicts
5. Liberation supporter	Support liberation movements without assuming formal responsibilities
6. Anti-imperialist agent	Act as agent of "struggle" against this evil
7. Defender of the faith	Defend value systems (rather than specified territories) from attack
8. Mediator-integrator	Reconcile conflict between other states or groups of states
9. Regional-subsystem collaborator	Honor far-reaching commitments to cooperative efforts with others
10. Developer	Assist underdeveloped countries with special skills
11. Bridge	Act as a translator or conveyor of messages
12. Faithful ally	Support the policies of another government
13. Independent	Determine own national interests rather than support others
14. Example	Promote prestige and influence by domestic policies
15. Internal development	Pursue involvement with other states only to further domestic development
16. Isolate	Minimize external contacts of any variety
17. Protectee	Affirm the responsibility of other states to defend them

Source: Holsti (1970).

First, we have calculated a Spearman's rho for the relationship between the actual rank order of the role-conception distributions for each nation and their "ideal rank order." For the Japanese the "ideal rank order" would be a descending distribution from the group end of

Table 7.3   Percentage distributions of Japanese
and French national role conceptions

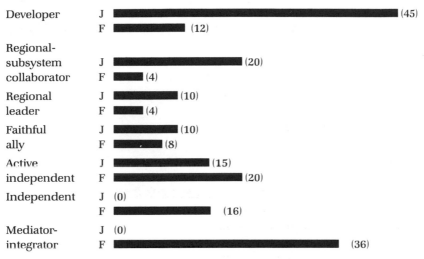

Developer	J	(45)
	F	(12)
Regional-subsystem collaborator	J	(20)
	F	(4)
Regional leader	J	(10)
	F	(4)
Faithful ally	J	(10)
	F	(8)
Active independent	J	(15)
	F	(20)
Independent	J	(0)
	F	(16)
Mediator-integrator	J	(0)
	F	(36)

Source: Adapted from Holsti (1970); N = 25 (France) and 20 (Japan).

the scale to the individual end. In the French case, the "ideal rank order" distribution would descend from the individual to the group end of the continuum. The Spearman's rho for Japan is + .75, while the rho for France is + .57. These results indicate that each nation's configuration of national role conceptions corresponds well to the hypothesized ideal distribution for each one. The Japanese configuration resembles its hypothetical ideal more closely than does the French distribution, but both patterns are relatively robust ones which approach the maximum possible Spearman's rho of + 1.0 for a perfect direct relationship.

Second, we have calculated a Spearman's rho between the actual Japanese and French distributions of national role conceptions. This measure will estimate the degree of contrast between them. This rho is −.38, which indicates that there is a moderately strong inverse relationship in the rank order of their role conception frequencies along the group-individual scale; a completely opposite rank order between the two distributions would generate a Spearman's rho of −1.0. The likelihood that the actual difference in the variation of their rank orders is due to chance is only p = .025 (one-tailed), estimated by the Wald-Wolfowitz Runs Test (Blalock 1972, 249−55; Watson and McGaw 1980,

Table 7.4 National role conception distributions along the group-individual scale

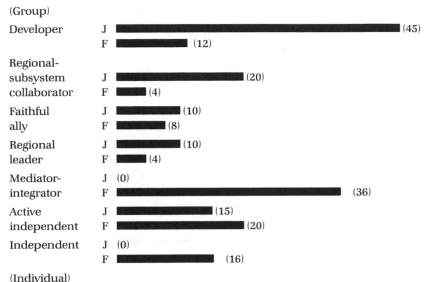

(Group)

Developer	J	(45)
	F	(12)
Regional-subsystem collaborator	J	(20)
	F	(4)
Faithful ally	J	(10)
	F	(8)
Regional leader	J	(10)
	F	(4)
Mediator-integrator	J	(0)
	F	(36)
Active independent	J	(15)
	F	(20)
Independent	J	(0)
	F	(16)

(Individual)

Source: Adapted from Holsti (1970); N = 25 (France) and 20 (Japan).

276–78). Consequently, we are reasonably confident that this evidence is strong enough to support our central hypothesis and its corollary.

In order to assess the impact of culture upon the actions as well as the role conceptions of Japanese and French foreign policy, we shall now examine some relevant properties associated with their foreign policy behavior. Earlier, we hypothesized that cultural norms would overlap with the norms embodied in national role conceptions. Role conceptions would then act as procedural, normative constraints upon the range of acceptable goals and the variety of appropriate means in the domain of foreign policy. Our analysis of the normative properties shared by the cultures and role conceptions, respectively, for each nation has supported part of this argument. Japan's national culture and national role conceptions share a group-oriented norm, while the French nation has an individualistically oriented culture and repertoire of role conceptions.

Consequently we would expect to find similar patterns for the foreign policy behaviors of the two countries. M. Hermann (1982a) has completed an analysis of thirty-eight nations, including Japan and France, in which she reports variations among these cases along an independence/interdependence of action scale for the period 1959–68. This time period overlaps the 1964–67 period covered in Holsti's (1970) analysis of national role conceptions and corresponds as well to a period of continuity in the leadership of Japan and France under the liberal democratic and Gaullist regimes respectively. We might expect, therefore, that there will be a pattern along the independence/inter-dependence of action scale for the two countries that corresponds to the pattern associated with their respective national role conceptions and national cultures.

Specifically, we shall hypothesize that the group-oriented norm associated with Japanese national culture and role conceptions will make Japanese foreign policy behavior high in interdependence of action. The individualistically oriented norm identified in French national culture and role conceptions, on the other hand, will drive French foreign policy behavior toward independence of action. To test these hypotheses, we shall calculate a difference-of-means test between each nation's mean scale score (Watson and McGaw 1980, 256–60, 267–71). M. Hermann's (1982a, 248) scale assigns a score of one to actions coded as unilateral initiatives and indicates an independent action. Actions that are assigned a score of two may be either unilateral reactions or multilateral initiatives; either type of action is a "mixed" action. A score of three is assigned to multilateral reactions and indicates an interde-pendence of action. The rationale for these scaling decisions is reported fully in M. Hermann (1982a) and is part of the larger CREON (Comparative Research on the Events of Nations) data collection effort at Ohio State University (Callahan, Brady, and Hermann 1982).

The results of our difference-of-means test show that the Japa-nese (N = 271) mean score of 2.34 with a standard deviation of .71 is significantly greater (p <.001 one-tailed) than the French (N = 855) mean score of 2.07 with a standard deviation of .81 (Watson and McGaw 1980, 267–71). The validity of this finding is reinforced by the difference in the rank order of the two scores; France is the ninth most indepen-dent nation on this scale, whereas Japan ranks twenty-fourth in inde-pendent action out of thirty-eight nations (M. Hermann 1982a: 251–52). Two other interesting results also emerge from the CREON data. Japan is significantly above (p <.001 one-tailed) the mean as well for interde-pendence of action scores among this set of nations, while France is indistinguishable from the average nation (Watson and McGaw 1980, 256–60). The mean and standard deviation for the entire set of thirty-eight nations is identical to the corresponding scores for France to the second decimal place (Hermann 1982a, 252–53). This finding has two possible implications. One is that either individualistic cultural norms or other variables drive many countries toward independence of action. The other one is that other characteristics of France are suppressing the impact of its individualistic culture. However, if one views the actions of Japan and France as two matched groups, that is, as the respective actions of a pair of nations with several shared characteristics, then it is possible to attribute the significant difference in their mean scores as directly associated with the corresponding differences in their national cultures and national role conceptions (Watson and McGaw 1980, 271–72).

We have already argued in our discussion of the logic of a "most similar systems" research design that the high degree of similarity between the two nations along other dimensions rules out those dimensions as competing sources of explanation (Przeworski and Teune 1970, 31–46). We can also infer with some theoretical justification from this argument that the results of our difference-of-means tests correspond to the conditions necessary to interpret them as a matched group test. "The *matched group test* utilizes a different methodological approach in which observations from the two separate groups are purposely matched on various relevant variables" (Watson and McGaw 1980, 271; see also 271–72). The groups in our interpretation are the two sets of foreign policy actions by Japan (N = 271) and France (N = 855), respectively, which are two groups of observations that share matching relevant variables according to the logic of our "most similar systems" research design. The only three characteristics which they do not share closely in our research design are their different country names, their different national cultures, and the different relative frequencies of their national role conceptions. We have already argued that the latter two characteristics differ significantly in degree and in a theoretically consistent fashion. The results of our statistical analysis of the CREON data reinforce this interpretation and extend it to include foreign policy behavior.

Japan and France: Differences Between "Most Similar Systems"?

The results of this study imply that cultural characteristics of the policymaking process in Japan and France affect policy outputs in these two nations. Although we base this conclusion upon a limited number of observations, the pattern is strong enough to warrant the inference on statistical grounds. The similarity of the two cases across a number of other potentially confounding dimensions also allows us to rule them out as competing sources of explanation for our observations. This result suggests that further work is worth doing on this topic.

In regard specifically to France and Japan, the design of this study controls for bases of power by comparing two nations that are at the wealthy, industrial/post-industrial end of the continuum. It could be argued that the study has not really addressed the implications of what choices the leaderships of those nations made over a period of decades about the use of that power and wealth, specifically the French choice to spend large amounts on its military and the Japanese choice to forego a military long after the United States had begun to encourage greater Japanese defense expenditures. Along those lines the rival hypothesis to our argument is that differing French and Japanese role conceptions stem from differences in the availability of military force. Whether that possibility supports or confounds the general argument in this chapter requires consideration.

If the cultural influences in these two nations were reversed, would Japan have sought ways to revive its military at a sub-superpower level and France instead have devoted more attention to economic issues and intra-Europe cooperation? Both nations were devastated by World War II. Algeria and Dien Bien Phu could have been powerful incentives for demilitarization by France. Similarly, the American search for military allies in the Pacific during the Vietnam war and the Nixon Doctrine could have been opportunities for Japan to increase its military. Instead each nation has persisted with patterns set down at the end of World War II.

Regarding the larger argument, that roles and cultural influences on decision making are related, there are other considerations. Japanese and French decision-making practices appear to be opposite ends of a continuum. Research is needed on the policies and decision processes of states that are within those extremes, less centralized than France and less decentralized than Japan. There is not a lot of related work to which these results can be compared. Wish (see chapter 6) reports that a nation's size and level of economic development are related inversely to individualistic role conceptions and directly correlate with the degree of dominance and the size or domain of influence reflected in the content of a country's role conceptions. Her sample of seventeen nations includes France but not Japan, and her role-conception data are not drawn from the Holsti (1970) data set.

It is not possible, therefore, to make direct comparisons between

Wish's results and ours. However, our findings lead us to speculate that cultural norms may be an important intervening variable that mediates the impact of size and economic development upon national role conceptions. These attributes of a great power may dispose a nation to conduct a more active foreign policy with greater scope, but cultural norms may very well leaven the role conceptions which shape its behavior and give meaning to its activities.

It should be noted that this paper is a first cut at a topic that is more elaborate than either the data set employed or the conceptual framework developed in the present paper. It is likely that cultural elements of organizational behavior influence policy activities in ways not captured in the data set that we have used. Patterns of timing, implementation problems or lack thereof, and aspects of policy style can be inferred from the cultural characteristics of the decision processes; they may well be significant components of a state's orientation toward the international system but are not entirely reflected in the Holsti data. A concern with these characteristics in this study has pushed the Holsti conceptualization in directions consistent with, yet somewhat unlike, prior work on role theory.

It would be helpful to achieve a better understanding of the circumstances under which these kinds of influences interact with role conceptions to produce patterns of foreign policy behavior. Traces of such influences do exist in the CREON data set. Swanson (1982, 235) reports the difference between the means for Japan and France along a specificity-of-action scale, while Hermann (1982b, 270) reports differences in the mean scores of the two nations on a feedback scale. Japan's actions are more specific ($\bar{X} = 1.35$) than the actions of France ($\bar{X} = 1.05$), and the ratio of positive-to-negative feedback experienced by Japan ($\bar{X} = 3.60$) is greater than the ratio ($\bar{X} = 2.32$) for France. An extended investigation of the interaction between these influences and role conceptions to produce patterns of foreign policy behavior is one avenue for further research. We base this suggestion upon our demonstration that there are some theoretically consistent statistical relationships between culturally induced characteristics of organizational behavior and the foreign policy outputs of Japan and France.

8

Foreign Policy Role Orientations and the
Quality of Foreign Policy Decisions

Margaret G. Hermann

Research examining the relationships between political leaders' personal characteristics and their governments' foreign policy behavior (for example, Crow and Noel 1977; Driver 1977; Falkowski 1978; M. Hermann 1977, 1980; Winter and Stewart 1977; Ziller et al. 1977) has shown the following six traits can impact on what governments do: nationalism, belief in one's own ability to control events, need for power, need for affiliation, conceptual complexity, and distrust of others. Moreover, these characteristics appear to interrelate in shaping political leaders' foreign policy orientations, their predispositions when faced with a foreign policymaking task (see M. Hermann, 1976, 1978, 1980). Political leaders' beliefs and motives — illustrated here by nationalism, belief in ability to control events, need for power, and need for affiliation — affect the content of the foreign policy orientation.

A grant from the National Science Foundation (GS-SOC76-83872) supported the research in this chapter.

Beliefs and motives aid leaders in interpreting their environment; they provide leaders with maps for charting their course, suggesting appropriate strategies for achieving goals and, at times, the nature of the goals. Political leaders' decision and interpersonal styles—illustrated here by conceptual complexity and distrust of others—influence the style of their foreign policy orientations. These styles indicate the leaders' usual ways of making decisions and interacting with others that carry over into the foreign policy arena.

These six personal characteristics interrelate to form six foreign policy role orientations. Before describing the orientations, however, let us briefly define the six personality traits that comprise the orientations:

Nationalism. Nationalism is conceptualized as a view of the world in which one's own nation holds center stage. There are strong emotional attachments to the nation-state; one's own nation is perceived as the best while other nations are perceived in less positive terms. Moreover, there is an emphasis on the importance of maintaining national honor and national sovereignty.

Belief in one's own ability to control events. By belief in one's own ability to control events is meant a view of the world in which one perceives some degree of control over the situations in which one is involved. What happens to an individual is contingent on his/her own behavior and characteristics.

Need for power. Need for power refers to an individual's concern for "establishing, maintaining, or restoring one's own power—that is, one's impact, control, or influence over another person, groups of persons, or the world at large" (Winter 1973, 250).

Need for affiliation. Need for affiliation is conceptualized as a concern with "establishing, maintaining, or restoring warm and friendly relationships" (Atkinson 1958, 685) with other persons or groups.

Conceptual complexity. Conceptual complexity refers to the degree of differentiation which a person shows when observing or contemplating his environment (cf. Crockett 1965; Scott 1963). The individual who is high in conceptual complexity can see varying reasons for a particular position, is willing to entertain the possibility that there is ambiguity in his environment, and is flexible in reacting to objects or ideas in the environment. The person who is low in conceptual complexity classifies objects and ideas into good-bad, black-white, either-or dimensions; is unwilling to perceive ambiguity in the environment; and tends to react unvaryingly to objects and ideas in the environment.

Distrust of others. Another name for this personal characteristic is suspiciousness. By distrust of others is meant a general feeling of doubt, uneasiness, misgiving, and wariness of others—that is, an inclination to suspect the motives and actions of others.

Many of the ideas for the particular orientations examined here come from the foreign policy literature, particularly that literature concerned with national role conceptions (for example, K. Holsti 1970; Wish 1977) and with the operational code (for example, O. Holsti 1977; Johnson 1977). Each orientation is perceived as setting the tone for the foreign policy behavior that leaders will urge on their governments, and each orientation is characterized by a specific strategy and style. The six orientations we will consider are the expansionist, active independent, influential, mediator-integrator, opportunist, and developmental orientations.

Much like the names suggest, the expansionist is interested in gaining control over more territory, resources, or people, while the active independent is inclined to participate in the international community on his own terms without engendering a dependent relationship with another country. The influential is concerned with having an impact on other nations' foreign policy behavior—in playing a leadership role in regional or international affairs. The mediator-integrator is oriented toward reconciling differences between other nations and, thus, in resolving problems in the international arena. The opportunist has an aptitude for taking advantage of present circumstances, whereas the developmental's interest is in continued growth and development of his nation through the cultivation of useful and rewarding relations with other countries or international organizations.

Appendix 2 describes these orientations in more detail, indicating the way in which the individual traits are combined to determine the six role orientations, the foreign policy the leader with each orientation is likely to urge on his government, how he is likely to organize and operate in a decision-making situation, and the types of regimes where we are likely to find leaders with the various orientations. Table 8.1 presents a summary of how the individual traits combine to form the orientations and some examples of heads of government having these role orientations. The data for determining a particular head of government's orientation were acquired through content analysis of press interviews with that leader. The coding schemes and procedures

Table 8.1 Bases for determining the foreign policy role orientations
and examples of heads of government exhibiting orientations

			Persona
Orientation	Nationalism	Belief in own ability to control events	Need power
Expansionist	Hi*	Hi	Hi*
Active independent	Hi*	Hi*	Lo
Influential	Lo	Hi*	Hi*
Mediator/integrator	Lo	Hi	Lo
Opportunist	Lo	Lo	Lo
Developmental	Hi*	Lo	Lo

*These traits are weighted more heavily in determining the orientations.

that were used in ascertaining the scores for the personal characteristics and orientations are available from the author. The leaders listed in table 8.1 have among the highest scores on the role orientations.

Linkages between Role Orientations and Decisions

We have described a series of foreign policy role orientations which indicate political leaders' predispositions toward behavior in the international arena. What are the linkages between the quality of foreign policy decisions and these role orientations? The criteria which form the focus of attention in discussions of ways of improving the quality of foreign policy decisions have generally evolved from considerations

Need affiliation	Conceptual complexity	Distrust of others	Leaders exhibiting orientation
Lo	Lo	Hi*	Castro (Cuba) Kaunda (Zambia) Nasser (Egypt)
Hi	Hi*	Lo	Eshkol (Israel) Gandhi (India) Lin Piao (China)
Hi	Hi	Lo	Zhou En Lai (China) Kenyatta (Kenya) Nkrumah (Ghana)
Hi*	Hi*	Lo	Diefenbaker (Canada) Frei (Chile) Sato (Japan)
Lo	Hi*	Lo	Eisenhower (U.S.) Erhard (W. Germany) Nehru (India)
Hi*	Hi	Lo	DeGaulle (France) Franco (Spain) Toure (Guinea)

of the relationships between goals and actions, the way information is processed, means of dealing with conflict, and ways of dealing with value complexities (George 1975; Holsti 1977; Janis 1972; Jervis 1976; Murphy Commission 1975). We will examine how leaders' orientations to foreign affairs impact on their goal-directed activities, information processing, and ways of dealing with conflict. We will also explore which means for improving the quality of foreign policy decision making would probably be perceived as feasible by leaders with specific orientations.

In considering whether or not a foreign policy action is effective, analysts often examine whether the action moves the government toward its goals or objectives. Given a certain stated policy objective, does the activity aid the government in achieving or working toward that goal? Foreign policy actions are called rational when they maximize movement toward the goal while minimizing the costs involved in such movement (see, e.g., Allison 1971; Verba 1969). The "best" alternative is thereby selected. But as George (1975) has observed, foreign policymakers often do not have enough information to know what their range of options is or to formulate what the consequences of the options are. It is thus hard to choose a "best" alternative. In effect, policymakers operate most of the time with information uncertainty. How the policymaker views the situation and his preferred decision-making styles and strategies can affect the way in which he/she deals with such uncertainty and, in turn, how rational a decision is likely to be.

George (1974, 1975) has proposed some strategies that are commonly used in coping with incomplete information. Such strategies include: satisficing (selecting a "good enough" alternative rather than the "best" alternative), incrementalism (focusing on marginal as opposed to dramatic change by considering a narrow range of alternatives), seeking consensus (acting on what others will support), using an historical analogy (what previous situation does the present one resemble), and relying on a set of principles (a set of maxims that differentiate a "good" from a "bad" alternative). Although these strategies can help policymakers use what information they do have more effectively, the strategies can also become crutches that are relied on, leading to a minimal search for more information or options.

For example, a policymaker can satisfice for the first alternative which shows some positive benefits without considering if there are any other alternatives suggested by the information with even better payoffs. Similarly, consensus can be sought for an option without consideration of the effectiveness of the option for movement toward a goal. Consensus can be attained for that option, so why consider others? What policymakers are like—whether or not they have certain beliefs, their motivations, their preferred decision styles—can suggest which of these strategies for dealing with uncertainty they are likely to choose and if the strategy will become a crutch.

Another factor that impacts on how policymakers deal with information uncertainty involves the nature of the decision-making group in which they find themselves. Foreign policy decisions are generally not made by single policymakers in isolation. If nothing else, there is consultation between a leader and a trusted confidante before a decision is made. What often appears to be the case is that foreign policy decisions are made by small groups embedded in large organizations.

C. Hermann (1978, 1979) has proposed a typology of the small groups involved in foreign policymaking, suggesting that they differ in the way power is distributed among the members of the group and the degree to which members respond and identify with groups outside the present one.

This typology has implications for our discussion in that it identifies groups in which there is likely to be disagreement or conflict over substantive matters (goals, definitions of the situation, alternative courses of action, expected consequences of actions) in the course of making a decision and over the ways in which such conflict is handled. When disagreement is present policymakers are forced to consider a wider range of alternatives and more facets of the situation than when disagreement is not present. But decision making is not possible if the disagreements or conflict cannot be resolved. How conflict is resolved gives us an indication of how much of the available information is actually used. Leader's preference, unanimity, use of a working majority, and a formal vote are all ways of resolving conflict and are indicative of whose information is considered and how available information must be distorted for a decision to occur.

The typology in table 8.2, inspired by C. Hermann (1978, 1979), illustrates the types of groups that result from the combination of the two decision-structure dimensions—power distribution and membership identity/loyalty. The typology also suggests whether disagreement or conflict occurs in the group and the ways in which such disagreement or conflict is handled. This typology builds on material from C. Hermann (1978, 1979) and C. Hermann et al. (1979). It indicates how different the decision process and output can be, depending on the nature of the small face-to-face group engaged in the policymaking. What policymakers are like will influence whether or not they will tolerate conflict and their preferred means of handling conflicts when such arise. If the policymakers are in leadership positions, their characteristics will probably have an impact on the type of decision unit in which they will prefer to work if given a choice.

One last factor that can influence how policymakers deal with information uncertainty involves their general operating goals or reasons for being actors in the political arena. Are they primarily concerned about maintaining (or advancing) themselves in their office or position of power and influence? Is there a specific problem or area of concern which they are committed to solving? Are they interested in furthering a certain ideology or set of beliefs about how things should be done? Or are they interested in the public support and adulation that their

Table 8.2   Processes and behaviors that occur in decision units where power distribution and role of members differ

Power distribution	Delegates from autonomous organizations (Positions depend on those of external organization; little latitude to change position)	Leaders from autonomous organizations (Initial positions depend on those of external organiza-tion but can change if so desire)	No external autonomous unit membership (Positions shared by group members, can change if all are so disposed)
Predom-inant leader (Power lodged in one person)	(Interagency bu-reaucratic task force with head of gov-ernment)[a] Delegates feel pres-sure not to lose too much; often engage in pre-meeting coalition building; if cannot build coalition will exag-gerate differences in positions; often accept status quo, stating any deci-sions in broad, vague terms.	(Ministerial cabinet in dictatorship) Some disagreement is tolerated; use advocacy process, presenting informa-tion favoring posi-tion if not too diver-gent from leader's position; members can shift positions on basis of argu-ments; advantages and disadvantages of various positions will be presented as positions are debated; innovative behavior is possible.	(Head of govern-ment with staff of advisors) Members of group seen as advisory to leader; little dis-agreement generally tolerated, with members reinforcing leader's views; minimal information gathering done; if disagree with leader's position members use infor-mal persuasion to gain some change; can make quick decisions but are often of a less cautious, less conservative nature than if consultation was more widely undertaken.

Table 8.2   (continued)

Power distribution	Delegates from autonomous organizations (Positions depend on those of external organization; little latitude to change position)	Leaders from autonomous organizations (Initial positions depend on those of external organization but can change if so desire)	No external autonomous unit membership (Positions shared by group members, can change if all are so disposed)
Subset of dominant leaders (Power held by minority subset of group)	(Interagency coordinating committee with powerful co-chairpersons) Delegates are likely to ally with leader having position closest to that of their organization; leaders will seek coalitions with delegates to increase their influence, probably through side payments; conflict may arise over how decisions are made with leaders' preferences prevailing if leaders form coalition; if leaders differ, may be push to refer problems to another group; decisions may be slow and change in nature depending on winning coalitions which allow delegates to claim some victories with some losses.	(Cabinet in parliamentary system) Coalition building is a predominant activity of this group, the less powerful members of the group playing broker or mediator roles among the more powerful; if leaders can agree on decision they will push for a working majority as the means for resolving conflict; time will be spent in "behind the scenes" power plays as leaders may threaten to reconstitute group toward their own ends; can take fairly bold actions if working majority in place.	(Legislative committee with seniority system) Leaders establish coalition framework through log rolling, trade-offs, side payments, and compromise to insure a working majority; rules as to how decisions are made are set in place with rewards for seeing they are implemented; advocacy of differing alternatives is sanctioned if not too deviant from position of working majority.

Table 8.2 (continued)

Power distribution	Delegates from autonomous organizations (Positions depend on those of external organization; little latitude to change position)	Leaders from autonomous organizations (Initial positions depend on those of external organization but can change if so desire)	No external autonomous unit membership (Positions shared by group members, can change if all are so disposed)
Approximate power parity (Power dispersed across members of group)	(Interagency work group) Members experience cross pressures of loyalty to external organization and group; engage in slow, incremental bargaining with trade-offs, log rolling, and compromise; may seek outside information to aid in deliberations; extreme behavior highly unlikely, as response often is qualified or limited to take in the varying positions; decisions are often postponed or referred to other groups; deadlock is a definite possibility.	(Military junta) Although have initial loyalty to external organization, soon learn that only way can make decisions is if become a cohesive unit; time is spent in designing decision rules to maintain cohesiveness; information is often distorted to enable consensus to be achieved; problems that have the possibility of leading to disagreement are avoided; tendency to accept options on which can build consensus regardless of consequences.	(Autonomous board, commission, or court) Because support and respect from other members is important to being able to make decisions, have high concern for group welfare and cohesiveness; attempt not to put person in position of "loser" but if take deviant position too often will be isolated; develop impersonal decision rules as "split the difference" and "let external developments dictate our choice"; can lead to highly assertive, high-commitment behaviors.

[a] Examples of each type of decision unit are listed in parentheses before the description of processes and behaviors.

position brings them? Literature on who becomes a political leader (for example, Barber 1965; Burns 1978; M. Hermann 1977; Paige 1977) indicates that these are basic motivating factors explaining why persons seek political office.

These goals can have far-reaching consequences for how the policymaker will deal with information uncertainty. The goals can affect what information is perceived as relevant, how it is interpreted, and what alternatives are seen as worth pursuing. Thus, a political leader interested in public support and adulation may focus only on those problems which the polls indicate people find him/her addressing effectively, putting off issues where support is not forthcoming. How much support a particular option would receive becomes a major criterion for its selection or rejection.

As with other factors affecting how policymakers deal with information uncertainty, these basic operating goals are in part dictated by the policymaker's personal characteristics. We would like to argue that the role orientations derived from personal characteristics largely help to define which of several ways of dealing with information uncertainty will be used. Table 8.3 presents the proposed linkages between these two sets of variables. Based on this information, let us examine how leaders with each orientation deal with uncertainty and what might be considered by them a high-quality decision.

Expansionist Role Orientation

From table 8.3 we note that the leader with an expansionist role orientation is guided by a set of principles or beliefs. This set of beliefs primarily concerns the power of the nation. Power is linked with expanded resources and territory. "The more one has, the more powerful one is." There is a certain messianic spirit about expansionist leaders in that they are convinced of the correctness of their position and of the strategies for pursuing their goal. They will gather around them highly loyal staffs who will be consulted at times but whose primary function is seen as implementation. Information is sought that complements the goal and preferred alternatives. There is a certain self-fulfilling prophecy about what information is assimilated and what situations pose problems.

If an effective decision is one where there is movement toward a goal, the decisions that expansionist leaders make will meet this criterion. At least each decision will be intended to lead to some improvement in the nation's power position. In a sense the decisions

Table 8.3 Proposed linkages between ways of coping with information uncertainty and the foreign policy role orientations

Orientation leader has	General operating goal[a]	George's (1975) commonly used strategies for coping with uncertainty[b]
Expansionist	Maintain self in office; further ideology or set of beliefs	Rely on set of principles; use historical analogy
Active independent	Further ideology or set of beliefs	Rely on set of principles; use incrementalism
Influential	Maintain self in office	Seek consensus; satisfice
Mediator/integrator	Solve societal problems	Seek consensus
Opportunist	Seek public support	Seek consensus; use incrementalism
Developmental	Solve particular societal problem	Use incrementalism; satisfice

[a] The four general operating goals being considered here are maintenance of self in office, in est in furthering ideology or set of beliefs, interest in solving a societal problem(s), and des for public support and adulation. See earlier discussion of these goals.
[b] The commonly used strategies referred to here are: satisficing, use of incrementalism, seek consensus, use of historical analogy, and relying on a set of principles. These are discussed more detail earlier in the paper.

will be fairly rational since the leader is likely to be calculating in thinking about which among the alternatives considered would be the best. But given the closed system in which the expansionist leader is operating, the range of alternatives considered is likely to be narrow, the information search concerned with defining the problem and situ-

Willingness to tolerate substantive disagreement or conflict[c]	How resolve substantive disagreement or conflict when arises[d]	Type of decision making units likely to prefer[e]
Lo	Leader preference	Predominant leader in group with no external membership
Hi	Leader preference; reconstitution of decision making unit; dissolution of decision making unit	Predominant leader in group with leaders from autonomous organizations
Mo	Unanimity; working majority	Predominant leader in group with leaders from autonomous organizations
Lo	Working majority; formal voting	Groups with approximate power parity and no external memberships or leaders from autonomous organizations
Mo	Unanimity; outside referral of problem	Groups with approximate power parity or subset of dominant leaders that comprise delegates from autonomous organizations
Lo	Leader preference; working majority	Prefer group with no external memberships; can tolerate any power distribution

he abbreviations here stand for high (Hi), moderate (Mo), and low (Lo).
he categories listed here build on a discussion of ways of handling decision-unit conflict
scribed in C. Hermann (1979).
efer back to appendix 2 for descriptions of the behavior in the particular decision units noted
re.

ation is likely to be limited, and the consequences of the decision for other sectors of society are unlikely to have been carefully thought through. The leader works in a relative information vacuum. Moreover, with the expansionist's low tolerance for conflict and preference for a leader-staff decision group, the situation is ripe for the operation of the processes of groupthink (Janis 1972) and the malfunctions in the advisory system which George (1974) has described.

Are there ways of improving the expansionist leader's use of information? Data linking the expansionist orientation to foreign policy behavior shows less impact for this predisposition the more training in foreign affairs the leader has had. The expansionist leader appears to learn from his/her mistakes and to gain a wider repertoire of behavior with experience. A similar thing also happens with interest in foreign affairs. The more interested the expansionist is in foreign affairs, the wider his/her repertoire of behavior. With increased interest, the expansionist leader works harder at making sure he/she is considering the "best" alternative for the situation. Given the tight control that such leaders maintain over the foreign policymaking process, it is difficult to increase the diversity of the decision-making group. However, an alert special assistant (or two) could increase the information being considered by couching additional information in terms of the power goal.

Active-Independent Role Orientation

Turning to the leader with an active independent role orientation, we note again a reliance on a set of principles for guiding behavior—the need to remain independent and unaligned. The active independent leader, however, seeks out information to make sure all bases are covered, that all options are considered so as to insure no loss in independent status. The possible outcomes or consequences of options are a particularly salient focus in such an information search. The active independent leader is willing to take small steps if there remains any uncertainty about the possible consequences of a larger initiative. This type of leader finds a closed group of advisors stifling because there is always the fear of missing something and being caught in a dependent relationship.

It is the aim of active independent leaders to make decisions that insure movement toward a goal and to make decisions that are as rational as the circumstances allow. They are interested in high-quality decisions. But often due to their own uncertainties, such leaders settle for less than best if they can be sure of the outcome. To a certain extent their motto is, "it is better to be safe than sorry."

Are there ways of increasing the active independent leader's trust in the information at hand? One way might be to institutionalize a multiple advocacy system (see George 1972, 1975) where the leader is assured of certain types of information on a regular basis from a wide range of groups within the government. With constant monitoring by the leader, such a system might be molded so that it provides the depth of information the active independent needs to make a rational and effective decision.

Influential Role Orientation

For leaders with influential role orientations, maintaining themselves in office is of major importance so that they can continue to exercise influence in the international system. An important part of keeping one's self in office involves maintaining a degree of consensus among key individuals in government that one is making appropriate and helpful decisions. The perceptions of others are important to the influential leader, particularly the perceptions of those others whose support is necessary for staying in power. Alternatives and options are unlikely to be given careful consideration if they are unpopular among these individuals. In effect, consideration of domestic outcomes of foreign policy alternatives become as important (at times even more important) than consideration of outcomes in the international arena. The influential leader wants to know how important others are defining the situation before he/she will act on it.

For leaders with an influential orientation, an effective decision is one that gains them support—or, at least, does not lose them support —among those in the environment whose support is necessary to stay in office. In making decisions the pros and cons of a particular option affecting the leader's power base are as much a consideration as the pros and cons of the option for solving the problem at hand. Rationality calculations are compounded. Moreover, problems are not addressed and decisions are postponed if the political climate is not right.

With the leader with an influential orientation we confront the issue of the leader who actually leads versus the leader who follows. The policymakers with this orientation are unlikely to take many stands that they perceive are not condoned by the important members of their constituencies. If it were possible for these leaders to separate out the calculations with regard to the problem from the calculations with regard to political support, they could discover which of their foreign policy decisions actually have implications for their domestic political support and which do not. By classifying the different types of decisions, they could focus more directly on the foreign policy problems unaffected by political support issues while picking and choosing among the foreign policy problems that are affected by political support issues.

Mediator-Integrator Role Orientation

The leader with a mediator-integrator role orientation is genuinely interested in seeing that problems are solved. Compromise is always possible and these leaders are facile at finding such compromises or at setting mechanisms into motion that permit compromise. Leaders with this orientation are agitated by conflict and disagreement. But here as with the leader having an influential orientation, problems are perceived in terms of people's positions rather than for their substantive content. Questions such as who will support what option and how an option must be modified to receive support are more likely to be addressed than the question of whether the option will move them toward a particular goal.

For leaders with a mediator-integrator orientation an effective decision is one which resolves a disagreement or conflict between two or more parties. Considerations of the nature of the decision are of less consequence than the fact that a resolution was possible and was achieved. In other words, they are not very interested in how rational the decision was. These leaders are likely to work with the information on hand rather than seek more information unless there is no alternative available to work with that would receive enough support. These leaders perceive themselves as grand negotiators.

How can leaders with this orientation be induced to pay more attention to the nature of the decision as well as the fact that a decision can be reached? Leaders with a mediator-integrator orientation might benefit from having on their staff a form of devil's advocate whose role was to raise questions about the consequences of the various options for solving the problem given the goals of the parties involved. Such an individual would have to be highly regarded by the leader and tenacious in carrying out his/her duties for the information to make a difference.

Opportunist Orientation

Leaders with an opportunist role orientation take their cues from others, being interested in ascertaining what will receive widespread public support. These leaders will make only marginal moves without knowledge that there is support "out there" for a specific action. They seek out information about the public's opinions. For such leaders an important consequence to consider for any option being scrutinized is what is the degree of public support it is likely to generate. Moreover, problems that are agitating the public become important issues for these leaders to try to solve.

An effective decision for leaders with an opportunist orientation is one which generates wide public support. The long-term consequences are less germane if the decision has an immediate payoff that is perceived by the people as good. Although information is widely sought and disagreement is fostered to some degree, the information of interest is concerned with support rather than the substance of the problem.

More sensitive assessment of support might aid leaders with an opportunist orientation to pay more attention to the substance of the problem and options. Instead of merely ascertaining whether persons would support X or Y option, one might also seek the reasons for such support and the circumstances under which individuals would change their support. Answers to questions like these provide information about support while also indicating something about the substance of the issue. For substance to be considered in any great detail by leaders with an opportunist orientation it must be intertwined with answers to questions of support. The best possible outcome with such leaders would be for them to make decisions on seeking support based on substantive arguments.

Developmental Role Orientation

Leaders with a developmental role orientation have a particular interest in holding office—a desire to improve their nation, to see it reach its potential. They often have definite ideas about how this can be done and are not highly tolerant of persons who do not perceive the problem as they do. What these leaders want are individuals around them who are interested in taking action and implementing their schemes for national improvement. Leaders with developmental orientations are willing to move incrementally toward their goal as long as there is some continual movement.

Leaders with a developmental orientation are obsessed with "effective" decision making or, in other words, movement toward their goal. But because they want continual movement toward the goal, they often settle for less than the "best" option. Such leaders seek options that are implementable, being highly perceptive as to what can and cannot be done rather quickly with some payoff in the international arena. Problems sometimes arise, however, because leaders with this orientation translate most stimuli as having something to do with issues of development and treat them accordingly.

The question can be asked of leaders with a developmental orientation, how they could be persuaded to consider alternatives with long-term as opposed to short-term gains. Such might begin to happen if these leaders would consider a review process following the postulation of alternatives in which the purpose was to see if any options with long-term gain had been excluded from discussion just because they did not show immediate payoffs. Alternatively the task of the review group might be to ascertain what long-term benefits are associated with each of the options perceived as providing short-term gains. The leader might be persuaded that he/she would make a more effective decision by selecting that alternative with both long-term and short-term benefits and by avoiding options with short-term gains but long-term costs. The review process would be viewed as setting the decision-making situation into perspective.

Implications

The descriptions of the role orientations presented here are idealized and certainly need to be elaborated by case materials and further systematic study. Nevertheless this intuitive analysis suggests that political leaders with these six foreign policy role orientations deal with information uncertainty in different ways. The goals of the various types of leaders differ as do their means of resolving conflict, their preferred decision units, their tolerance of disagreement/conflict, and their use of George's (1975) strategies for coping with uncertainty. The bases for what is considered effective or could be considered rational, therefore, differ with the various orientations. Moreover, in order to get the leaders to use more of the information available to them, we would need to employ different techniques. It may take information about the impact of such things as leaders' foreign policy role orientations before we can develop adequate criteria for deciding what is effective, rational, or high-quality decision making.

9

Role Sets and Foreign Policy Analysis

in Southeast Asia

Stephen G. Walker and Sheldon W. Simon

In this paper we attempt to use concepts associated with role theory to describe and understand the dynamics of foreign policy selection and implementation in Southeast Asia. For this task we make the presumption that "role" is identical in important respects with "policy" and, therefore, the intellectual processes associated with role analysis lend themselves readily and usefully to policy analysis. Specifically, we will argue that *role enactment* as a concept used to describe behavior should also be applicable to the description of policy implementation, while *role location* as a concept employed to analyze the selection of one or more roles among many possibilities should be valuable in understanding the adoption of policies. Briefly, the rationale for this argument rests upon two points (see also Walker 1979, 1981).

First, the concepts "role" and "policy" have similar normative characteristics. A role is a set of norms which prescribe behavior in a given situation toward the occupants of other roles which collectively constitute a role set. A policy is also defined in terms of norms which prescribe behavior toward others in a situation. Role analysis and policy analysis, therefore, both involve the assessment of behavior in terms of the norms associated with particular roles or policies.

Second, role analysis goes beyond classical policy analysis in that the norms associated with role analysis encompass more than the ends/means norm of rationality associated with conventional policy analysis. Rational policy analysis tends to appraise behavior by the criterion of whether it protects or achieves the goals articulated in the norms that constitute the policy. Role analysis goes beyond this assessment to include whether the behavior meets the *role expectations* of other members of the role set (the targets of the policy), the *demands* of the audience (third parties in the policy situation), and the *role conceptions* of the individual or group enacting the role (implementing the policy).

Consequently, in the context of role theory, a good foreign policy is one that not only protects or achieves its goals but also meets the expectations and demands of others in the situation. Although this set of criteria is ipso facto more difficult to satisfy, it is our contention that these norms are precisely what participants in foreign policy often strive to meet. Since role expectations, demands, and role conceptions do not always coincide, policymakers often find themselves experiencing *role conflict*. Role theorists have advanced several strategies for dealing with role conflict, defined as a situation in which multiple roles are elicited by competing or conflicting expectations, cues, and conceptions (Sarbin and Allen 1968, 538). In addition to the enactment of one role at the expense of another, they are:

1. the *merger* of two or more roles so that they are indistinguishable in terms of role enactment within the period of observation
2. the *interpenetration* of roles without their merger in behavioral terms within the period of observation
3. the *alternation* of two or more roles within the period of observation
4. *altercasting*, that is, responding to cues and expectations with behavior that creates a reorientation of the target's role expectations

The elicitation of multiple roles may take two basic forms: *bilateral* in which two or more competing roles are elicited toward the same target; *multilateral*, in which two or more competing roles are evoked toward two or more targets. Depending upon the form which role conflict assumes, one can hypothesize that different strategies may be appropriate to deal with it.

H1: If the form of role conflict is bilateral, then the strategy tends to be either merger or interpenetration.
H2: If the form of role conflict is multilateral, then the strategy tends to be either alternation or altercasting.

These hypotheses presume that merger and interpenetration strategies are response patterns which mirror the mixture of cues emanating from a single target, while alternation and altercasting strategies resemble the more easily differentiated patterns of cues from multiple targets.

If it is true that policymakers strive to meet the simultaneous sources of norms represented by expectations, demands, and conceptions, then a third hypothesis is also in order:

H3: Regardless of whether the form of role conflict is bilateral or multilateral, the strategy of enacting one role at the expense of another will tend to be avoided.

However, if the preferred strategies associated with each form of role conflict are inadequate and it becomes necessary to enact one role at the expense of another, which one will be selected?

The possibilities include enacting the role that conforms to conceptions, expectations, or demands. These sources of influence, in turn, can have two locations: domestic and international. If the role enactment conforms to the conceptions of the policymaker or to the demands of his domestic constituency, then domestic sources of influence are decisive. On the other hand, if the enactment meets the target's expectations or the demands of third parties either within or external to the region, then international sources determine the resolution of role conflict. One criticism of role theory has been that it lacks a set of propositions which resolve role conflict when one role must be enacted at the expense of others (Walker 1979, 176).

Elsewhere, one of us (Walker, 1983b, chapter 4 in this volume) has argued more generally that the domain of political behavior, defined as the process of authoritatively allocating values for a society (Easton 1953), has characteristics implicit in this definition which make exchange theory the most appropriate source of propositions to inform the concepts of role analysis and meet this criticism. According to Easton "authoritative allocation" is the core of the political process.

Exchange theory systematically articulates the logic of allocation as a theory of exchange, an explanation of the act of giving or taking one thing in exchange for another. Depending upon the domain, the scope of exchange theory broadens from the exchange of concrete commodities (economics) to the exchange of behaviors that may be beneficial to one or more of the participants in the exchange (politics) (Walker 1981, 274; see also Baldwin 1978; Homans 1961, 1974; Blau 1964; Emerson 1972a, 1972b).

An exchange theory of global politics implies at least six types of roles in the exchange process: consumer, producer, belligerent, hegemone, facilitator, and provocateur. The consumer role refers to the behavior of one state associated with gaining or maintaining assistance from another state, while behaviors which supply such assistance are manifestations of a producer role. A belligerent role involves either resisting requests for assistance or pressing demands for assistance in the face of resistance (Walker 1983b, 14). If the outcome of the ensuing conflict results in a one-sided exchange relationship, the dominant nation is enacting a hegemonial role. A facilitator role is one in which a state attempts to establish or maintain an exchange among other states, while a provocateur role involves disrupting or preventing an exchange relationship among other states (Walker 1983b, 14; Hudson et al. 1982; Wilkinson 1969, 12-13).

These six roles encompass the major dimensions of political behavior implicit in Easton's (1953) definition of the political process as the authoritative allocation of values. Also implied in this definition are four subprocesses: the exchange process, the role-location process, the conflict process, and the institution-building process (Walker 1983b, 7–8).

1. The *exchange process* refers to the actual allocation of values among the individuals and groups in the political process.
2. The *role-location process* refers to the authoritative establishment of a shared set of expectations regarding the terms of allocation.
3. The *conflict process* refers to the creation of adversary relations among individuals or groups regarding the terms of allocation and/or the set of shared expectations regarding the terms of allocation.
4. The *institution-building process* refers to the formalization of the terms of allocation and the set of shared expectations over a long period of time.

There is also a major proposition which functions as a general law regarding each subprocess (Walker 1983b, 7–14):

1. *Exchange proposition.* A state's foreign policy tends to be an instrument for the pursuit or maintenance of domestic policy goals; international exchange relationships tend to consist of the giving and taking of resources between states to solve their respective domestic problems.

2. *Role-location proposition.* In the event that a state cannot avoid the enactment of one international role at the expense of another one, the resolution of role conflict will tend to be in favor of the role that most enhances domestic policy goals.

3. *Origins-of-conflict proposition.* Conflict situations among states tend to occur when (a) the terms of the allocation have not been established among the states in the exchange process, or (b) the existing set of shared expectations among the states in the exchange process breaks down. Then states in conflict tend to adopt policies to protect against armed attack, severe economic dislocation, and the loss of cultural or territorial identity.

4. *Institution-building proposition.* States tend to behave toward one another in accord with a pattern of conduct whose basis in an exchange relationship may no longer exist.

Propositions 1 and 3 account for the existence of consumer, producer, and belligerent roles in the international political process, while the second proposition resolves role conflicts. A fifth proposition accounts for the existence of facilitator and provocateur roles:

5. *Linkage proposition.* In order to pursue or maintain domestic policy goals, a state may act to establish, maintain, or disrupt a shared set of expectations or the allocation of values among other states.

A theoretical justification for these propositions is the subject of an earlier paper by one of us (Walker 1983b), which appears as chapter 4 in this volume. We hope to demonstrate the utility of these propositions for understanding foreign policy through role analysis by employing them as guidelines in the conduct of a theoretically informed historical interpretation of the regional foreign policies of selected states in mainland Southeast Asia between 1975 and the present. We will focus our attention upon China, Vietnam, Cambodia, and Thailand as core actors plus Japan, the United States, the USSR, and the ASEAN bloc as peripheral actors.

Our focus upon a region in the Third World should prove to be particularly interesting because in the aftermath of decolonization we should be able to observe attempts by these states at the formation of new role sets, that is, the establishment of a series of new exchange relationships accompanied by sets of shared expectations among them. With the aid of our five exchange propositions and the hypotheses dealing with role conflict, we hope to be able to interpret variations in the foreign policies of these states and also diagnose the extent to which they have formed new role sets since 1975.

Role Theory and Foreign Policy Analysis

The history of Southeast Asian international relations reveals three major relationships which have been important structural components of the total network of relations among the countries in the region (Simon and Walker 1983, 7–15). They are: (1) Sino-Southeast Asian relations, (2) Vietnamese-Thai relations and their relationships with the smaller entities located between them in what is now Laos and Cambodia, and (3) relations with outside powers, such as France, Russia, and the United States, who have intermittently intruded into the region—sometimes at the invitation of one of the local powers. In our examination of post-1975 relationships, we will focus primarily upon the axes provided by Sino-Vietnamese and Thai-Vietnamese relations, but it will also be necessary to remain sensitive to the potential impact of governments outside of the region.

We begin our analysis with a dissection of Vietnamese foreign policy because the logic provided by our theory of foreign policy makes a Vietnamese focus most likely to be fruitful. Proposition 1 informs us that a state's foreign policy tends to be an instrument for the pursuit or maintenance of domestic policy goals. A corollary of this proposition is that among a set of states, the one with the most pressing domestic problems (defined as an imbalance between the resources necessary to handle these problems and the available domestic resources) is the state most likely to take the initiative in requesting assistance from abroad and establishing exchange relationships with other countries. Vietnam is clearly the state in the region with the most volatile combination of domestic problems and incentives to seek external assistance in the aftermath of the most destructive war in its history.

The traditional sources of external resources for Vietnam have been the development of trade ties with China and the expansion of Vietnamese dominance westward into the remainder of Indochina (Simon and Walker 1983, 8–10). The latter response was, if anything, reinforced by the French colonial experience. The French used Vietnamese officials to administer Laos and Cambodia. In addition two contemporary external sources of assistance exist in the form of the United States and the Soviet Union. However, to establish exchange relations with either superpower would violate the traditional role expectations of China regarding Sino-Vietnamese relations and, in the context of existing Sino-Soviet relations, place Vietnam in danger of becoming embroiled in the Sino-Soviet conflict. The expectations of each Communist giant toward Vietnam might, therefore, create a multilateral role-conflict situation for Vietnamese leaders.

In fact the Hanoi government had faced this type of dilemma during the Vietnam War as they tried to maximize aid from both China and the USSR in their prosecution of the war. We have argued earlier (see hypotheses 2 and 3) that states will tend to avoid resolving a role-conflict situation by selecting one role at the expense of another. Decision makers will attempt either to alternate, merge, or interpenetrate the conflicting roles or to respond by creating a reorientation of the role expectations held by at least one of the sources of the role conflict. According to proposition 2, however, in the event that a state cannot avoid the enactment of one international role at the expense of another, the resolution of role conflict will tend to be in favor of the role that most enhances domestic policy goals. In this case China and the Soviet Union each wanted Vietnamese support against the other in return for their aid against the United States and the Saigon regime.

During the course of the Second Indochina War, Hanoi initially used alternating and altercasting strategies to resolve role conflict (Simon 1982, 140–46). During the 1965–75 decade, North Vietnam was pressured by both the Chinese and Soviets to side with each against the other. Adroitly refusing to play this harmful political game, Ho Chi Minh maneuvered between Moscow and Peking, while urging them to settle their differences and consolidate their support behind Vietminh efforts to defeat the United States and South Vietnam. Since the DRV's primary goal was to maximize military assistance, it leaned toward a particular partner during the war only when its adversary seemed to be obstructing aid. Thus, in the 1960s, Hanoi opposed China's obstruction of Soviet rail shipments through the PRC.

The Vietnamese communists carefully avoided the appearance of excessive dependence on either supplier, however, for fear that the other would reduce its aid. From China came light arms and construction personnel to maintain transportation routes between the two countries. The USSR provided the heavy equipment to prosecute the war as it moved from guerrilla to conventional tactics. Only in the last stages of the conflict and its aftermath did Hanoi opt for Soviet support over the Chinese, for at that point only the Russians could provide the necessary armor and artillery for the final assault on the South in 1975. Thus Vietnam reluctantly abandoned the alternating and altercasting strategies associated with multilateral role conflict (hypothesis 2), knowing that to do so would lead to the loss of a major ally (hypothesis 3).

When Hanoi chose to meet the expectations of Moscow at the expense of those emanating from Peking, this choice was consistent with propositions 2 and 3. The Vietnamese domestic goals at stake were the threat of armed attack, the possibility of severe economic dislocation, and the potential loss of cultural and territorial identity. Soviet military and economic aid was vital and could not be matched by an outmoded Chinese military and economic resource base. In exchange, the USSR demanded the use of port facilities in Vietnam, which violated traditional Chinese expectations regarding the intrusion of external powers into the region and created a corresponding reduction in Chinese status. In the case of the Soviet Union and their demands for naval bases, Chinese security from armed attack was also affected adversely.

The origins of the current Sino-Vietnamese conflict, therefore, are also to be found in the logic of proposition 3: conflict among states tends to occur when (a) the terms of allocation have not been established among the states in the exchange process, or (b) the existing set of shared expectations among the states in the exchange process breaks down. China was unable to meet the domestic needs of Vietnam either during or following the Vietnam War and, consequently, an exchange relationship along traditional lines was not viable. Under these circumstances the set of shared expectations between them broke down as the Vietnamese sought assistance from other states. The refusal of the United States to participate in the postwar reconstruction of Vietnam restricted further the range of external options available to Vietnam and amplified its dependence upon the Soviet Union.

In addition to resources for economic reconstruction and development, Vietnam needed external sources of food. The ravages of the war had reduced the capacity of the country to feed itself. Cambodia was a logical external source of supply. In contrast to Vietnam, it has a low ratio of population-to-rice productive capacity. However, the external chaos created in Cambodia by the spillover of the Vietnam conflict and Kampuchean revolution made the Pol Pot regime an unpredictable neighbor. In this environment of political uncertainty, the high domestic stakes for Vietnam and the traditional Vietnamese hegemonial role toward Cambodia combined to create a volatile, tense relationship between the two countries at the end of the Vietnam War (Simon and Walker 1983, 9–10).

The Kampuchean government under Pol Pot tended to define the relationship as a belligerent one without exploring the possibilities of a stable exchange relationship in which they would supply food in return for a Vietnamese guarantee to respect the national autonomy of Cambodia. Given the level of domestic dissatisfaction with Pol Pot's government, the accompanying exodus of refugees, and the government's own announced policy of guaranteeing their revolutionary society from contamination by outsiders, this bargain was not likely to be explored. When Cambodia engaged in preemptive strikes into Vietnam as a deterrent tactic to lend credibility to their desire for self-imposed isolation, these belligerent cues reinforced the Vietnamese tendency to equate their security with a hegemonial relationship over Cambodia (Simon and Walker 1983).

The military response from Vietnam, therefore, expanded into an all-out invasion and occupation. This development forced Pol Pot's Khmer Rouge administration to seek external aid from China and from Thailand via sanctuary in Thai border enclaves. It also brought the Soviet-North Vietnamese relationship closer together, as Vietnam required Soviet military supplies to maintain its occupation of Cambodia. The Soviet-Vietnamese axis, in turn, created a further incentive for China to support the Cambodian rebels against the Vietnamese invaders. In accord with proposition 3, the Chinese subsequently adopted a producer role toward the Khmer Rouge.

The consequences of the Vietnamese invasion also provoked a Thai response, as refugees poured across the Thai border from Cambodia. Their presence represented a threat to Thai security from armed attack, possible cultural disruption, and potential economic dislocation. The Bangkok government encouraged economic assistance from international agencies to feed the refugees and pushed for their relocation to other countries. While the Thais publicly insisted that the refugee camps would not serve as external sanctuaries for Cambodian rebels, in fact, some of these camps have served in that capacity.

Bangkok also sought assurances of support from the United States and China in the event of a Vietnamese attack. The U.S. response was ambivalent, but the Chinese signaled their resolve to oppose any expansion of Vietnamese hegemony. The most dramatic manifestation of Peking's policy came in the form of the Sino-Vietnamese War in 1979. The PRC also exerted pressure upon the Vietnamese border in 1980, 1983, and 1984 when VPA attacks spilled over into Thailand, thus upholding China's pledge to Bangkok.

Since the Chinese incursion into northern Vietnam and subsequent withdrawal, relations in Indochina have shown little change. China and Vietnam maintain belligerent roles toward one another, while Vietnam has adopted the multiple roles of hegemone and belligerent toward Cambodia. Interdependence characterizes the relationships between China and the deposed Cambodian government, while an interdependent relationship exists between Vietnam and the Soviet Union. Thailand has pursued a policy best characterized as a facilitator role regarding Chinese assistance to the Khmer Rouge and a provocateur role vis-à-vis Vietnamese efforts to dominate Cambodia.

We have made no attempt to provide a detailed account of Southeast Asian relations in the post-1975 period. Instead we have tried to delineate the development of the structural features which characterize these relations and give a theoretically informed interpretation of the generation of these relationships. The five propositions which guided this analysis provide keys to identify and place into perspective the important aspects of the complex set of interactions that have occurred since the end of the Vietnam War. The analysis, however, has not been a test of these propositions or the implicit research hypotheses that they contain.

We will now attempt to specify the theory in a more testable form by using its propositions to hypothesize changes in the structural relationships represented in the Southeast Asia role set. We shall define "structural change" as a shift in the roles of those countries vis-à-vis one another; for example, a change from mutual belligerency to an interdependent or hegemonial relationship between China and Vietnam would be an instance of structural change. By extension, we may define "extensive structural change" in terms of the number of dyadic changes that occur.

Role Conflict and Structural Change

The source of structural change is the development of role conflict, which is created when the expectations of more than one member of a role set conflict and it becomes necessary to enact a new role at the expense of the existing one. This point is reached for a given member of the role set when the merger, interpenetration, alternation, and altercasting strategies fail to deal with role conflict. In Southeast Asia the ASEAN countries have experienced role conflict in the form of competing expectations from Beijing and Moscow as the role set among the belligerent states in Indochina has evolved.

The initial ASEAN response to this multilateral form of role conflict conformed to our role-conflict hypotheses. They tried to avoid endorsing the regional preferences of either one (hypothesis 3), and offered ZOPFAN as a means of resolving tensions. The ZOPFAN initiative, a proposal to create a Zone of Peace, Freedom, and Neutrality, was an instance of altercasting (hypothesis 2). It called for denying outside powers military access to the region. However, Hanoi's security treaty with the Soviet Union in 1978 and the ensuing war between Vietnam and Cambodia undermined this policy.

> The ASEAN states were particularly incensed at Vietnam's action because they violated Hanoi's pledge only a few months earlier not to interfere in the region by force or to aid insurgents. Equally appalling from the ASEAN perspective was Hanoi's invitation to Moscow to enter the region as a security collaborator. Not only was hope for ZOPFAN destroyed, but the ASEAN states were forced to turn once again to what they saw as a less than reliable United States for protection as well as increase their own military budgets at a time they preferred to concentrate on economic growth. (Simon 1983, 309)

Specifically, escalating conflict in Indochina aroused anxieties in Malaysia and Indonesia. They feared an increase in Chinese influence over Thailand as a consequence of Bangkok's reliance upon Beijing to deal with the Vietnamese presence in Cambodia. The leaders in Kuala Lumpur and Jakarta were suspicious of China's willingness to intervene in other countries with important Chinese minorities. This possibility threatened their security, since both nations have important Chinese minority groups. Consequently the two governments met at Kuantan in March 1980 and proposed the following: China would reduce its pressure on Vietnam in exchange for a loosening of Vietnam's ties with the USSR, and renewed bonds with ASEAN, the West, and Japan. Hanoi would remove its forces from the Thai-Cambodian border, and Bangkok would recognize the Heng Samrin regime in Phnom Penh (Simon 1983, 310–11).

This altercasting arrangement would reduce overt Soviet and Chinese influence in the region, an outcome compatible with the previous ZOPFAN proposal. The Kuantan initiative would also recognize Vietnam's expansion into Cambodia, thereby transforming Thailand into a buffer state between Hanoi and Beijing on the north versus Malaysia and Indonesia in the south. This alternative set of role relationships would satisfy Vietnam's domestic needs for external economic assistance, a friendly government in Phnom Penh, and access to Cambodian resources. However, the Thais would have to accept the disappearance of Cambodia as a buffer state between them and the Vietnamese. To date the belligerents have not responded positively to the Kuantan initiative.

Nevertheless, it remains the only plausible alternative to the status quo (Simon 1983, 310). If it should be implemented, the result would be the occurrence of extensive structural change, which we have defined as a shift in a large number of bilateral role relationships in the Southeast Asian role set. A comparison of the structure of the status quo with the structure of the Kuantan alternative appears in figure 9.1. There are sixteen role relationships associated with the Kuantan proposal; there are eight interdependent, cooperative relationships (+'s), four belligerent, conflictual ones (–'s), and four uninvolved neutral ones (o's). Twelve of the sixteen relationships (75 percent) are shifts from the status quo, which amounts to extensive structural change. Vietnam is the most involved member of the role set and, along with China, would contribute most heavily to the over-all change in the role set envisioned in the Kuantan proposal. Vietnam, China, Thailand, and ASEAN would experience the most change in their foreign policy roles among the core actors in the region. What is the likelihood that the decision makers in Beijing, Hanoi, and Bangkok will make these changes in response to the altercasting strategy of the ASEAN states?

According to proposition 2, a state's foreign policy tends to be an instrument for the pursuit or protection of domestic policy goals. Proposition 3 identifies three core domestic goals to be protected: cultural and territorial identity, economic stability, and physical security. We may deduce from these two propositions that the status quo roles and relationships in figure 9.1 will persist so long as they protect or achieve these goals. Alternatively we may infer that the key to forecasting changes in international roles is to specify the domestic changes which will prompt international change and, if possible, the conditions under which the domestic change will occur. One obvious domestic change is a change of

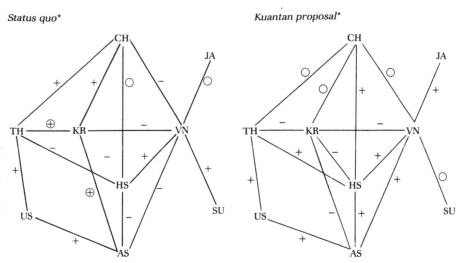

Figure 9.1   Alternative role sets in Southeast Asia

	Actor's involvement in role set[1]		Actor's contribution to role set change[2]		Change in actor's roles[3]	
Vietnam (VN)	(6/16)	38%	(4/12)	33%	(4/6)	67%
China (CH)	(4/16)	25%	(4/12)	33%	(4/4)	100%
Thailand (TH)	(4/16)	25%	(3/12)	25%	(3/4)	75%
ASEAN (AS)	(4/16)	25%	(3/12)	25%	(3/4)	75%
Khmer Rouge (KR)	(5/16)	31%	(3/12)	25%	(3/5)	60%
Heng Samrin (HS)	(5/16)	31%	(3/12)	25%	(3/5)	60%
Japan (JA)	(1/16)	6%	(1/12)	8%	(1/1)	100%
Soviet Union (SU)	(1/16)	6%	(1/12)	8%	(1/1)	100%
United States (US)	(2/16)	13%	(0/12)	0%	(0/2)	0%

* + = cooperative; − = conflictual; ○ = uninvolved; ⊕ = formally uninvolved and informally cooperative.
[1] measured by dividing the total number of roles by the actor into the total relationships for the role set
[2] measured by dividing the number of changed roles for the actor into the total number of changes in the role set
[3] measured by dividing the number of changed roles for the actor into the actor's total number of roles.

regime in one or more of the countries. We shall not focus upon that change per se; we will regard it instead as at most a symptom of more important domestic changes which may or may not lead to a change in leadership or foreign policy in every case.

If we may take the status quo set of relationships in figure 9.1 as a given, what are some potentially important domestic changes that could occur in Vietnam, China, Cambodia, and Thailand? What would be likely sources of change? The preceding analysis has interpreted the policies of the latter three states as essentially reactions to the initiatives undertaken by Vietnam for domestic reasons. Unless their responses have created important domestic problems, the probability of structural change emanating from these sources is relatively low. The belligerency of Chinese policy is unlikely to decrease because the present level of involvement does not create domestic problems for China. On the other hand, an increase in the belligerency of Chinese policy toward Vietnam would incur substantial domestic costs.

Unless Vietnam invades Thailand, Chinese and Thai support for Cambodia is very unlikely to increase. Structural change in the roles of Thailand and the PRC, then, is not likely unless either the roles of Cambodia or Vietnam undergo structural change. Vietnam is unlikely to invade Thailand because of both international and domestic constraints. Leaving aside the latter for the moment, the major external constraint is the probable Soviet veto. Vietnam would have to rely upon an increase in Soviet aid already estimated to be at least $3 million per day. There are no payoffs and many negative outcomes for the USSR associated with an attack upon Thailand. It would destroy Soviet relations with the ASEAN countries, exacerbate the Sino-Soviet conflict, and provoke a confrontation with the United States.

A change in Cambodia's role is also unlikely. The Cambodian rebels do not have the capability to expel the Vietnamese. On the other hand the Khmer Rouge faction is strong enough to block a diplomatic settlement in which the two other resistance factions would form a "Grand Coalition" government with the Vietnamese puppet regime in exchange for the withdrawal of Vietnam's forces. The Grand Coalition is not strong enough to dominate the Khmer Rouge without Vietnamese troops.

The most likely source of structural change, therefore, is Vietnam. If Hanoi takes the initiative, the other nations in the region are likely to respond, just as they reacted earlier to other Vietnamese initiatives. The question, then, is in what direction and under what conditions are Vietnamese initiatives likely to occur? In addition to the probable

Soviet veto of a wider war, there are domestic obstacles against an initiative in that direction. The necessity to pursue the war in Cambodia and also station troops along the Chinese border increases Vietnam's reliance upon Soviet military aid and reduces the domestic resources available for economic reconstruction and development. Either an intensive escalation of the conflict within Cambodia or an expansion of the war into Thailand would exacerbate the costs associated with a belligerent-hegemonial policy.

On the other hand, abandonment of the Vietnamese occupation of Cambodia also appears unlikely. Although VPA forces invaded Kampuchea to secure their country from armed attack, the domestic consequences of occupation make withdrawal unattractive. Because of an ill-administered reconstruction effort within Vietnam, which has affected rice production, among other crops, an exodus has occurred from some rural areas into eastern Cambodia. Several tens of thousands of Vietnamese now live in Cambodia; and the potential exists for a net Vietnamese gain in agricultural and aquatic resources from Cambodia once the latter begins to repay Hanoi's generous aid program (*Indochina Report* 1984).

The impact of these developments upon Vietnam's willingness to withdraw from Cambodia can be presented in graph form. It is possible to project some hypothetical points when Hanoi's role should be more likely to shift away from the belligerent hegemone toward the interdependent relationship with Cambodia envisioned in the Kuantan proposal and its subsequent variants. These projections appear in figure 9.2, which graphs the relationships between Vietnam's dependence upon Cambodian land for Vietnamese emigrants and crops for import into Vietnam versus the rate of economic recovery and the development of administrative efficiency in the management of Vietnam's economy.

Two points in figure 9.2 (A and B) divide the periods in which Vietnam is either more or less likely, respectively, to change its present roles of belligerent-hegemone. The area to the left of point A represents the period between 1975 and the immediate future. In the short run the graph indicates that Cambodian resources (CR) are becoming more important more rapidly than Vietnam's internal recovery (VR) can compensate. Paradoxically, the SRV's reconstruction is actually impeded by the allocation of Vietnamese resources to aid in Cambodia's recovery from the Pol Pot devastation (McWilliams 1984). As more Vietnamese migrate, the burden on the SRV's economy is reduced and Vietnam's productivity rises. However, the emigrants are reportedly transmitting

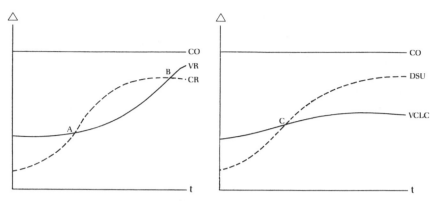

Figure 9.2 Trends and turning points in Vietnam's foreign policy

a substantial portion of their crops and fish into Vietnam's economy, making it increasingly dependent upon Cambodian resources.

The area between A and B represents a period in which Vietnam is most unlikely to change its policy. Until the SRV's domestic productivity increases significantly, it is unlikely that point B will be realized. Vietnam, therefore, is unlikely to withdraw from Cambodia once point A is reached until its neighbor becomes significantly less important as a source of agricultural and aquatic resources (the area beyond point B). Even if Hanoi's economy becomes self-sufficient or develops enough to trade for these commodities with Cambodia or other suppliers, withdrawal may not follow. The migration of Vietnamese into Cambodia expands the SRV's psychological boundaries, making Kampuchea less a buffer with Thailand and more an extension of Vietnam.

Another important set of trends is the relationship between the Vietnamese capital and labor consumed by their occupation of Cambodia (VCLC) versus the increase in their dependence upon the Soviet Union (DSU) for the development of Vietnam and the provision of resources for the friendly regime protecting Vietnamese living in Cambodia. The trade-off between these two trends is divided by point C. The area to the left of point C is the period when dependence upon the USSR has not reached the point (C) where the Soviet contribution to the Cambodian operation and Vietnamese development efforts is greater than Vietnam's. This point may occur during the upward slope of VCLC, increasing in probability as the depletion of Vietnam's resources results in the VCLC's slope flattening and, finally, turning downward in the face of continued Cambodian opposition (CO).

Prior to the time represented by point C, Vietnam is unlikely to change its role of belligerent-hegemone. However, as point C approaches, the Vietnamese face the prospect of surrendering control over their domestic and foreign policies to the USSR. The probability of a change in Vietnam's role should first increase as this point is approached and then decrease again as point C passes and Vietnam's control over their own affairs passes increasingly into Soviet hands.

Depending upon the relationship among points A, B, and C, therefore, one can predict with varying degrees of confidence whether there will be a structural change in Vietnam's international role toward Cambodia. These predictions are stated in the following hypotheses. Assuming a constant level of Cambodian opposition (CO):

H4: If point C becomes imminent prior to point A, then Vietnam's role is likely to change prior to point A.

H5: If point C approaches between point A and point B, then Vietnam's role is less likely to change than if C precedes A.

H6: If point C becomes likely to occur after point B, then Vietnam's role is most likely to change after point B and prior to point C.

H7: If point C does not occur, then a change in Vietnam's role is most likely after point B, less likely prior to point A, and unlikely between point A and point B.

These hypotheses reflect the presence of different combinations of antecedent conditions. Hypothesis 4 addresses the situation when Cambodia has not yet become a major supplier of resources for Vietnam, but dependence upon the USSR has become a threat to Vietnamese autonomy. Under these circumstances Hanoi is likely to change its role. Hypothesis 5 specifies the situation when Cambodian resources have become important to Vietnam, but the cost of maintaining access is the threat of Soviet domination. How the Vietnamese would resolve the trade-off between the risks of severe economic dislocation and the loss of autonomy is unclear. Hypothesis 6 refers to the situation when access to Cambodian resources is no longer so vital and the cost is likely to be excessive dependence upon the USSR. Under these conditions a change in Vietnam's role is very likely. Hypothesis 7 states the likelihood of a role change in the absence of high dependence upon the Soviet Union under varying conditions of dependence upon Cambodian resources.

At the present time the conditions specified in hypothesis 7 appear to be present. Cambodia is not presently a major supplier of resources for Vietnam, and Vietnamese dependence upon the USSR does not appear to be close to point C. Consequently, our short-range forecast is for no structural change in Vietnam's role toward Cambodia. Unless point C or point B is reached, our long-range forecast is the same as for the short run. Finally, the occurrence of point A would strengthen the forecast of no structural change.

To the extent that role change by other states in the region is a function of Vietnamese change, extensive structural change is also relatively unlikely. The Kuantan role scenario, therefore, is an improbable one unless changes in the domestic conditions of other Southeast Asian states or in Sino-Soviet relations occur. The collapse of the Cambodian resistance movements, for example, would reduce Vietnam's dependence upon the USSR and could make the Kuantan formula more attractive to Hanoi. This contingency might accompany a Chinese decision to seek a rapprochement with Vietnam in exchange for a reduction in Soviet-Vietnamese ties. This chain of events in turn could decrease Hanoi's willingness to maintain close relations with Moscow. Changes in the Soviet view of Vietnam's worth as an ally also could lead to a loosening of the Moscow-Hanoi axis. Any of these developments could create the possibility of resurrecting the Kuantan alternative.

In 1985, however, Vietnam predicted that even if there is no negotiated settlement between ASEAN and the Indochinese states over Cambodia's future, the Phnom Penh regime will be sufficiently capable by the end of the decade so that Hanoi can withdraw its forces from Cambodia. Underlying this prediction is Hanoi's belief that once the resistance components are separated from their Thai sanctuaries and supply lines, they will atrophy, leaving ASEAN and China with no one left to support. Successful Vietnamese raids during the 1985 dry season on all resistance base camps along the Thai border generated this optimism in Hanoi; they believe that the Cambodian problem will be resolved on the ground with no need for Vietnamese concessions. By 1990, then, Hanoi's own projection is that Cambodia will become a docile political client and resource supplier as well as, perhaps, a magnet for surplus Vietnamese peasant farmers, fishermen, and tradespeople (FBIS 1985, H1; Quinn-Judge 1985).

Conclusion

In this essay we have applied role analysis to the study of foreign policy and international politics in Southeast Asia. This task has required us to address three questions. What role(s) may a country enact in the conduct of its foreign policy? What are the sources of these roles? What kind of role sets are established and maintained as countries interact with one another? We have identified several roles enacted by the Southeast Asian role set, including consumer, producer, belligerent, hegemone, facilitator, and provocateur. The sources of these roles are either domestic or international, depending upon the location of the immediate cue for enacting the role. The structure of the role set is a product of this role-location process, as countries enact roles and attempt to cope with role conflict via merger, interpenetration, alternation, and altercasting strategies of role enactment.

In Southeast Asia Vietnam pursued an alternation strategy toward China and the Soviet Union until the end of the Vietnam War. The ASEAN states have selected an altercasting strategy in response to cross-pressures from China and Vietnam generated by the Sino-Vietnamese conflict over Cambodia. Neither of these role-conflict strategies has been successful. Vietnam eventually abandoned their strategy in favor of an unabashed cooperative-interdependent relationship with the USSR, which contributed to the development of a Sino-Vietnamese belligerent relationship. We attribute the tilt toward Moscow to the decisive influence of domestic political goals, which is consistent with our hypothesis that domestic sources are more influential than international ones in the resolution of role conflict. Our analysis of the ASEAN altercasting strategy yields the prediction that it will also fail. Even though the ASEAN states may continue to push for a diplomatic resolution of the Cambodian war along the lines of the Kuantan or ZOPFAN proposals, the domestic sources of Vietnam's belligerent-hegemone roles are likely to remain too strong for these altercasting initiatives to be successful.

IV Role Theory and Foreign Policy Dynamics: The African Arena

10

Assessing the Foreign Policy Role Orientations of Sub-Saharan African Leaders

Margaret G. Hermann

When we think about Sub-Saharan African politics, leaders' names become synonymous with countries, for example, Houphouet-Boigny with the Ivory Coast, Nyerere with Tanzania, Toure with Guinea. And as leaders change in this African scene so do the policies and, at times, the general direction of the government. As Jackson and Rosberg (1982) argue, the political systems in Black African countries are character-ized by personal rule. The political system is dependent on the "dispositions, activities, abilities, efforts, and fortunes of politicians —especially rulers. . . . [H]ow [the ruler] chooses to perform his role, how well he performs, and with what degree of fortune are crucial to the stability of the polity and the persistence of the regime" (Jackson and Rosberg 1982, 22).

The fact that most Sub-Saharan African leaders need not seek a

The author wishes to express her appreciation to Julie Kline, Kevin Richardson, and Eric Singer for their help in coding the interview responses of the leaders in this chapter.

contested reelection is evidence that they engage in personal rule. There are seldom constitutional time limits on their tenure in office. Most have established one-party systems in their countries with themselves as party heads. Moreover, other actors in the political system serve at the pleasure of the leader, their fortunes being dependent on how well the leader is faring and his disposition toward them. In effect, there are relatively few institutional checks and balances on the leader's behavior.

Thus, what a Sub-Saharan African leader is like has the potential of influencing both his government's domestic and foreign policy behavior. In the rest of this paper, we will explore how the personal characteristics of such predominant Black African leaders can influence their governments' foreign policy behavior. We will propose a model suggesting on what characteristics one should collect information and how the characteristics link to form role orientations to foreign affairs which in turn mold behavior. We will suggest how a leader's interests and experience in the foreign policy arena and his responsiveness to domestic and foreign political pressures can modify the relationship between his role orientation and the behavior he urges on his government. The model is applied to twelve Sub-Saharan African leaders.

The Model

Figure 10.1 displays the proposed model linking leaders' personal characteristics to governments' foreign policy behavior. As indicated in the figure, four broad types of personal characteristics seem to impact on the policymaking process. These four are the leader's beliefs about the world, his needs and desires, his preferred ways of making decisions, and the ways he interacts with others. A search of writings on political leaders, both journalistic and scholarly, suggests the importance of these four types of personal characteristics for the making and implementing of political decisions.

Beliefs about the world refer to the leader's fundamental assumptions about the world and, in particular, political reality. For example, does the leader assume that events are predictable, that conflict is basic to human interaction, that one can have some control over what happens, or that the maintenance of national sovereignty and superiority is the most important objective of a government? Beliefs are proposed by many to affect a political leader's interpretation of his environment and, in turn, the strategies he employs (DeRivera 1968; Frank 1968; George 1980; Jervis 1976; Walker 1977). Two beliefs that seem to

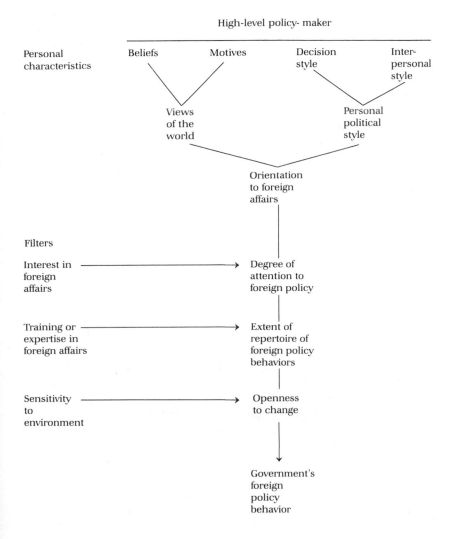

Figure 10.1   Summary of proposed relationships between personal characteristics of political leaders and their government's foreign policy behavior

have special relevance to foreign policymaking are nationalism and belief in one's own ability to control events. Nationalism is often used by journalists and policy analysts as one reason for a particular Third World leader's actions. A belief in the controllability of events is thought to be fundamental to how a leader defines his government's role in the international system (Holsti 1977).

It is hard to find political analysis that does not consider at some point the reasons why a political leader does what he does, that is, his motives. By examining a political leader's motives—his needs and desires—we can suggest what kinds of goals the leader will have and how situations will probably be interpreted. Need for power is certainly the most discussed motive when political leaders are the topic of conversation. Leaders high in the need for power have been found to be more aggressive in their foreign policy behavior than those low in need for power (Hermann 1980; Winter and Stewart 1977). McClelland (1975) and Winter (1980) have shown how need for power and need for affiliation interact to form an orientation to war in political leaders. Need for affiliation, because it indicates how interdependent leaders are willing to become in their foreign policy behavior, is an important motive to examine in and of itself (Hermann 1980; Winter and Stewart 1977).

Decision style refers to how a political leader goes about making decisions, his characteristic ways of approaching a policymaking task. Possible components of decision style are self-confidence, openness to new information, preference for certain levels of risk, ability to tolerate ambiguity or uncertainty, and willingness to compromise. By learning about decision style we gain information about what the decision will probably be like. Two aspects of decision style—self-confidence and complexity of information processing—in combination have been found to indicate how ideological or pragmatic a political leader will be (Ziller et al. 1977).

In contrast to decision style, interpersonal style suggests the leader's usual way of dealing with others, for example, advisors, other leaders, party personnel, and bureaucrats. Interpersonal style is often reflected in the style of behavior the leader urges his government to undertake in the international arena, other countries being treated like other people. One aspect of interpersonal style often discussed in relation to political leaders is paranoia or, in its less extreme form, distrust of others. Tucker (1965) has shown how paranoia is characteristic of the political leader with a "warfare personality"—the leader who is combative. Whether a leader chooses to emphasize task completion or constituent morale and satisfaction is another important aspect of interpersonal style with regard to political leaders. Byars (1973) has noted that a balance between emphasis on task completion and constituent morale is a measure of charisma. He also found that an emphasis on task completion as opposed to constituent morale differentiated leaders in industrialized societies from those of Third and Fourth World nations.

As figure 10.1 indicates, in the model we propose that beliefs and motives combine to determine how a political leader will view the world, that is, how he will interpret the political environment in which he finds himself. Beliefs and motives, in effect, provide political leaders with maps for charting their course, shaping the nature of the leaders' goals and appropriate strategies for achieving the goals. Beliefs and motives suggest what is important to the leader and what he will seek to work on while in office.

Decision style and interpersonal style combine to shape a leader's personal political style or the ways in which he will feel comfortable dealing with political problems and issues as well as the people he must work with on such problems. In effect, a leader's personal political style often shows through in the way he chooses to interact with leaders from other countries and how he involves himself in the foreign policymaking process. Differences in these stylistic characteristics are probably the first things noticed when political leaders change. In order not to incur the wrath of the political leader, subordinates often cater to these stylistic preferences knowing that their lives will be more pleasant in the process. And the styles of the leader become the styles of the government.

Figure 10.1 indicates that a leader's views of the world and personal political style interrelate to form an orientation to foreign affairs or, in other words, a predisposition regarding action when faced with a foreign policy problem. Leaders' orientations to foreign affairs reflect their personalities as a whole. Thus, orientations to foreign affairs have both substantive and stylistic aspects and are suggestive of certain goals and ways of approaching the goals.

The model proposes that leaders' orientations to foreign affairs do not have a direct effect on their governments' foreign policy behavior but rather are filtered by certain background or contextual factors. These filters amplify or diminish the relationship between orientation and government foreign policy behavior. Three such filters are noted as particularly important: interest in foreign affairs, training or experience in foreign affairs, and sensitivity to the environment.

Interest in foreign affairs enhances the effect of a leader's orientation on government policy. Interest acts as a motivating force, leading to increased attention to foreign policy issues and increased participation in making foreign policy decisions. The leader will want to be consulted on decisions and to be kept informed about what is happening in the foreign policy arena. Moreover, he may choose to have all foreign policymaking located within his office. The leader with little interest in foreign affairs is likely to delegate authority to other people, negating the effect of his orientation on the resultant policy except as the spokesman's orientation is similar to that of the leader.

Training or experience in the foreign policy arena, in contrast, has a dampening effect on the impact of a leader's orientation on government behavior. With experience the leader has some idea of what will work and not work in the foreign policy arena and what behaviors will have what effects on other governments and how other governments will behave in response. With experience leaders tend to have a wider repertoire of possible behaviors. At the least they have a sense of history in their relations with other governments which is probably more likely than their orientation to influence what they urge on their government. The leader with little experience in foreign affairs has little but his orientation to help guide his proposals regarding foreign policy behavior.

Sensitivity to the environment also has a dampening effect on the relationship between a leader's orientation and his government's foreign policy behavior. The more sensitive the leader is to cues from his political environment, the more likely other types of factors are to intervene in this relationship. The more sensitive the leader is to his political environment, the more likely he is to accommodate himself to new information and to the nuances of the situation, molding what he urges on the government to meet the demands of the occasion. The less sensitive leader, on the other hand, generally adjusts incoming political cues to fit his own point of view. Information is made congruent with the leader's orientation, and the leader acts on his orientation. The model in figure 10.1 is elaborated further in M. Hermann, C. Hermann, and Hagan (1987) and in M. Hermann (1980, chapter 8 in this volume).

Applying The Model To Sub-Saharan African Leaders

Information was collected on eight personal characteristics for the twelve Sub-Saharan African leaders noted below. These characteristics were nationalism, belief in one's own ability to control events, need for power, need for affiliation, conceptual complexity, self-confidence, distrust of others, and task orientation. As indicated in discussing the model, these eight characteristics have been found to influence foreign policy behavior in research on political leaders. The following are brief definitions of these traits:

Nationalism. A view of the world in which one's own nation holds center stage; there are strong emotional ties to the nation-state with one's own nation being perceived as the best while other nations are perceived in less positive terms; emphasis is placed on the importance of maintaining national honor and identity.

Belief in one's own ability to control events. A view of the world in which one perceives some degree of control over the situations in which one is involved; the perception that individuals and governments can influence what happens to them.

Need for power. A concern for establishing, maintaining, or restoring one's power; the desire to control, influence, or have an impact on other persons or groups.

Need for affiliation. A concern for establishing, maintaining, or restoring warm and friendly relations with other persons or groups.

Conceptual complexity. The degree of differentiation which an individual shows in describing or discussing other people, places, policies, ideas, or things.

Self-confidence. A person's sense of self-importance; an individual's image of his/her own ability to deal adequately with the environment.

Distrust of others. A general feeling of doubt, uneasiness, misgiving, and wariness of others; an inclination to suspect the motives and actions of others.

Task orientation. A relative emphasis in interactions with others on getting the task done as opposed to focusing on the feelings and needs of the others.

The eight personal characteristics interrelate to form leaders' orientations to foreign affairs. Nationalism and belief in one's ability to control events as beliefs, and need for power and need for affiliation as motives, help to define leaders' views of the world. Conceptual complexity and self-confidence as factors in decision style, and distrust of others and task orientation as aspects of interpersonal style,

Table 10.1 Descriptions of six possible orientations to foreign affairs

Orientation	Definition	View of world
Expansionist	Interest in gaining control over more territory, resources, or people	Perceive the world is divided into "us" and "them," each intent on improving its condition at the expense of the other; thus, conflict is inherent to functioning in the international system
Active independent	Interest in participating in the international community but on one's own terms and without engendering a dependent relationship with another country	Want to be self-reliant but perceive importance of other countries to one's own continued existence so are determined to maintain close control over interactions with other nations to avoid any kind of dependent relationship
Influential	Interest in having an impact on other nations' foreign policy behavior, in playing a leadership role in regional or international affairs	Perceive inability of nations to act alone, importance of acting together but such activity demands a strong leader; think time is right for such leadership; may have a particular ideology wish other nations to adopt but usually this is secondary interest to gaining leadership role
Mediator/ integrator	Concern with reconciling differences between other nations, with resolving problems in the international arena	Perceive some problems between other nations in international system can be resolved through third-party politics and that one's nation (and one's self) can gain prestige by playing a "good Samaritan" or peacemaker role

Style	Resulting foreign policy
A wariness of others' moves; attempt to keep one step ahead of those considered the enemy; directive and manipulative in dealing with others	Generally focused on issues of security and status; behavior often hostile in tone and directed toward the "enemy"; favor use of low-commitment actions unless perceived "backed into the wall"; not averse to using "enemy" as a scapegoat on which to blame problems; espouse short-term, immediate change in the international arena
Seek a variety of information before making a decision; examine carefully the possible consequences of alternatives under consideration for dealing with a problem; cultivate relationships with a diverse group of nations	Generally focused on economic and security issues; behavior is nonaligned in nature, directed toward a wide variety of governments; behavior is usually positive in tone but involves little commitment since shun commitments that limit maneuverability and sense of independence; espouse need for long-term change in international arena
Show interest in and seek information on problems of countries wish to influence; initiate collaborative activities with such countries and meet frequently with their leaders	Foster friendly relations with nations wish to have influence over; make necessary commitments to secure working relationships with such nations; act protectively toward such nations in their dealings with adversaries; behavior generally focused on status issues
Good listeners; able to see both sides of issues and raise options where few were perceived earlier; willingness to "take a back seat" in the policymaking process, having an impact without seeming to control or to interfere with others; uses consensus-building and group maintenance techniques effectively	Behavior is principally diplomatic in nature; have extensive activity in international and regional organizations which are used as practice arenas and places to develop a reputation for mediating skills; engage in collaborative activities with other nations to foster sense of mutual trust and understanding; behavior is generally positive in tone

Table 10.1 (continued)

Orientation	Definition	View of world
Opportunist	Interest in taking advantage of present circumstances, in dealing effectively with the demands and opportunities of the moment, in being expedient	Perceive foreign policy situations are generally unique— times change, goals change, and the views of other governments change; to be effective in the foreign policy arena one must deal with each situation according to its own merits
Developmental	Commitment to the continued improvement of one's own nation through the development of useful and rewarding relations with other countries or organizations in the international system; an interest in building up one's own nation with the best help available	Perceive nation has deficiency that can be improved with the aid of certain other countries or organizations in the international system; perceive it is important to seek out and establish relationships with other countries or organizations that can be helpful in dealing with one's deficiencies

help shape leaders' political style. The particular orientations we will examine in Sub-Saharan African leaders are described in table 10.1.

The role orientations we are focusing on come from the foreign policy literature, specifically that literature concerned with national role conceptions (Holsti 1970; Wish 1977) and with the operational code (Holsti 1977; Johnson 1977). Each orientation is perceived as setting the tone for the foreign policy behavior the leader is likely to urge on his government, and each orientation is characterized by a particular type of strategy or style. In addition to defining the orientations, table 10.1 describes the view of the world and style associated with each orientation as well as the foreign policy behavior leaders with each orientation are likely to urge on their governments. Table 10.2 shows how the personal characteristics are combined to determine each orientation and provides some examples of heads of govern-

Style	Resulting foreign policy
Seek out information from a variety of sources; try to ascertain early on what alternative will secure consensus; may use "trial balloons" to test others' responses; seek compromise if consensus is not possible	Focus of much behavior is on gaining information from the international arena, on keeping abreast of international events and attuned to other governments' actions and intentions; political resources are committed to keeping contacts open; an attempt is made to maintain a low positive profile in order to keep as much as possible on everybody's good side; encourage face-to-face diplomacy to learn about a situation firsthand
Develop relationships with others based on what can gain from relationship; constantly seeking information in area of perceived deficiency—appear almost to have a "one track" mind; try to maintain controlled dependence in relationships with others, that is, getting what is desired while not becoming dominated by the others	Behavior generally focused on economic or security issues; are quite friendly toward those seeking as benefactors; can be hostile, however, if others try to dominate or control the relationship; only those political resources are committed that are necessary to establishing a beneficial relationship; active in regional and international organizations in search of benefactors and beneficial relationships

ment that have been found to have each orientation in previous studies (Hermann 1977, 1980).

Interest in foreign affairs, training or experience in foreign affairs, and sensitivity to the environment are seen as enhancing or diminishing the influence of a leader's orientation on his government's foreign policy behavior. In applying the model to Sub-Saharan African leaders, we have tried to define and assess these filters with the African context in mind. For most Sub-Saharan African leaders interest in foreign affairs is almost forced on them as they try to keep their countries economically and politically viable. Instead of differences in degree of general interest in foreign affairs, the leaders exhibit interest in some issues more than others. In effect, as a result of their own interests, they become involved in some aspects of foreign policy more than others.

Thus, for example, for leaders of front-line states Southern African

Table 10.2 Bases for determining the foreign policy orientations and example from previous studies of heads of government exhibiting orientations

Person

Orientation	Nationalism	Belief in own ability to control events	Need power	Need affiliation
Expansionist	Hi*	Hi	Hi*	Lo
Active independent	Hi*	Hi*	Lo	Hi
Influential	Lo	Hi*	Hi*	Hi
Mediator-integrator	Lo	Hi	Lo	Hi*
Opportunist	Lo	Lo	Lo	Lo
Developmental	Hi*	Lo	Lo	Hi*

* These traits are weighted more heavily in determining the orientations.

liberation has been at times an all-consuming issue. With vacillation in the world prices of many of the resources African countries have for export and recurrent natural disasters, many Sub-Saharan African leaders have become intensely interested in economic development issues. By ascertaining leaders' orientations to foreign affairs by issue and by noting which issues seem of particular interest to each leader, we can make some proposals concerning the issues for which orientation is probably going to affect behavior and also the issues for which the influence will be less.

As with interest in foreign affairs, most Sub-Saharan African leaders have had training or experience in foreign affairs either through participation in struggles for independence and their consequent negotiations or as part of their tenure in office. For purposes of applying the model, we could consider that leaders who spent longer periods of time in achieving independence and those with a longer tenure in office had more training or experience in foreign affairs. And we could propose that these leaders' orientations would have less effect on their governments' foreign policy behavior than those of their counterparts with less time spent in achieving independence and a shorter tenure in office.

haracteristic

Conceptual complexity	Self-confidence	Distrust of others	Task orientation	Leaders exhibiting orientation
Lo	Hi*	Hi*	Hi	Castro (Cuba) Nasser (Egypt)
Hi*	Hi	Lo	Hi*	Gandhi (India) Lin Piao (China)
Hi	Hi	Lo	Lo	Zhou En Lai (China) Kosygin (Soviet Union)
Hi*	Lo	Lo	Lo	Diefenbaker (Canada) Sato (Japan)
Hi*	Lo	Lo	Lo	Erhard (W. Germany) Nehru (India)
Hi	Hi*	Lo	Lo	DeGaulle (France) Franco (Spain)

It may be, however, that with experience in foreign affairs orientations change. Through experience leaders learn that their views of the world and strategies are inadequate to meet present challenges. Or perhaps leaders find some orientations more useful as they are consolidating their power than later on. For those Sub-Saharan African leaders who have been in office for some length of time, it is possible to determine their orientations early on in their tenure and compare them with their orientations later. Moreover, for those Black African leaders with data available during the pre-independence period, it is possible to compare orientations during the liberation struggle with orientations once in office as head of government. If we find changes in orientations across time, it would seem safe to argue that the orientation will have its greatest influence on foreign policy behavior early in the time period in which it is held, diminishing in influence as the leader's experience based on that orientation grows or as the leader searches for another way of looking at the world.

There are many ways of being sensitive to the political environment. An easy way for us to assess sensitivity in the present study is to see if the personal characteristics of the Black African leaders in our sample

Table 10.3 The sample of Sub-Saharan African leaders

Leader	Country	Years in office through 1984
Amin	Uganda	January 1971–April 1979
Houphouet-Boigny	Ivory Coast	November 1960–1984
Kaunda	Zambia	October 1964–1984
Kenyatta	Kenya	June 1963–August 1978
Machel	Mozambique	June 1975–1984
Mobutu	Zaire	November 1965–1984
Mugabe	Zimbabwe	February 1980–1984
Neto	Angola	November 1975–June 1979
Nkrumah	Ghana	March 1957–February 1966
Nyerere	Tanzania	December 1962–1984
Obote	Uganda	December 1962–January 1971; December 1980–1984
Toure	Guinea	October 1958–1984

change with the context, for example, by topic, by audience, across time. The more characteristics that are influenced by aspects of the context in which the leader finds himself, the more situationally responsive the leader is and the less likely his orientations are to influence his government's foreign policy behavior.

In the present study we shall focus upon the personal characteristics and orientations to foreign affairs of a sample of Sub-Saharan leaders when they were heads of their governments. These twelve leaders in table 10.3 represent all the regions of Sub-Saharan Africa and different colonial legacies. Among the group are military leaders as well as those with primarily political backgrounds. The leaders represent those who have succeeded in having a long tenure in office as well as several who have been in power for only a short period of time. Among the leaders are some inclined toward the Western bloc as well as some inclined toward the Eastern bloc and toward nonalignment. Moreover, some of the leaders are in countries that were granted independence without violence, while others had to fight for independence. In addition to testing the model we proposed earlier, we will examine if there are differences in the orientations of the leaders in the sample as a result of these different background factors.

We shall use content analysis in assessing the personal characteristics of the Sub-Saharan African leaders in our sample. In the past decade a growing number of researchers have found content analysis useful in gaining personality information about political leaders, in particular, about heads of government, who are virtually inaccessible for personality testing or clinical interviewing (Axelrod 1976; Stewart 1977; Stuart and Starr 1981–82; Winter 1980). The present study follows in this tradition, content analyzing leaders' responses to reporters' questions in an interview setting.

Interviews with the twelve African leaders in our sample were sought in the following types of sources: Foreign Broadcast Information Service *Daily Report, New York Times, Washington Post, Le Monde, Jeune Afrique, Times* of London, U.S. weekly news magazines, newspapers from the leaders' countries such as the Zambia *Mail* and *Fraternité Matin*, and English-language surveys of Africa such as the *African Recorder* and *Africa Report*. Table 10.4 shows the number of interview responses that were content analyzed for each leader, the number of interviews from which these responses were drawn, the number of years the interviews covered, and the average number of words per response. Only verbatim interview responses were included in the analysis. Paraphrases and summaries of interview responses were avoided. And only responses that were at least fifty words were included. The cutoff date for interviews included in this study was October 1982.

We focus on interviews with the leaders because they appear to contain the most spontaneous public materials available on these individuals. Spontaneous material is desirable since it minimizes the effects of

Table 10.4 Nature of material used in content analysis

Sub-Saharan African leader	Number of interview responses analyzed	Average number of words per response	Number of interviews	Number of years interviews cover
Amin	63	88	14	4
Houphouet-Boigny	73	82	18	10
Kaunda	74	80	34	14
Kenyatta	73	84	44	14
Machel	83	102	21	6
Mobutu	103	90	26	10
Mugabe	82	88	36	8
Neto	92	81	19	7
Nkrumah	72	90	34	10
Nyerere	81	79	29	14
Obote	74	73	23	12
Toure	61	101	21	13

ghost writing and planned communication. Materials such as speeches and letters can be written for the leader by others and are generally designed to convey a specific image to a certain audience. As a consequence the researcher content analyzing these materials will learn what the ghost writer is like or what the image is which the political leader would like to reflect. In the interview setting, the leader is usually the author of his comments and has little time in which to plan a response. With the more spontaneous material there is a better chance for the leader's personality to be reflected in what he says. Several content analysis studies indicate that the link between personal characteristics and spontaneous material is stronger than that between personal characteristics and planned or controlled material (LeVine 1966; Osgood and Anderson 1957). On the average, 7,000 words were content analyzed for each leader. In completing the content analysis, only half of the available interview responses were coded for Kaunda, Mugabe, and Nyerere. For these leaders every other response of their approximately 150 were included in the analysis reported here.

Table 10.5 describes the coding procedures used in assessing the personal characteristics of the leaders. The table also indicates the score used in the present analysis and average intercoder agreement for each characteristic. The complete coding manuals for the eight personal characteristics are available in the *Handbook for Assessing Personal Characteristics and Foreign Policy Orientations of Political Leaders*, which can be acquired from the author. Emphasis in these coding schemes is on the number of times a leader could have exhibited a trait and the percentage of times he did exhibit it. The intercoder agreement figures listed in table 10.5 represent average agreement scores among the four coders involved in the study. The intercoder agreement figures are based on common coding of twenty interview responses from those which each coder analyzed.

In addition to content analyzing each leader's interview responses, the following information was acquired about the interview response: the nature of the topic being discussed, the place where the interview occurred, the nature of the interviewer(s), and the apparent spontaneity of the response. The topics could be classified into twelve broad categories, that is, economic development, security, political stability, colonialism/imperialism, quality of life of people, ethnic problems, struggles for liberation, relations with other countries, pan-Africanism, national pride, nonalignment, and the leader's background. Of interest concerning the place of the interview and nature of the interviewer was whether each involved the leader's own country, another African country, South Africa, a former colonial power, a Western bloc country, an Eastern bloc country, a nonaligned country, or an international/ regional organization. Even though we have made the argument that interviews with political leaders are more spontaneous, they too can differ in their degree of spontaneity. An effort was made to note when interviews were done "on the run" at airports or after meetings, when they were one-on-one with a reporter, and when they were called press conferences. Information on the date of the interview and the source in which it was found were also collected.

Results and Discussion

The results of the content analysis allow us to answer several questions. First we will examine the personal characteristic and orientation scores for each of the twelve Sub-Saharan African leaders in our sample. What is the personality profile each leader presents in his public statements? Second we will learn whether the leaders' orientations differ by topic and, thus, by area of interest. What can we propose regarding the effects of the leaders' orientations on their governments' foreign policy behavior given this information on orientation by topic? Third we will see if time in office or in a position of leadership has led to any change in orientation. Can we determine if experience has muted the leaders' orientations? Fourth we will explore how sensitive the leaders are to their political environments. What effects do sensitivity differences have upon their orientations? Finally, we will find out if different types of Black African leaders have different role orientations toward foreign affairs.

What is the personality profile each leader presents in his public statements? Table 10.6 reports the standard scores on each of the personal characteristics for the twelve leaders in our sample. The scores are standardized to a distribution with a mean of 50 and a standard deviation of 10. Standard scores make it possible to compare scores on the characteristics within and among leaders. The standard scores for each characteristic were based on the mean score and standard deviation for that characteristic across the twelve leaders. These means and standard deviations are listed at the bottom of table 10.6. To aid in interpreting the standard scores, we have noted in table 10.6 whether the score is one standard deviation or more below (L) or above (H) the mean of 50. Those characteristics on which a leader scores a standard deviation or more below or above the mean distinguish him from the others.

Table 10.5   Coding procedure, score used in analysis, and intercoder agreement for personal characteristics

Personal characteristic	Coding procedure	Score used in analysis	Average intercoder agreement[a]
Nationalism	Focus on nouns/noun phrases referring to nation; coded for nationalism if noun refers to own nation and is modified by favorable term, term denoting strength, or phrase suggesting importance of national honor or identity; also coded for nationalism if noun refers to another nation and is modified by hostile term, term denoting weakness, or phrase suggesting meddlesomeness in affairs of others.	% of references to own and other nations meeting criteria	.79
Belief in one's own ability to control events	Focus on verbs (action words); coded for this characteristic if context of verb indicates speaker (or group speaker identifies with) is accepting responsibility for initiating or planning the action.	% of verbs meeting criteria	.87
Need for power	Focus on verbs; coded need power if verb context meets any of six conditions indicated in Winter's need power coding scheme (Winter 1973).	% of verbs meeting six criteria	.83
Need for affiliation	Focus on verbs; coded need affiliation if verb context meets any of four conditions indicated in Atkinson's (1958) need affiliation coding scheme.	% of verbs meeting four criteria	.83
Conceptual complexity	Focus on sets of high-complexity words (e.g., may, possibly, sometimes, tends) and sets of low-complexity words (e.g., always, only, without a doubt).	% of complexity words that were high in complexity	.90
Self-confidence	Focus on pronouns referring to self—myself, I, me, mine; coded for self-confidence if self seen as	% of self-references meeting criteria	.92

Table 10.5   (continued)

Personal characteristic	Coding procedure	Score used in analysis	Average intercoder agreement[a]
	instigator of activity, authority figure, or recipient of positive feedback.		
Distrust of others	Focus on nouns/noun phrases referring to groups speaker does not identify with; coded for distrust if context showed indications of doubts or misgivings or suggested particular group was going to harm speaker or group with which speaker identifies.	% of nouns meeting criteria	.80
Task orientation	Focus on sets of task words (e.g., results, goal, solution, achievement) and sets of interpersonal words (e.g., sensitivity, understanding, appreciation, coordination).[b]	% of task plus interpersonal words that were task words	.91

[a] The figure listed here is a Scott's pi or percentage of intercoder agreement that exceeds chance (Scott 1955).
[b] This coding scheme represents a modification of a scheme developed for use with political material by Byars (1972), who based his categories on Bales (1951).

Before commenting on the scores for individual leaders, it is important to put these data into perspective. A comparison of mean scores at the bottom of table 10.6 with mean scores for a sample of fifty-three heads of government from around the world shows these African leaders as more nationalistic, lower in belief in their ability to control events, higher in their needs for both power and affiliation, comparable in conceptual complexity, lower in self-confidence, more distrusting of others, and less task-oriented than the other heads of government (Hermann 1980; Hagan et al., 1982). The following are the means for the fifty-three heads of government that have been studied previously: nationalism, .14; belief in ability to control events, .59; need for power, .20; need for affiliation, .07; conceptual complexity, .37; self-confidence, .87; distrust of others, .15; task orientation, .64. Included in these fifty-three heads of government were Castro, Nasser, DeGaulle,

Table 10.6 Standard scores on personal characteristics for African leaders

African leader	Nationalism	Believe can control events	Need power
Amin	40 (L)	47	47
Houphouet-Boigny	34 (L)	53	41
Kaunda	41	40 (L)	42
Kenyatta	60 (H)	72 (H)	66 (H)
Machel	51	59	59
Mobutu	38 (L)	36 (L)	35 (L)
Mugabe	52	46	57
Neto	67 (H)	41	41
Nkrumah	55	61 (H)	59
Nyerere	55	47	61 (H)
Obote	59	46	51
Toure	48	52	40 (L)
Mean actual score for sample of leaders:	.3825	.455	.427
Standard deviation for actual score for sample of leaders:	.108	.063	.139

Adenauer, Tito, Zhou En Lai, Trudeau, Marcos, Ulbricht, Bourguiba, and Khrushchev.

An examination of table 10.6 shows that Houphouet-Boigny, Kenyatta, and Toure have the largest number of low and high scores on these

Need affiliation	Conceptual complexity	Self-confidence	Distrust of others	Task orientation
49	54	46	39 (L)	41
70 (H)	39 (L)	64 (H)	42	40 (L)
34 (L)	49	47	41	58
49	65 (H)	52	61 (H)	50
46	38 (L)	33 (L)	54	65 (H)
41	42	39 (L)	45	57
51	55	50	51	60 (H)
51	56	63 (H)	66 (H)	40 (L)
47	44	52	53	47
47	61 (H)	45	55	49
47	60 (H)	45	60 (H)	60 (H)
68 (H)	36 (L)	65 (H)	33 (L)	34 (L)
.232	.351	.645	.358	.541
.063	.106	.197	.134	.061

personal characteristics and stand out on these particular traits from the rest of the group. Kenyatta is low on none of the traits and scores high on five of the characteristics—nationalism, belief in his ability to control events, need for power, conceptual complexity, and distrust of

Table 10.7 Standard scores on orientations
to foreign affairs for African leaders

African leader	Expansionist	Active independent	Influential	Mediator/integrator	Opportunist	Developmental
Amin	37 (L)	41	54	64 (H)	65 (H)	50
Houphouet-Boigny	40 (L)	45	60 (H)	67 (H)	42	60 (H)
Kaunda	42	42	39 (L)	42	63 (H)	43
Kenyatta	66 (H)	72 (H)	67 (H)	54	46	48
Machel	56	47	46	38 (L)	35 (L)	33 (L)
Mobutu	36 (L)	33 (L)	32 (L)	46	60 (H)	41
Mugabe	54	56	50	46	50	49
Neto	59	55	41	42	50	66 (H)
Nkrumah	60 (H)	50	57	42	38 (L)	46
Nyerere	54	50	52	49	57	46
Obote	55	60 (H)	42	45	54	49
Toure	42	50	59	64 (H)	41	67 (II)
Mean actual score for sample of leaders	600	600	499.75	499.75	499.75	550
Standard deviation for actual score for sample of leaders	54.95	31.40	43.14	28.77	34.70	51.08

others. At the other extreme is Mobutu who is low on four of the
characteristics—nationalism, belief in his ability to control events, need
for power, and self-confidence—and not high in any of the traits.
Looking for the leaders among this group of twelve who are highest
and lowest on each characteristic, we note: Neto is most nationalistic,
Houphouet-Boigny least; Kenyatta has the highest belief in his own
ability to control events, Toure least; Kenyatta is highest in need for

power, Mobutu lowest; Houphouet-Boigny is highest in need for affiliation, Kaunda lowest; Kenyatta is most conceptually complex, Toure least; Neto is most distrustful of others, Toure least; Machel is most task-oriented, Toure least; and Toure is most self-confident, Machel least.

In table 10.7 the personal characteristics are combined to form the six role orientations to foreign affairs described earlier (see table 10.1). The formulae used in combining the characteristics are available from the author. Once again standard scores are reported with a mean of 50 and a standard deviation of 10. As before, an L means at least one standard deviation below the mean, while an H indicates at least one standard deviation above the mean. Table 10.7 shows that for five of these African leaders their personal characteristics combine to form one fairly distinctive role orientation to foreign affairs. That is, only one of the orientations has an H score. Thus, Kaunda's public statements indicate an opportunist orientation as do Mobutu's. A developmental orientation characterized Neto; an expansionist orientation Nkrumah; and an active independent orientation Obote. Amin and Toure have two dominant orientations to foreign affairs. For Amin these are the opportunist and mediator/integrator; for Toure these are the developmental and mediator/integrator. For Houphouet-Boigny and Kenyatta three orientations predominate. Houphouet-Boigny's are the influential, mediator/integrator, and developmental; Kenyatta's are the expansionist, active independent, and influential. Three of the leaders—Machel, Mugabe, and Nyerere—have no high score. Mugabe's and Nyerere's scores hover around the mean, suggesting the presence of all the orientations to some degree for these leaders with no emphasis on any single one. Machel's scores indicate that he is unlikely to exhibit the mediator/integrator, opportunist, or developmental orientations but likely to reflect the expansionist, active independent, and influential orientations.

The results in table 10.7, therefore, indicate that no one role orientation is characteristic of Sub-Saharan African leaders. Indeed, all six orientations are found among the twelve leaders, each orientation characterizing at least two leaders. Among these twelve leaders there are those interested in gaining more control over others, in participating in the international arena but on their own terms, in playing a leadership role in regional affairs, in playing a peacemaker role, in taking advantage of present circumstances, and in developing useful and rewarding relationships. We should observe that these orientations are reflected in the leaders' public statements and suggest the kinds of roles these leaders would like to play in the international arena. Having the orientation does not necessarily insure one will be successful in implementing one's wishes. The orientations indicate what these twelve leaders will urge their governments to do in foreign policy, but they do not guarantee that the government will be successful in achieving the ends the leaders desire.

What are the effects of role orientations upon foreign policy behavior when the leader's interest in foreign affairs is taken into account? Most Sub-Saharan African leaders are interested in foreign affairs. Instead of general interest in foreign affairs differing among the leaders, they are more and less interested in particular issues. Table 10.8 shows the orientations to foreign affairs of the leaders in the present sample by issue or topic discussed in their interview responses. We have included in table 10.8 only those topics for each leader for which we have 500 words or more (around ten interview responses) to increase the stability of the data and to examine topics of interest to the leaders. These are the topics the leaders were willing to be interviewed on and on which they tended to focus in their interviews. We assume that these are the issues on which the leaders' orientations will affect their governments' foreign policy behavior. At least, these are the issues which appear to be of concern to the leaders and for which they are likely to be involved in the policymaking process. In table 10.8 we have indicated under the name of each topic the orientations for a leader that were one or more standard deviations above the mean. The scores on the orientations are indicated in parentheses after each orientation. Where none of the scores for the orientations was at least one standard deviation above the mean, we have noted in the table "none high."

These scores indicate that the leaders appear to differentiate among issues, adapting their orientations to the issue. Moreover, all leaders do not have similar orientations for similar topics, for example, expansionist for struggles for liberation. The orientations seem to be more leader-specific with some significant exceptions. Those leaders in the sample involved in military struggles for liberation—Machel, Mugabe, and Neto—do exhibit an expansionist orientation when dealing with this issue. For development as an issue, all but Houphouet-Boigny emphasize an active independent orientation. Houphouet-Boigny has remained a maverick on the African scene with regard to development issues, being willing to remain tied to France and to seek private investment as the means to economic growth (Jackson and Rosberg 1982; Woronoff 1972). We note from table 10.8 that the opportunist and developmental orientations are associated with development for Houphouet-Boigny.

Examining the data in table 10.8 for some of the leaders individually, we see that for Amin the mediator/integrator orientation is prominent for both discussions of relations with other countries and struggles for liberation. Although highly ineffective, Amin spent a lot of his foreign policy effort on offering both his services and advice to other countries to help them deal with their problems. The Foreign Broadcast Information Service *Daily Report* is full of his telegrams and messages to other heads of government commenting on their problems. As Gwyn (1977) observed, Amin was in a constant search for recognition. Amin was interested in being an important player in the international arena and did not perceive how his tyrannical governance of Uganda diminished his credibility elsewhere.

For Kaunda the struggles for liberation in Southern Africa have been of particular importance. Since Zambia is a land-locked country, he is dependent on maintaining working relations with the countries around Zambia to assure export of its materials. Moreover, he has been striving to reduce Zambia's dependence on South African trade. Much of Kaunda's behavior during the long struggle for majority rule in Southern Africa fits with the opportunist orientation we observe for him for this topic in table 10.8—trying to take advantage of what he perceived the situation to be to negotiate with South Africa, to take a hard line with the other front-line states, or to move on his own (Anglin and Shaw 1979).

It is interesting to note that although Machel, Mugabe, and Neto have expansionist orientations when focusing on their colonial situations, they become less hard-line when considering relations with countries other than their colonial powers, exhibiting orientations that seek out positive ways of interacting with these others. With the exception of South Africa, which still remains the enemy in the liberation struggle, there is some inkling in these results that these leaders "forgive and forget." In seeking to govern their newly independent countries, these leaders realized quickly the importance of friends.

Once more for Nyerere none of the orientations has a score that is one standard deviation above the mean. As before he is about as likely to rely on one orientation as another. We do note, however, that Nyerere scores 58 on the opportunist orientation when focusing on struggles for liberation and 58 on the expansionist orientation when focusing on relations with other countries.

For eight of the African leaders in our sample political stability is an

Table 10.8 Leader's orientations by topics discussed in interview responses

Amin	Houphouet-Boigny
Quality of life of people: opportunist (91)	Development: opportunist (80), developmental (60)
Struggles for liberation: influential (77), mediator/integrator (83)	Relations with other countries: influential (79), mediator/integrator (93), developmental (74)
Relations with other countries: mediator/integrator (83)	Pan-Africanism: active independent (73), influential (70), mediator/integrator (73)

Kaunda	Kenyatta
Development: active independent (79)	Development: active independent (81)
Political stability: expansionist (61)	Political stability: active independent (72), influential (73)
Nonalignment: none high	Struggles for liberation: expansionist (67), active independent (66), influential (61)
Struggles for liberation: opportunist (62)	

Machel	Mobutu
Development: none high	Development: active independent (73)
Colonialism/imperialism: expansionist (69)	Political stability: expansionist (74), active independent (69)
Struggles for liberation: none high	Relations with other countries: mediator/integrator (62)
Relations with other countries: mediator/integrator (84), influential (68)	Pan-Africanism: opportunist (70)

Mugabe	Neto
Development: active independent (60)	Security: expansionist (69), active independent (68)
Political stability: mediator/integrator (77), active independent (62), influential (64)	Political stability: opportunist (61), developmental (78)

Table 10.8   (continued)

Struggles for liberation: expansionist (66)	Struggles for liberation: expansionist (66)
Relations with other countries: opportunist (75), mediator/integrator (82)	Relations with other countries: opportunist (61), developmental (80)

Nkrumah	Nyerere
Political stability: expansionist (64)	Development: none high
Struggles for liberation: expansionist (63), influential (65)	Struggles for liberation: none high
Pan-Africanism: influential (73)	Relations with other countries: none high

Obote	Toure
Political stability: expansionist (60)	Political stability: active independent (116), expansionist (73)
Struggles for liberation: mediator/integrator (61), developmental (71)	Relations with other countries: mediator/integrator (113), developmental (100)
Relations with other countries: expansionist (69), active independent (62), opportunist (63)	Pan-Africanism: opportunist (62), mediator/ integrator (63), developmental (64)

issue of importance. And these eight leaders have had to pay attention to maintaining themselves in office given a large number of coup or assassination attempts, the presence of entrenched ethnic groups, or the need to bring previously warring guerrilla movements together. Often for these leaders the stability issue has involved other countries that are homes for dissidents. Table 10.8 suggests that these eight leaders have chosen different methods of tackling their stability problems. Some—Kaunda, Mobutu, Nkrumah, Obote, and Toure—have operated from an expansionist orientation, opting to crush or suppress any opposition. Others—Kenyatta, Neto, and Mugabe—have adopted orientations more likely to involve the opposition in the government. They have been interested in coopting the opposition or, at the least, in courting important elites so as to isolate or highlight the differences between themselves and the opposition.

Table 10.9   Correlations between leaders' orientation scores and three types of foreign affairs experience

Orientation	Type of experience		
	Years spent seeking independence	Years spent as head of government	Years spent in specific foreign affairs positions before assuming office
Expansionist	.44	− .46	.66**
Active independent	.70**	− .25	− .15
Influential	.53*	.20	.35
Opportunist	− .06	.03	− .69**
Mediator/integrator	.23	.50*	− .35
Developmental	.20	.18	− .06

* $p < .10$
** $p < .05$

Had more interview responses been available dealing with the issues of struggles for liberation and relations with other countries for each leader, we might have been able to see if the orientations are linked to certain target nations or groups. Thus, where two or more orientations are high for these two types of issues, one orientation might be directed toward one target, for example, South Africa, and the second orientation toward another target, say, a former colonial power. We were prevented from doing this in the present study because of the small number of interview responses available for each leader toward any one target.

Can we determine if experience has affected the role orientations of these leaders? There are at least three ways in which the African leaders in our sample have gained experience in foreign affairs. They gained experience through their struggles for independence from colonial power, through being heads of government and having to deal with other countries, and through specific foreign affairs positions prior to assuming office. Table 10.9 presents product moment correlations between the leaders' scores on the orientations and their years of experience of each of these three types. The data in Table 10.9 suggest that different kinds of insights result from these three types of experience. The longer the independence struggle, the greater the leader's interest is in going it alone—in keeping one's independence once it is gained and in being as self-reliant as possible. And with a long struggle for independence comes an interest in being influential in regional politics, perhaps to assure one's independence with a greater control over events.

With a longer tenure in office there appears to be a growing interest in trying to solve the problems between other countries that may be affecting you. Self-reliance and gaining more power become less important. Specific foreign affairs training such as designated negotiator with a colonial power seems to increase the leaders' interest in gaining more power or control; the leaders gain a sense of how it is to try to function effectively in the international arena without it. Specific foreign affairs training also relates to a diminished interest in being merely expedient. There may be a feeling that without some sort of plan, small, underdeveloped countries like theirs can become pawns of the superpowers or be buffeted about in the rapid changes than can occur in Africa.

Table 10.10 indicates the leaders' orientations to foreign affairs by time periods both just prior to and during their tenure as heads of government. The orientations listed in Table 10.10 are those with a score one or more standard deviations above the mean. The standard scores for the orientations listed are found in parentheses following the name of the orientation. Where no orientations meet this criterion, the words "none high" are indicated in the table. For some of the time periods, a brief description of what is happening in the leaders' countries is indicated under the dates.

The cases in table 10.10 suggest that some of the leaders have a repertoire of orientations among which they move back and forth depending on the events facing their nation. For example, three orientations are indicated for Houphouet-Boigny—influential, mediator/integrator, and developmental. These three orientations appear, disappear, and reappear across the time periods listed in table 10.10. When there is an abrupt shift in orientations for some leaders such as Mobutu and Nyerere, there is a period where no orientation is high before the change. Table 10.10 also indicates that the orientations characteristic of the leaders during the periods in which they are consolidating their power are not those held as the leaders move on to deal with their countries' problems. Similarly, the orientations leaders used in their struggle for independence do not seem to carry over to the post-independence period.

The leaders appear to accommodate to experience, changing their orientations as the situation changes. Some of the leaders appear to

Table 10.10 Leaders' orientations by time periods during and just prior to their tenure in office

Amin	1971–75	influential (65), opportunist (65), mediator/integrator (60) (consolidation of power)
	1976–79	none high (declared president for life)
Houphouet-Boigny	1951–60	influential (75), mediator/integrator (74) (pre-independence)
	1961–69	mediator/integrator (108), developmental (69)
	1970–74	influential (74), mediator/integrator (95), developmental (71) (initiative toward South Africa)
	1975–79	developmental (71)
	1980–82	influential (60), mediator/integrator (64) (questions on succession)
Kaunda	1960–67	none high (consolidation of power)
	1968–70	opportunist (66) (Mulungushi Declaration and Lusaka Manifesto)
	1971–76	opportunist (62) (overtures to South Africa)
	1977–82	opportunist (61) (active front-line state)
Kenyatta	1953–63	influential (61), mediator/integrator (65) (pre-independence)
	1964–69	active independent (66), influential (66) (consolidation of power; Mboya assassinated)
	1970–78	expansionist (73), active independent (79), influential (71) (revered leader)
Machel	1970–74	expansionist (60) (pre-independence)
	1975–82	none high (post-independence)
Mobutu	1965–70	expansionist (60) (consolidation of power)
	1971–75	none high (launched "authenticity" program)
	1976–78	none high

Table 10.10   (continued)

		(Zaire defaults on loans; invasions of Shaba Province)
	1979–82	opportunist (60)
		(tightening of political control; search for foreign investment and aid)
Mugabe	1975–79	expansionist (68)
		(pre-independence)
	1980–82	none high
		(post-independence)
Neto	1971–74	expansionist (67), active independent (66)
		(pre-independence)
	1975–79	developmental (63)
		(post-independence)
Nkrumah	1953–60	expansionist (61), influential (64)
		(consolidation of power)
	1961–65	influential (62)
		(assumes absolute control; Nkrumahism promulgated; pushes Pan-Africanism)
	1966	none high
		(post-coup)
Nyerere	1960–66	influential (60)
		(consolidation of power)
	1967–76	none high
		(first decade following Arusha Declaration)
	1977–82	opportunist (64)
		(second decade of Ujamaa)
Obote	1962–66	developmental (61)
		(consolidation of power)
	1967–71	expansionist (64), active independent (65)
		(move to left; successful coup by Amin)
	1979	opportunist (60)
		(seeking power after overthrow of Amin)
	1980–82	active independent (61), influential (60)
		(returns to power)
Toure	1958–66	developmental (71)
		(consolidation of power; emphasis on self-reliance)
	1967–74	influential (61), mediator/integrator (64), developmental (71)

Table 10.10   (continued)

	(several coup attempts; authenticity program launched; less emphasis on self-reliance)
1975–82	influential (68), mediator/integrator (77), developmental (71)
	(end to isolation; increased search for foreign investment)

move among a set of orientations that are readily available while others appear to change from one orientation to another after a period of time in which they search for what seems appropriate or what seems to work. Experience has more of an effect on this latter group, causing them to rethink their views of the world and strategies. Thus for certain periods of time their orientations will have little effect on their governments' foreign policy behavior as they test new thoughts and ideas. The orientations of those leaders with a readily available repertoire are more likely to influence their governments' foreign policy behavior, although even here the situation seems to determine which orientation will prevail.

How sensitive are these leaders to their political environments and what are the effects upon their role orientations? To some degree we have already been talking about sensitivity to the environment in examining the effects of interest and experience in foreign affairs upon the orientations. We have seen how orientations change in response to what the issue is and to outside events. The data in table 10.11 allows us to explore sensitivity to the environment directly by indicating the number of times the personal characteristics scores of the twelve African leaders changed in response to the topic in the interview, to the nature of the interviewer, to the period of time when the interview occurred, and to the degree of spontaneity called for by the interview setting.

In determining the effects of these various aspects of the interview situation on the personal characteristics of these leaders, a series of one-way analyses of variance were performed for each leader looking for significant ($p < .05$) differences among topics, types of interviewers, time periods, and how spontaneous the interview was. To be included in these analyses a category (topic, type of interviewer, time period, type of interview) had to include ten interview responses. Table 10.11 indicates the number of personal characteristics out of the eight examined for which significant differences were found. The final column in table 10.11 sums the significant differences across topic, interviewer, time period, and degree of spontaneity. The total possible number of significant differences is 32.

Among the twelve African leaders in table 10.11 Mugabe is the most sensitive to the situation, while Neto and Nyerere are the least sensitive. For Mugabe 11 out of 32 (34 percent) possible differences were significant whereas for Neto and Nyerere only 2 out of 32 (6 percent) were significant. We would, therefore, expect Mugabe to test his orientation to foreign affairs against any situation before applying it. Neto's and Nyerere's orientations are more likely to be applied regardless of situation. Some of the leaders are differentially sensitive to their environments. Thus, we note in table 10.11 that Mobutu and Toure are more sensitive to changes in issue than to differences in people or events. Mugabe is more sensitive to issues and events than to people. Nkrumah and Kaunda show the most sensitivity to people, that is, to who is addressing them or with whom they are carrying on a conversation.

These data suggest that particular leaders will pay attention to

Table 10.11 Sensitivity of leaders' personal characteristics scores by topic, interviewer, time period, and degree of spontaneity in interview

| | Number of Significant Differences | | | | |
Leader	by topic	by interviewer	by time periods	by degree of spontaneity in interview	Total number of changes
Amin	0	2	1	0	3
Houphouet-Boigny	2	2	2	0	6
Kaunda	2	3	2	0	7
Kcnyatta	3	2	2	1	8
Machel	2	1	1	1	5
Mobutu	4	2	2	0	8
Mugabe	5	1	4	1	11
Neto	1	0	1	0	2
Nkrumah	0	4	3	1	8
Nyerere	0	1	1	0	2
Obote	1	2	3	0	6
Toure	5	0	0	1	6

different aspects of the situation that is facing them. Moreover, they will seek out information about different aspects of a situation. Thus, for example, while Kaunda is interested in what people will benefit and who is concerned about what is going on, Mobutu will want to know specific details about what is happening, where, with what economic consequences. By learning about a leader's areas of sensitivity to the political environment, we become attuned to the kinds of information that are going to be important to the leader and about which he is going to want to be kept informed. In effect, we begin to map the influences on the leader that will affect whether and how his orientation is used in attacking a specific foreign policy problem.

Finally, let us ask whether different types of Black African leaders have different role orientations. The twelve African leaders in the present sample represent several different types of leaders. There are leaders with a military background and those with a primarily political background; some have been in office for very long periods of time—up to two decades in several instances—while others have served in office for only a short period of time. The leaders have different colonial legacies and represent different regions of Sub-Saharan Africa. Moreover, some have pro-East leanings while others are pro-West and still others profess nonalignment. Table 10.12 shows the mean scores on the six orientations of these various types of leaders. Given the small sample sizes for the various groups of leaders, these results should be seen as suggestive rather than definitive.

Table 10.12 indicates that the military leaders in the sample only scored higher than the nonmilitary leaders on the opportunist orientation. Moreover, we note that the opportunist orientation is most characteristic of the military leaders. The nonmilitary leaders scored highest on the average on the influential orientation and lowest on the opportunist orientation. With little political experience, the military leaders appear to perceive expedience as the best course of action. Leaders who have been in office a short time also scored higher than those who have held office for a long time on only the expansionist orientation, which is where they scored the highest. Still in a period in which they are consolidating their power, short term leaders have reason to focus on expanding their base of power. Other concerns can occupy the leaders who have been in office for some time.

An examination of the effects of different colonial experiences show leaders from former British colonies scoring higher on the active independent and opportunist orientations. Leaders from former Portu-

Table 10.12   Mean orientation scores for
the African leaders by type of leader

Type of Leader[a]	Expan-sionist	Active inde-pendent	Influ-ential	Oppor-tunist	Mediator/integrator	Develop-mental
Military background (N = 5)	48.4	46.4	44.6	52.0	47.2	47.8
Nonmilitary background (N = 7)	51.2	52.7	53.7	48.7	51.9	51.3
Long term in office (N = 7)	47.9	50.3	50.1	51.9	52.4	50.6
Short term in office (N = 5)	53.2	49.8	49.6	47.6	46.4	48.8
British colony (N = 7)	52.6	53.0	51.6	53.3	48.9	47.3
Portuguese colony (N = 2)	57.5	51.0	43.5	42.5	40.0	49.5
French colony (N = 2)	41.0	47.5	59.5	41.5	65.5	63.5
West African (N = 3)	47.3	48.3	58.7	40.3	57.7	57.7
East African (N = 4)	53.0	55.8	53.8	55.5	53.0	48.3
Front-line state (N = 6)[b]	50.2	47.2	43.3	52.5	43.8	46.3
Pro-East (N = 2)	57.5	51.0	43.5	42.5	40.0	49.5
Pro-West (N = 4)	49.3	52.5	50.3	50.5	53.0	49.5
Nonaligned (N = 6)	48.2	48.2	51.8	52.3	51.2	50.2

[a] Background data on the twelve leaders comes from Legum (1969–81); Kurian (1978); *Africa biographies* (1967); Dickie and Rake (1973); Jackson and Rosberg (1982).
[b] Nyerere is counted here as both an East African and front-line state leader.

guese colonies score higher on the expansionist orientation, and leaders from former French colonies score higher on the influential, mediator/integrator, and developmental orientations. These results suggest more of an interest on the part of leaders of former French colonies in playing a leadership role in Africa, whereas leaders with the other two colonial legacies seem more concerned with their own interests and "making it on their own."

Studying the results for leaders from various areas in Sub-Saharan Africa, we note that West African leaders score higher on the influential, mediator/integrator, and developmental orientations while leaders from East Africa score higher on the expansionist, active independent, and opportunist orientations. Leaders from front-line states do not score higher than these other two types of leaders on any of the orientations. However, their highest scores across the orientations occur for the expansionist and opportunist orientations. Here we observe leaders from West African countries having orientations indicating an interest in working on common problems with other countries, while leaders from the other two areas are more predisposed to orientations that focus inward on themselves.

Grouping the leaders according to their preferences on East-West issues, we observe in Table 10.12 that those who are pro-East score highest on the expansionist orientation. Those who are pro-West score highest on the active independent and mediator/integrator orientations, and those who are nonaligned score highest on the influential and opportunist orientations. All three types of leaders score almost alike on the developmental orientation. It may seem odd, given the definition of the active independent orientation, to have leaders with pro-East and pro-West ties scoring higher on this orientation than the leaders who consider themselves nonaligned. Such an orientation on the part of these pro-East and pro-West leaders, however, may indicate their perception that though accepting aid from one side or the other predominantly, they are not tied to those countries—that they are still in charge of their own destiny and can and will change if circumstances indicate such is important. They perceive there is less attachment to one side or the other than the East and West blocs may be counting on. On four of the orientations—expansionist, influential, opportunist, and mediator/integrator—the nonaligned and pro-West leaders are very much alike and both quite different from the pro-East leaders. There is less focus on power and capabilities among the pro-West and nonaligned countries and more focus on being alert to and taking advantage of opportunities.

Conclusions

The Sub-Saharan African leaders we have been examining in the present study are dominant leaders. They are heads of government for the most part in one-party states; others in the government serve at their pleasure. What these leaders are like can influence what their governments do in the foreign policy arena. We have tried to suggest the kinds of personal characteristics of these leaders which are likely to impact on their governments' foreign policy behavior. Moreover, we have proposed that these traits combine to predispose the leaders to different role orientations to foreign affairs, that is, to certain views of the world and preferred political styles that act as a guide to behavior. Six such orientations were described and assessed in the twelve African leaders under study, and all six orientations were found among the leaders—there being no particular African orientation.

Included in the description of each role orientation was a description of the foreign policy behavior a leader with each orientation is expected to urge on his government. Support has been found for the linkages between the role orientations and specific foreign policy proposals in previous research. Thus, knowing what orientation a leader has, we have some idea about what kind of foreign policy behavior he will urge on his government.

The link between role orientation and a government's foreign policy behavior is not automatic, however, even for a dominant leader. The leader's interests in the foreign policy arena, his experiences, and what kinds of information he tends to monitor in making foreign policy decisions help to dictate whether and how his orientation will influence his government's foreign policy behavior. And, indeed, for most of the leaders the dominant orientation changed with different interests and experiences. These African leaders tended to tailor their orientations to the issues they were facing. Thus, for example, the role orientation organizing information about development problems was not similar to that depended on for organizing information on relations with other countries. The subtle changes in the leaders' beliefs, motives, decision style, and interpersonal style in response to various types of problems was reflected in the responsiveness of their orientations to changes in issue—particularly issues of interest to them on which they were likely to focus a lot of energy.

Changing experiences also led leaders to reorient themselves. For some of the African leaders in our sample, this meant moving among a repertoire of role orientations, experience dictating which orientation was relevant under which circumstances. For other leaders, there were periods in which no orientation dominated as the leader experimented with ideas and strategies, seeking some feedback from the environment. Moreover, orientations relevant at one point during a leader's tenure in office appeared to become less relevant at other points, for example, as the leader moved from a period of consolidating power to one of building his nation's economy.

By ascertaining what kinds of information a leader is going to be sensitive to in his environment, we can look for the forces that will influence the role orientation the leader will form and apply in developing the foreign policy he will urge on his government. Is it opposition that the leader feels he must be responsive to; is it an ideology he has built his reputation on; is it dependence on events transpiring in another country? We began such a mapping for the twelve leaders in the present study.

The present study is only a first step in examining factors in foreign policy leadership in Sub-Saharan Africa. It is important as a next step to see if there is a relation between the leaders' role orientations found here and their governments' foreign policy behavior. In specific situations when we know the leader's orientation and the kinds of information to which he is particularly sensitive, can we indicate with some degree of accuracy if the leader's orientation will have any effect on his government's foreign policy behavior and, if so, what kind of effect? The answer to this question will suggest the relevance of further examination and monitoring of African leaders' orientations to foreign affairs.

11

Role Sets and African Foreign Policy Behavior: Testing an External Predisposition Model

Eric G. Singer and Valerie M. Hudson

The effects of the international or external environment on African states has received considerable attention from both Africanists and developmentalists. For the last twenty-five years or so, scholars have been debating these effects with little to show for their efforts. On the one hand, those who subscribe to the dependency school (for example, see Wallerstein 1974) claim that constraints are placed on African states by the world economic structure, which is designed to benefit the interests of the advanced capitalist states and contradict the interests of underdeveloped states. Through cooptation of African elites and a continued grip over the institutions and structure of the world economy, African states are thus destined to remain impoverished and on the periphery of global development.

On the other hand, proponents of the decolonization school (for example, Zartman 1982) assert that North-South relationships are in an "evolutionary process" by which facets of colonial influence are being replaced by multilateral relations characteristic of an interdependent world. Although the process may not exhibit immediate change, changes are occurring. The achievement of political independence has created an atmosphere for military disengagement, reduction in settler populations, opportunities for economic interaction on a mutually beneficial basis, and a resumption of cultural pride.

The two schools of thought seem irreconcilably at odds over the effects of the external environment's influence on African societies. The decolonizationists agree that a degree of dependence exists (Zartman 1982), but they argue that it is a transitory phase and can be a positive factor. In addition, they view the notion of a conspiracy between First and Third World elites as exaggerated. In contrast, the dependency school opines that not only is there an alliance of the elites, but also that the structure and institutions of the international system deprive African states of autonomy and access to those resources necessary for development.

Despite these contrasting positions, both schools of thought are in essential agreement on the fact that the external environment is an important element in the activities and policies of African states—the decolonizationists see it as facilitating development and interdependence, while the dependency school views it as retarding development and fostering marginality. The importance of the external environment necessitates a search for alternative means of examining its effects. We believe the debate between the decolonization and dependency schools, while incorporating both attractive and plausible insights, fails to offer cogent explanations of the day-to-day behavior of African states in the international environment. Both schools emphasize macro, long-term explanations which, when applied to specific instances of African foreign policy behavior, may be unsatisfactory.

In our investigation we introduce a technique by which the role of the external environment on the discrete foreign policy activities of African states may be studied. This effort is intended as a preliminary test of the usefulness of this technique, role analysis, in the explanation and prediction of foreign policy behavior. While the model we propose includes facets of the explanatory variables of both schools mentioned above, it also offers explanations of discrete events, something the two schools are unable to provide. Our model proceeds on the assumption that knowledge of the externally defined decision-making situation may be especially valuable if one theorizes that certain nations' behaviors may be to a significant extent a function of the external environment. As the analysis of the dependency and decolonization schools indicate, this view prevails among at least these Africanists.

Role Analysis and Foreign Policy Behavior

Role analysis is a technique derived from the theater; it has been used in various forms by anthropologists, sociologists, and psychologists. The basic premise of role analysis is that social behavior is in large part a function of the expectations attached to or associated with individuals on the basis of their locations or positions in social systems. Around this position (called a "status" by Linton) converges a collection of rights and duties. A role, then, is a status put into action. Incorporating the work of such scholars as Linton (1945), Gross et al. (1958), Nadel (1957), Banton (1965), Goodenough (1965), and Goffman (1961), the behavior of individuals in a social system can be explained by reference to the concept of "role behavior," that is, actual performance that relates to the norms and expectations of the role of the individual. This role behavior is enacted within the context of a "role set," that is, the set of relevant others and their roles within the system.

Explanation by reference to role behavior actually involves more than one step and also a controversial assumption. The steps are as follows: identify the expectations associated with the roles the individual plays; observe behavior of the individual and see if it is consonant with any of the role expectations; if it is, explain the behavior by asserting the individual is playing out that role. The controversial assumption is that the individual will conform to the norms and expectations of the role. Explanation by role is explanation by reference to norms.

Obviously, normative expectations about behavior may not result in accurate predictions of behavior for several reasons: There may be role conflict; the individual may be playing a different role than the researcher believed; the individual may be making a "mistake"; the individual may "misunderstand" how to implement the expectations. In addition, many times the role expectations are in fact the researcher's and not the role occupants'. The role expectations in that case become the hypotheses that the researcher will test by his research. Despite the problematic nature of this assumption, its adoption gives one a powerful tool for understanding and even generating expectations about an individual actor's behavior.

In attempting to use role analysis to explain the behavior of nations, a key question must be addressed: can one transfer the concept of "role" from the individual level, where it is defined, to the national level? Can nations or governments have roles? Those who answer in the affirmative usually posit one of two arguments: either nations can be "reduced" to individuals (for example, leaders) and therefore there is no problem at all; or the international system is in some sense equivalent to the notion of a social system, and nations make up the "individuals" of that particular system. In this research effort, our sample of nations (Ivory Coast, Guinea, Ghana, Uganda, Kenya and Zambia) can, in large measure, be "reduced" to individuals because the leaders of all six nations dominate their respective political environments. As Jackson and Rosberg (1982, 22) argue, the political system of these types of states is dependent on the "dispositions, activities, abilities, efforts, and fortunes of politicians—especially rulers.... [H]ow the [ruler] chooses to perform his role, how well he performs, and with what degree of fortune are crucial to the stability of the polity and the persistence of the regime."

In probably the best known work relating roles to foreign policy (Holsti 1970), the author content analyzed the speeches of leaders to identify seventeen types of national role conceptions. Subsequent works in this area (Walker 1979; Wish 1980) have relied on Holsti's basic typology. The national role-conception scheme of Holsti is based on two interesting assumptions: first, that a national role conception should be defined as the leader's role conception for the nation (this assumption, as noted above, is also adopted for this effort); second, that nations have a well-defined cross-time repertoire of roles.

This last assumption is not demanded by role analysis. One could argue that there are really two levels of national roles. The first represents the broader ideological and instrumental beliefs of a national regime and corresponds to Holsti's framework as well as the concept of "regime orientation" developed in Hagan, Hermann, and Hermann (1982). The second identifies situationally defined roles that shift as the situation does. The outcomes of the actor's role-playing in these situations can be seen as shaping the broader roles. We will utilize situationally based roles in this research.

One last underlying assumption that must be made explicit is that nations act in foreign affairs only in response to a problem or opportunity they recognize. A problem or opportunity can be seen as any perceived discrepancy between present or anticipated states of affairs and what is envisioned as desirable (see Hermann 1978). The problem, as defined by the acting nation, identifies who and what is important in each circumstance, thus defining the relevant role set for each situation. A specific problem thus provides the means for establishing a set of roles and enables one to determine the entities occupying those roles. From the perspective of the acting regime or leader (the actor), every recognized problem will produce a role set that includes a "source" role and a "subject" role—and possibly "facilitator," "aggravator," or "potential facilitator/aggravator" roles as well:

Source. Every problem has an inferred source, or a cause. The occupant of the source role is that entity perceived by the actor as responsible for the immediate problem (regardless of whether such perceptions are accurate). Human entities may be regarded as the source by the acting national government; so might nature, or the will of God. The actor may recognize multiple entities as constituting the source. Moreover the immediate problem might be seen as flowing from a prior problem.

Subject. Every problem also has a perceived subject role. The subject is some collective entity that suffers or is deprived—or will be in the future—by problems. As with sources, a problem as perceived by the actor may define multiple entities as the subject.

Actor. The third role in every problem is the actor, which for this project is the national government whose behavior we seek to explain. The individuals in the acting national government with the authority to allocate resources to foreign policy are the policy-makers from whose perspective the source and subject are identified.

Each role may be occupied by one or more separate entities. The same entity may also appear in several roles. The actor, for example, may also be the subject, or the source, or both. The latter situation is analogous to the individual deciding how to treat his own injury after shooting himself in the foot. This international equivalent of shooting oneself in the foot would not be a foreign policy occasion unless there was some other role involving a foreign entity in addition to those mentioned. For this and a number of other kinds of situations two others roles may be present in the problem environment. In contrast to the three previously mentioned roles, facilitator and potential facilitator may not always be involved.

Facilitator. This entity, or entities, is perceived by the actor as aiding or assisting the actor or the entities in one of the other two roles. It is recognized not to have caused the problem and not to be suffering—at least directly—as a result of it. Nevertheless, the facilitator supports one or more role occupants.

Potential Facilitator. This role differs from the facilitator in that it refers to an entity the actor perceives as having the ability to assist one of the other role occupants in the immediate future. Thus, a facilitator is one who already has offered assistance and a potential facilitator is one who could offer assistance.

For every problem, then, the actor identifies specific entities for each role. As a consequence, one can imagine that the context of the problem provides various types of situations depending upon the actor's relationship to the source and subject. There are four broad types of situations representing all possible configurations of roles. Each type of situation may be defined as posing a distinctive question for the decision makers in the acting government. The question that defines each type of situation appears summarized below.

Type I—*Confrontation.* How can we (the actor) reduce the adverse effects that the other entity in the problem creates for us?

Type II—*Intervention.* Should we (the actor) intervene in this problem on one side or the other, and if so, in what manner?

Type IIIA—*Assistance.* Who can give us (the actor) assistance in reducing the adverse effects of the problem we are experiencing?

Type IIIB—*Assistance.* Should we (the actor) provide assistance to those who are experiencing the adverse effects of a problem?

Type IV—*Collaboration.* Can we (the actor) reach a substantive agreement with those with whom we share this problem?

To elaborate this classification of situations let us limit discussion to the three necessary roles (actor, source and subject) and postulate three possible nations or other international entities: the actor (A), nation X, and nation Y.

Types of Situations   In a confrontation type of situation the actor also assumes one of the other roles—either source or subject. The actor, therefore, is directly affected by the problem—either having created it or being deprived by it. Another entity is in the third role. From the actor's perspective, then, this type of situation can be regarded as a confrontation—someone is posing a problem for the actor. It can be summarized as taking one of the following two forms:

Actor	Source	Subject
Nation A	Nation X	Nation A
Nation A	Nation A	Nation X

In an intervention type of situation separate entities occupy each of the three basic roles. The actor is a third party and observes that some external entity has created a problem for another external entity. The issue for the actor is whether to become involved; thus, we can characterize an intervention situation and diagram it as follows:

Actor	Source	Subject
Nation A	Nation X	Nation Y

Actually there are two different types of assistance configurations, but we have grouped them together because they share a concern with assistance or support. In one situation the actor is also the source and subject, that is, it has created its own problem and is seeking a solution. (In identifying the source of the problem as the actor we are including with the actor natural or societal conditions within the actor's nation that generated the problem.) A nation faced with sagging economic development would be assumed to fit this category. This subtype, our type IIIA, can be diagrammed as follows:

Actor	Source	Subject	Facilitator
Nation A	Nation A	Nation A	Nation X

There is also a second subtype of assistance situation, type IIIB. A nation other than the actor is both the source and subject of the problem and is turning to the actor for assistance.

Actor	Source	Subject
Nation A	Nation X	Nation X

In a collaboration type of situation the actor shares both other roles with another entity. The actor jointly with another nation is the source and subject of the problem and they are negotiating or collaborating over its treatment. The outcome of such a situation might be a communiqué or treaty. The diagram for this situation would be:

Actor	Source	Subject
Nation A	Nations A + Y	Nations A + Y

Several additional points about these configurations of situations should be noted. First, the other roles do not have to be nation-states;

they can be any type of international entity. Second, more than one entity can assume the roles we have illustrated with nations X and Y. For example, a problem could result from the behaviors of multiple nations acting separately or in concert. Third, we have not introduced the roles of facilitator or potential facilitator in the presentation of the four situations except for type IIIA because they do not alter the logic that underlies each basic configuration and need not be present, with the one noted exception.

The question that each type of situation frames is the fundamental task the actor must address. In estimating the response to that task it becomes essential to understand certain dimensions of the relationship between the actor and the other role occupants in the problem. From the problem it is possible to determine the actual international entities occupying each role and then to estimate their relationship with the actor. We propose three relational dimensions that shape the actor's behavior in the various situations: prior affect, salience, and relative capabilities.

Relational Dimensions   As the name implies, prior affect relates the affective history between the actor and each of the entities occupying the roles. Affect is expressed feeling ranging from extreme hostility to unequivocal friendship. The accumulated manifestations of affect in previous interactions that the actor has expressed toward a relevant other and has received from it comprise prior affect. An oversimplified statement of the idea that will be developed later is that if the acting regime's affective history has been positive with a given role occupant, then the regime is more likely to be supportive of that entity whether it is the source, subject, or facilitator of the current problem. If prior affect has been negative, the actor's present disposition is likely to be nonsupportive.

An actor may have a record of negative feelings toward another entity but be restrained from acting upon them in the present situation because of its dependence upon or need of that entity. This illustration introduces salience as a second dimension of the relationship among occupants of the set of roles in a foreign policy problem. Salience for the actor is the degree to which the explicit or tacit support or concurrence of a specific external entity is necessary for the regime, or its society, to realize basic values. In other words, the well-being of one nation is contingent upon the resources or agreement of another. Together with prior affect, salience can be understood to influence the predisposition of the actor to align with or against others in the problem or to remain neutral.

Prior affect and salience provide an actor with the motivation to support or oppose another entity. Calculations of how that motivation might be acted upon involve comparisons of relative capabilities with respect to the others involved in the problem. Exactly what capabilities are applicable depends upon the nature of the immediate situation and particularly the nature of the problem. For our purposes it is sufficient to differentiate problems according to basic values they involve. The deprivation that is part of every problem can be understood as interfering with the present or future enjoyment of some basic values by the entity being deprived. Thus we classify problems according to which of the following broad value areas they concern: security/physical safety, economic wealth, respect/status, well-being/welfare, and enlightenment. To promote these basic values, virtually all societies have developed human skills, physical resources, and institutions that collectively can be regarded as comprising the capabilities in each value area.

It is the comparison of capabilities associated with the basic values affected by the problem that form the third dimension of the relationship between the actor and the other role occupants. When the actor is motivated (by prior affect and salience) to side with one or another of the roles associated with the problem, it is the strength of the actor's capabilities relative to the others that shapes its predisposition to act.

Decision Logics   With these definitions of role, situation, affect, salience, and relative capabilities we will construct a model that integrates multiple variables through role analysis to explain foreign policy behavior. We call this model the "external predisposition model" because it addresses the question: how does the immediate nature of the problem and the resulting configuration of roles establish a general predisposition for a regime to act in a given way? In order to use roles, types of situations, and relational variables to explain behavior, it is first necessary to adopt a convention for using foreign policy behavior to describe role enactment.

Briefly foreign policy behavior may be described by answering the question, "who does what to whom, how?" For our present research, we have chosen four dimensions from Callahan et al., *Describing Foreign Policy Behavior* (1982) that will comprise our description of an acting nation's behavior:

Recipient. To whom is the behavior directed?

Affect. Where along the continuum of hostility/friendliness does the behavior lie?

Commitment. Does the actor engage in pledging behavior, or is there significant allocation of resources in implementing this behavior?

Instrumentality. What tools of implementation are employed in this behavior?

We contend that every foreign policy behavior can be described as a set of values on these four behavioral dimensions. Given our set of independent variables (roles, situations, relational dimensions) and our set of dependent variables (the four behavior attributes), the last step in the construction of the external predisposition model is the creation of "logics" linking the former to the latter. These logics can then be used as both a source of explanation and a means of prediction. How is this accomplished?

As we have seen, each situation establishes a frame in which the actor can be expected to try to resolve a basic question about its own behavior. Because the frame and its associated question or task change from one situation to another, the reasoning or logic advanced to estimate the actor's behavior also varies. For each type of situation, therefore, we have created a decision tree and an associated reasoning process for its choice points. The choice points in each decision tree are determined by the three relational dimensions—prior affect, salience, and relative capabilities—and by the presence or absence of facilitators and potential facilitators. The outcome at the end of each branch of the reasoning process is a specific type of behavior, which is a combination of the four behavior attributes noted above. Each branch is, in effect, a hypothesis about how the particular values of the independent variables lead to particular values of the dependent variables.

Because of the multiplicity of paths or branches through each of the decision trees, it is not possible to reproduce here the complete set of choice points and their associated arguments. The complete set can be found in Hudson (1983). Instead, we will illustrate one branch of one decision tree with an historical example and examine the reasoning and the prediction associated with that branch. The briefly sketched historical example of the Zambian-Rhodesian dispute over Rhodesian railways and the corresponding branch in its decision tree will neither reveal all possibilities nor the adequacy of our reasoning as a whole. However, we hope that it will demonstrate the general process in use and permit an initial judgment as to its utility.

The Zambian-Rhodesian problem is illustrative of those situations that pit the actor (Zambia) against another entity (Rhodesia) which the actor regards as the problem source. This is a type I confrontation situation. In an effort to comply with the United Nations sanctions against Rhodesia (following the latter's unilateral declaration of independence), Zambia decided in April 1966 to block all further payments from the railway account at Broken Hill (Zambia) to that at Bulawayo (Rhodesia). Rhodesia responded by refusing to transport Zambian imports and its copper exports to and from the Mozambican and South African ports along its rail line. At that time 90 percent of Zambia's imports and exports were transported through Rhodesia.

From Zambia's perspective this problem was caused by Rhodesia, thus making it the source of the problem, and Zambia perceived itself to be the subject, as it was already directly affected by Rhodesia's actions. It should be noted that Zambia precipitated this event just after the British Labour Party's decisive victory in the general elections of March 1966. Hall (1969, 138) contends that the timing of this event was not coincidental, "since Zambian leaders now expected the British government to act more resolutely against the rebel regime."

On the basis of the predispositional model, what would be Zambia's expected behavior? The answer can be found by examining the segment of the confrontation decision tree presented in figure 11.1. First, we will describe why in this case Zambia's hypothetical role-location process can be characterized by the branch or path shown in figure 11.1. Then we will review the argument that suggests why this configuration of positions on the key variables should make probable the behavior properties stipulated as the pattern for Zambia's role enactment.

With respect to the first question, there can be little doubt that the prior affect between Zambia (both the actor and the subject) and Rhodesia (the source) had been negative prior to 1966. The white-controlled government of Rhodesia and the newly independent country of Zambia each generated negative feelings for the other that characterized most of their interactions. The basic value involved in railroad payment transfers was economic, and with respect to economic capability it must be concluded Zambia was at a decided economic disadvantage compared to Rhodesia. Thus, with respect to the second question of relative capabilities (are the actor's relative capabilities greater?), the answer must be no. The third question in figure 11.1 concerns the presence of facilitators for the actor. Although Britain is a potential source of assistance for Zambia, neither Britain nor any other country had aligned itself with Zambia on the railroad issue.

Because there are no actual facilitators, the next choice point con-

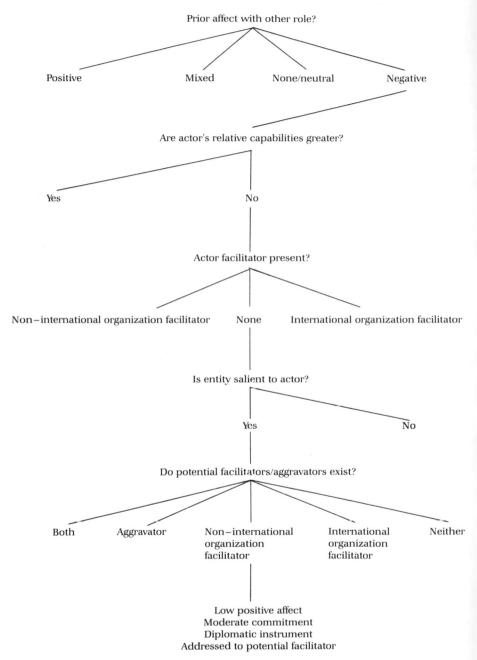

Figure 11.1   "Soliciting external support to offset a stronger enemy," branch of the decision tree for confrontation situations (type 1)

cerns salience. As the railroad issue clearly demonstrates, Rhodesia was highly salient for Zambia's economic well-being in 1966. As a poor; totally landlocked country, Zambia was often reliant upon its bordering states. As we noted earlier, Britain was the colonial power that occupied Zambia before its independence. Britain also contested Rhodesia's unilateral break from British rule and thus appeared as a potential source of assistance to Zambia—particularly the new Labour government which was expected to be sympathetic. On this issue no outside entity appeared as a potential aggravator for Zambia, although on other matters South Africa certainly assumed that role.

Tracing through this path in figure 11.1, we would expect Zambia's external predisposition (or that of any government in the same circumstance) to call for behavior addressed to the potential facilitator (Britain) using diplomatic instruments and expressing low positive affect and moderate commitment (conditional/unconditional policy statement by high-level official). In fact President Kaunda appealed to Britain to resolve the problem as it was still legally responsible for the governing of Rhodesia.

Why should this path yield this particular configuration of behavior properties? If the actor is in a confrontation situation facing as the source an entity who is clearly a stronger enemy, then the actor faces a serious predicament. Because the acting government believes it is being deprived by a long-standing adversary, the actor would like to take strong action against the source, but its capability disadvantage renders the success of such a venture unlikely. The salience of the source only compounds the difficulty of the actor's situation. Because of the acting government's reliance on the source, even if it could force a satisfactory resolution of the immediate issue, reprisals by the adversary might be possible due to the actor's dependence on it.

An actual facilitator might change the discouraging calculus if its capability in the relevant area could reliably augment the actor's. As we noted, however, Zambia had no facilitator. Under such circumstances, the presence of a strong potential facilitator presents an opportunity to avoid humiliation and submission to the source. All possible efforts to acquire the support of the potential facilitator to the actor's cause will be undertaken. If such support is forthcoming, the actor may be in a better position to press subsequently for a more advantageous solution than might otherwise be expected.

As a consequence, the actor will address the potential facilitator with positive affect but with low intensity befitting an entreaty of support. Commitment will be moderate due to the likely involvement of high-level officials anxious to take steps to persuade the other entity to support them. Given the nature of the appeal, diplomatic instruments will be the most likely vehicle. The behavior strategy suggested by this path does in fact correspond to the tone and content of President Kaunda's appeal.

The type of reasoning process illustrated in this example was used to construct the other hypotheses or branches in the model. The external predisposition model contains 221 hypotheses, and covers all types of situations and combinations of the values of the relational variables. Its comprehensive nature thus permits a more rigorous evaluation than the examination of the one example above. We will illustrate this potential by reporting the results of a postdictive test of those hypotheses that frame the foreign policy behaviors of six African nations between 1959 and 1968.

Conducting a Postdictive Test

A test of postdiction involves "hiding" the past from ourselves and attempting to "predict" it on the basis of our model. The postdictions can then be compared to actual history to assess the utility and accuracy of our model. Our test of postdiction is straightforward and comprises the following steps:

1. Perform the role-assignment coding to reconstruct the situations of 622 events of the Ivory Coast, Guinea, Ghana, Uganda, Kenya, and Zambia for the decade 1959–68. Coders specially trained in a country's history were used for each nation. Since some of these nations were not independent during the first part of the decade, events for only the latter part of the decade for those nations were used. Intercoder reliability ranged from .80 to .85; the coding rules and training of coders are in Hudson (1983).

2. Operationalize and collect the data on prior affect, relative capabilities, and salience for these six nations. The operationalizations are discussed in detail in appendix 3.

3. Use the knowledge of type of situation derived from the role assignment coding, plus the data on prior affect, salience, and relative capabilities to determine which branch/hypothesis of the decision logics is applicable in each of the 622 cases.

4. Compare the prediction of affect, commitment, instrumentality, and recipient offered by the appropriate branch of the decision logics with the actual behavior (affect, commitment, instrument, and recipient), as coded by the CREON data set. (See Hermann et al. 1973).

Table 11.1   Breakdown of predictive success
by behavior attributes (N = 622)

Behavior attribute	Predictive success	Probability of success by chance
Affect	51.3%	33%
Commitment	20.9%	25%
Instrumentality	67.4%	33%
Recipient	60.9%	10%

Let us begin our discussion of the results by first examining the predictive accuracy of the model in reference to the 622 cases taken together. Table 11.1 presents predictive accuracy broken down by the four individual behavior attributes. Alongside the success rate is presented the probability of successfully predicting that attribute by chance. The chance figure is, naturally, derived from the number of possible values the particular variable can assume.

Immediately noticeable is that the model appears to do very well in predicting instrumentality and recipient, fairly well in predicting affect, and fairly poorly in predicting level of commitment. This pattern may be because the external environment has more to do with shaping the instrumentality and type of recipient than it does with expressed affect and commitment, which may be more heavily influenced by the internal decision-making environment. Still, the success with respect to affect is significant when one keeps in mind that predicting affect correctly is in part a function of correctly predicting recipient first. Given that recipient is correctly predicted about 61 percent of the time, predicted success for affect cannot exceed that level.

Despite our relative success in predicting to affect, instrumentality, and recipient, our showing on commitment is poor—the success rate is even lower than the chance rate. In our opinion this indicates that either the reasoning process used to estimate level of commitment is flawed or prediction of level of commitment by the examination of only externally defined variables is not a useful enterprise.

Table 11.2 presents a different perspective on the predictive accuracy of our model. The prediction for each of the 622 cases was a score on each of the four behavior attributes. Therefore it is possible to characterize a case where the model predicted all four attributes as a completely successful prediction, and a case where the model did not predict any of the attributes as a completely wrong prediction, with gradations in between. Table 11.2 thus reports the percentage of the

Table 11.2   Number of correctly predicted
attributes per case (0–4) (N = 622)

Number correct per case	Percentage correct	Cumulative percentage
4	8.0%	8.0%
3	25.2%	33.2%
2	32.3%	65.5%
1	28.0%	93.5%
0	6.4%	100.0%

time we predicted none, one, two, three, or four of the behavior attributes correctly per case.

If we assume that getting three or four out of the four possible attributes correct as being either totally correct or very much within the ballpark, then our model appears to be on target 33.2 percent, or roughly one-third of the time. The contingent probability of getting three or four out of four correct by chance is, in comparison, 5.6 percent. The model gets two or more of the behavior attributes correct just about two-thirds of the time (65.5%). Finally, the model is totally wrong less frequently than it is totally right (6.4 versus 8.0 percent), which is encouraging. We view these results as promising, since the model only examines external variables. This can also be regarded as evidence that these external variables do play an important role in the shaping of African foreign policy behavior.

Are there any interesting results when the six nations are examined individually? One striking finding is in contrast to one's initial presupposition that these six states, all being newly independent, relatively underdeveloped African nations, would be facing similar sorts of external environments during this decade. The nations' situational profiles actually fall into three general sets, as shown by table 11.3. The largest set, composed of Ghana, Guinea, Uganda, and the Ivory Coast find themselves engaged for the most part in assistance consideration and intervention type situations, which upon closer examination turn out to take place in multilateral settings. This is perhaps corroboration of East's (1973) hypothesis that small, poor nations find this type of activity the least expensive and the easiest sort of diplomacy in which to engage.

Zambia, on the other hand, falls into a class of its own by virtue of its situational profile. Almost half of Zambia's events are responses to confrontation type situations, which reflects the overwhelming impact of the Rhodesian unilateral declaration of independence on that nation and suggests that the external environment facing Zambia was markedly different from that faced by the other nations. Kenya, too, has a unique profile: a much greater proportion of its events (relative to the other five nations) occur in intervention type situations. One possible explanation may be that Kenya's president, Jomo Kenyatta, actively participated in issues of liberation relative to other external matters, especially in multilateral diplomatic contexts. While the other leaders also may have been actively involved, Kenyatta devoted a great deal of attention in the Commonwealth, OAU, and other forums to the liberation of African states still under colonial domination.

Thus we see that the external predisposition model is able to discriminate between more typical and more unusual sets of external circumstances confronting arguably similar types of actors. It is likewise interesting to note in table 11.4 that our predictive success rates for Zambia are the highest of the sample, whereas for Kenya they are the lowest. This difference suggests that our logics for the circumstances Zambia finds itself confronting are probably better than those in which Kenya is frequently involved. Indeed, an examination of the most frequent intervention situation (branch number 2001, which con-

Table 11.3   Frequency distribution
for each actor by situation type*

| | Situation type | | | | |
Actor	Confron- tation	Interven- tion	Assistance requesting	Assistance consider- ation	Collabor- ation
Ivory Coast					
N = 92	(1) 1.0%	(30) 32.6%	(1) 1.0%	(46) 50.0%	(14) 15.2%
Guinea					
N = 139	(6) 4.3%	(55) 39.5%	(12) 8.6%	(44) 31.6%	(22) 15.8%
Ghana					
N = 189	(13) 6.8%	(85) 44.9%	(9) 4.7%	(73) 38.6%	(9) 4.7%
Uganda					
N = 81	(8) 9.8%	(29) 35.8%	(3) 3.7%	(30) 37.0%	(11) 13.5%
Kenya					
N = 60	(9) 15.0%	(31) 51.6%	(7) 11.6%	(8) 13.3%	(5) 8.3%
Zambia					
N = 61	(26) 42.6%	(14) 22.9%	(8) 13.1%	(8) 13.1%	(5) 8.2%

* Total N = 622

Table 11.4   Predictive success rates for each African nation*

Nation	Predictive success
Ivory Coast	31.5%
Guinea	31.7%
Ghana	30.7%
Uganda	38.3%
Kenya	25.0%
Zambia	49.2%

* Predictive success, being defined as percentage of times the number of attributes correctly predicted per case, was either three or four out of four possible. The number of cases (N) for each nation is reported in table 11.3.

tained 10.3 percent of all cases in the sample), reveals the difficulties inherent in this type of role-analytic model.

In this particular intervention situation the actor, regardless of its capabilities, prior affect, and salience with the two opposed entities (source and subject roles) will appeal to a potential facilitator to intervene instead of itself actually intervening. The most prevalent events falling into this case are ones where the actor is asked to vote on an issue involving two other entities in which a third entity can be called upon to facilitate the resolution of the issue. In the African context, the substance of the events was overwhelmingly questions of liberation debated within the setting of an international organization. For example, before Rhodesia declared UDI, a number of resolutions were introduced into the General Assembly of the United Nations calling on Great Britain to intervene on behalf of the majority of Rhodesian citizens.

Overall, our hypothesis as to what the ensuing behavior on the part of the actor would be in this particular situation fared poorly, correctly predicting only three out of sixty-four cases. The most cogent explanation for this showing may be found in the coding of the roles in these cases. Recall that the most problematic assumption that must be made in analytic role theory is that the role expectations identified by the researchers are identical to those which the actor holds. By examining these cases in detail, it became clear to us that the inaccuracy of the hypothesis could be traced to this problem. The coders tended to regard the existence of an entity able to facilitate resolution of the problem as a facilitator. However, the African states almost always regarded these entities as aggravators, possibly because the role occupants were usually colonial powers.

As a contrast to the problems of this intervention hypothesis, we can offer a brighter picture of assistance consideration logics. In fact, one branch in this type of situation (number 4003) accounted for 23.1 percent of all the African cases, and the percent of three or more matches per case was a healthy 45.8 percent. Events falling into this category generally involved governmental officials indicating their policy preferences in response to conference communiqués or United Nations resolutions. So many cases in this particular branch relative to the overall number of cases suggests the preeminence of multilateral settings for African external activities. This feature is particularly true for the Ivory Coast, which almost totally avoids any type of unilateral behavior. Only two Ivory Coast events out of ninety-two occur in types of situations characterized by unilateral behavior—confrontation and assistance requesting. Finally, the substantive nature of the resulting behavior by the African states consisted of a lot of verbal diplomacy; they seldom opted to engage in behavior that involved the commitment of resources.

Next Steps

In this research effort we have attempted to show how the concepts and techniques of role analysis can be used in both a conceptual and applied manner to explain and predict how the external environment will shape foreign policy behavior. We have applied these concepts to African foreign policy behavior, as many students of Africa have felt that the external environment plays an especially significant part in molding the policy of those nations.

Our empirical results have shown that as a predictive tool, the external predisposition model can account fully for one-third of the behavior of our sample of six African nations. Furthermore, the model can provide useful information for almost two-thirds of their behavior. As a tool of description, our model is able to discriminate meaningfully among the external environments of nations through the examination of their situational profiles. Patterns that are more typical can be distinguished from profiles that are more unusual, even for nations which may be more or less similar on the surface.

Lastly, our model exhibits how role concepts can be used to explain and predict discrete temporal events, which may be of more utility than approaches which are only able to offer explanation and prediction in very macro and very long term contexts. Not only may the type of approach used in this paper be more relevant to policymakers, but it is also a way for contending theories about the behavior of African states to be made testable in an empirical sense.

The external predisposition model, however, is neither complete nor perfect. Errors resulting from misplaced role expectations must be weeded out and corrected. Variables from the internal decision-making context might be added to shore up some of the model's weaknesses —notably in the area of predicting the level of commitment that will be chosen. More extensive empirical testing, perhaps even in a predictive rather than a postdictive mode, might also bring to light particular branches or hypotheses whose reasonings are inadequate.

Overall, we do feel that the success of this model makes plain that role analysis is useful for the study of international behavior, that it can be applied and tested empirically, and that a model built upon its foundations can provide surprisingly accurate explanations and predictions of discrete behavior. Apart from the technique itself, the model has shown that the external decision-making context is a significant and valuable variable in understanding the behavior of nations, perhaps especially so for the behavior of nations long hypothesized to be particularly vulnerable to the effects of the external environment.

12

Superpower Involvement with Others: Alternative Role Relationships

Charles F. Hermann

Certain actions of governments in foreign policy seem expected. As relations between the United States and Ethiopia soured in 1976–77, many were not surprised to see the Soviet Union seek to replace the United States as Ethiopia's patron. Nor were those persons familiar with the Reagan administration surprised that it refused to make many concessions to Third World countries at the Law of the Sea conference regarding the right of private companies in industrialized nations to engage in deep-sea mining. When such actions occur observers are inclined to say that they were predictable or, at least, not surprising. There are many reasons why some actions of governments may be expected. One potential source for explaining such actions is role theory. National governments, it can be suggested, have certain roles that they assume in world affairs. When we know the roles, and governments actually act to fulfill those roles, then the actions should be expected. This idea is appealing. If we had systematic knowledge about government roles in foreign policy, it could be an important source of explanation.

This potential of role theory has encouraged a number of scholars to explore its development in systematic research, including Holsti (1970), Wish (1980), and Walker (1979, 1981). The Comparative Research on the Events of Nations (CREON) project also has sought to incorporate role conceptions in its model building. In fact, CREON uses role in two separate ways, each of which is intended to contribute to an integrated explanation of foreign policy behavior.

One approach (see Hermann and Hermann 1979; Hudson, Singer, and Hermann 1982; and Singer and Hudson, chapter 11 in this volume) employs role as a basic element in establishing the relationship of other international entities to the acting government in dealing with transitory situations. Although the roles are defined from the perspective of the actor, it might reasonably be said that this is an international system perspective on the use of role.

The second CREON application of role is in the process of decision making. More specifically, national role is used as part of a larger conceptual structure to establish the shared preferences of policymakers for foreign policy. The larger construct in CREON is called regime orientation. It can be defined as the shared political system belief of authoritative decision makers about their country's relationship to its external environment and the roles of government appropriate for pursuing the belief. In other words, in this framework national foreign policy roles are determined by the beliefs of a regime's authoritative decision makers. These are the individuals in a state that, with respect to foreign policy issues, have the ultimate authority to commit the resources of the government. A foreign policy core political system belief is a conviction that is shared by the authoritative decision makers (a) about their own nation and its relationship to other entities in the world and (b) about how the international system operates. Roles are these decision makers' expectations about the pattern or configuration of foreign policy activity that their government will follow in certain situations in support of their beliefs. Thus a regime's authoritative policy makers may share a common belief about another nation's commitment to destroy their society. In certain situations involving that other nation, the regime leaders would expect their government to assume a certain role to resist that opponent. In different situations with the opposing nation, the regime leaders' expectation about their government's activity (that is, their sense of its role) may vary, although their belief remains constant.

Regime orientations are not applicable in all foreign policy decision-making circumstances. The regime's authoritative decision makers may have differing core political system beliefs on a particular subject. These may not exist on an experiential base—that is, a set of comparable previous circumstances—sufficient to generate expectations about how the government should act. Finally, even when regime orientations do exist other factors may cause the government to act in ways contrary to the authoritative decision makers' normal expectations. For example the government may not appear to the policymakers to have sufficient capability to make the role feasible, or strong domestic opposition may lead them to alter their course. The CREON associates regard regime orientation, and the national foreign policy roles which are elements in these orientations, as *one* of the various features that can form a nation's foreign policy in response to a given kind of problem.

This essay attempts to advance the theoretical underpinnings necessary for using regime orientation beyond the level previously reported in Hermann, Hermann, and Hagan (1982). It is concerned with three questions:

1. when a regime's leaders have more than one shared core political system belief about foreign affairs, which one applies?
2. When a government has multiple foreign policy roles appropriate for a given political belief, which one applies?
3. With a given foreign policy role, what is the probable foreign policy behavior?

Although the conceptual work advanced here is intended to be capable of systematic empirical investigation, no such analysis is presented here. (Regime orientation coding instructions are available from the author.) The immediate concern is with the regime orientations of the Soviet Union and the United States toward Third World countries. Although the CREON project is concerned with the explanation of foreign policy in a number of contemporary national governments, the present concentration on the USSR and the United States occurs for several reasons beyond strong intrinsic interest. First, it makes a more manageable focus for a paper-length exploration. Second, regimes in both countries have multiple core system beliefs about foreign policy and multiple roles for their beliefs. Third, actions of the superpowers toward Third World countries might reasonably be expected to engage a substantial variety of those different beliefs and roles (as, say, compared to those used with their bloc allies) because of the great heterogeneity of Third World countries. Thus, superpower relations with the Third World highlight the concerns this paper seeks to address.

Ordering Multiple Sets of Beliefs

In constructing core political system beliefs, the CREON project has chosen to conceptualize beliefs so that they can apply to a number of regimes, not just those in a single country. We recognize, however, that there are other important basic beliefs about foreign policy that may be held by only one regime. Although the empirical work is not complete for determining which specific regimes hold the general categories of beliefs that we have constructed, our preliminary work provides strong clues. It suggests that Soviet and American regimes during the 1960s each held at least four core political system beliefs applicable to Third World countries. Two sets of beliefs were common to both countries and two others were distinctive for each nation. The political system beliefs are:

1. *Anti-communism* (USA). A belief that political systems ruled by communist parties are inherently dangerous to the actor nation's interests. Unless communist political systems are held in check, they will undermine democratic political processes and capitalist, free enterprise economic activities in and between other countries by all means possible including extralegal and illegal operations extending to the use of military force.

2. *Communism/anti-Western capitalism* (USSR). A belief that political systems with a capitalist or quasi-capitalist economic system will, in the interests of their economies, attempt to destroy communist (socialist) political systems. Because political and economic systems gradually evolve through history with capitalism only as a stage in the evolution toward communism, capitalists will resist by all possible means the progression toward communism that would mean the loss of their control. Western capitalist states will attempt to undermine and discredit communist parties everywhere and particularly parties which exercise political rule. These attempts to destroy communism must be vigorously resisted.

3. *Oppose traditional enemies* (USA, USSR). The regimes and political elites in certain countries are enemies of the acting nation as a result of historical experience and tradition, religion, ideology, or falsely held views about injustice done that country by the actor's nation. This enemy seeks the destruction of the acting country,

the overthrow of its political system, or other unacceptable ends such as the acquisition of certain territories. Continuous vigilance is necessary to hold the enemy in check and whenever possible it is necessary to take the initiative with offensive actions to weaken its ability to harm the actor's country. This belief has two subdivisions: zero sum and non-zero sum beliefs. Zero sum beliefs about the traditional enemy conclude that the conflict is indivisible (which leads to denials of the enemy's right to exist, the inevitability of war, and so on). Non-zero sum adherents hold that the conflict is real and dangerous, but that under some realizable circumstances an accommodation can be reached that will permit the continued existence of both sides under acceptable conditions.

4. *International cooperation through centralized/planned economies* (USSR). A belief that the well-being of the nation depends upon its ability to engage in economic transactions with other international actors not under its political jurisdiction. Such transactions must be conducted with the government as the agent that determines such things as the terms of trade, rates of currency exchange, and the kinds of international specialization and future economic commitments countries should undertake.

5. *International cooperation through developed market economies* (USA). A belief that the well-being of the nation depends upon its ability to engage in economic transactions with other international actors not under its political jurisdiction. The government should promote and maintain international institutions that enable full participation by the private sector in international trade and investment opportunities. The government should establish such financial and monetary arrangements as are necessary to facilitate successful and stable private-sector economic transactions. Additionally, the government should act to protect necessary domestic industries from unfair competition at home while promoting their success abroad.

6. *Subsystem solidarity* (USA, USSR). A belief that it is essential for the government to develop and maintain a cohesive alignment of countries which share with the acting nation certain fundamental values and interests. The common interests may result from geographical proximity, shared cultural or religious heritage, trade interests, or nation-shaping historical experiences. The government must give attention not only to efforts at building the coali-

Table 12.1   Core political system beliefs and their associated roles in CREON regime orientations*

Anti-communism	*Anti-Western capitalism*	*Oppose traditional enemy*
Defender of the faith	Defender of the faith	Combatant
Donor	Donor	Conciliationist
Godfather/protector	Godfather/protector	Defender of the faith
Mediator	Liberator	Opponent
Policeman	Mediator	Policeman
Recruiter/promoter	Policeman	
	Recruiter/promoter	*International cooperation through centralized/planned economies*
Subsystem solidarity		
Contending leader	*International cooperation through developed market economies*	
Defender of the faith		
Leader		
Mediator	Bilateralist	Bilateralist
Member	Donor	Donor
Recruiter/promoter	Mediator	Mediator
Reluctant ally	Multilateralist	Multilateralist
	Protectionist	Protectionist
Nonalignment		
Contending leader	*Development*	*Colonialism*
Defender of the faith	Defender of the faith	Defender of the faith
Donor	Donor	Donor
Leader	Foreign assistance seeker	Godfather/protector
Mediator	Protectionist	Mediator
Member	Self-reliance/ independent	
Recruiter/promoter		
Anti-colonialism	*Conflict resolution*	
Defender of the faith	Defender of the faith	
Liberator	Mediator	
Mediator	Peacekeeper	
Recruiter/promoter	Recruiter/promoter	

* For an explanation of all the core beliefs and roles mentioned in this table, see Hermann, Hermann, and Hagan (1982).

tion but also to discouraging those parties who may be antithetical to the subsystem.

Recall that the above beliefs are not intended to be exhaustive. They represent efforts to capture beliefs that several regimes shared during the 1960s and, in the case of these six, they are beliefs assumed to be held by either the United States or the Soviet Union which might pertain to the Third World. Table 12.1 offers a somewhat broader context in which to consider the described beliefs. It shows them to be part of a larger set of beliefs identified by the CREON project as applicable to various regimes. In addition the table shows that for all core beliefs there are a number of roles that a government might follow in realizing its beliefs. Before examining roles in more detail, attention is addressed to the first question posed in this paper.

Assuming that Soviet and American regimes in the 1960s held multiple core beliefs, which ones may have influenced decision making at any one point in time? In the simplification of reality that is the CREON model, it is assumed that only one belief is applicable in the consideration of a given problem. (This may not be quite as restrictive as it first seems when we note in table 12.1 that some roles appear under several different beliefs.)

To establish which beliefs prevail, a set of decision rules have been stipulated that depend upon systemic roles and the basic values involved in a foreign policy problem. Before introducing the decision rules it will be necessary to describe the CREON concepts of systemic roles and basic values.

The CREON project assumes that foreign policy behavior results only after a nation's authoritative decision makers have perceived a problem. As defined by the decision makers, every problem has a source (who caused the problem) and a subject (who is deprived by the problem). In addition, some problems have actual or potential facilitators and aggravators. Source, subject, facilitator, and aggravator are systemic roles in the problem. This is the other conception of role in the CREON project developed in the external predisposition component (see Hudson, Singer, and Hermann 1982). Any international entities may be perceived by the actor as occupying one of these roles. The decision rules about core beliefs depend in part upon which nations are occupying these roles for a specific problem.

To a lesser extent the decision rules also depend upon the basic values in the problem. When we want to estimate behavior the first task is to determine the problem from the actor's perspective. Once established, any problem can be coded for the basic values it entails. From the value constructs of Harold Lasswell (1971) a set of five foreign policy basic values have been derived: (a) military security/physical security, (b) wealth/economic condition, (c) respect/diplomatic status, (d) social well-being/welfare, and (e) education/enlightenment.

These systemic roles and basic values are used in the following decision rules for establishing the priority of alternative political beliefs.

1. *Oppose traditional enemy*. If the traditional enemy is the source or subject, it is the only entity in that role, and the basic value of the problem in a collaborative situation (defined below) is not economic, then traditional enemy belief prevails.

Justification: The powerful nature of the threat posed in any situation in which that entity alone plays a dominant role should override other beliefs. The instinct of survival is assumed to be most basic.

2. *Anti-communism (anti-Western capitalism)*. If source, subject, or facilitator roles are occupied by communist bloc [Western capitalist bloc] members and (a) the basic value is not wealth/economics and (b) the traditional enemy condition above is not fulfilled, then the anti-communist [anti-Western capitalist] belief prevails.

Justification: For those with this belief set, it has much of the same threat motivation as traditional enemy. Therefore, it can be expected to exercise more influence than any beliefs other than traditional enemy if the appropriate actors appear in the problem. The exception involving the basic value of wealth deals with cross-bloc negotiations on economic matters. Special roles under the international economic cooperation beliefs cover such situations.

3. *Subsystem solidarity*. If the source and the subject are both subsystem members or if either the source or the subject consists exclusively of multiple subsystem members and the other role occupants are either friendly countries or former bloc members (who are not currently traditional enemies), then subsystem solidarity applies. (Note: If the subsystem is primarily economic in function the international economic cooperation roles are added to those normally listed under subsystem solidarity.)

Justification: These beliefs are engaged in problems that occur among subsystem members or between them and potential or former bloc members. When hostile blocs or traditional enemies do not intrude into such situations, the beliefs about subsystem solidarity can be expected to be a powerful influence.

4. *International cooperation through centralized/planned economies (international cooperation through developed market economies)*. If the basic value is wealth/economics and none of the roles is occupied by a traditional enemy in other than a col-

laborative situation, then the international economic cooperation beliefs prevail.

Justification: The circumstances under which beliefs about international economic cooperation are likely arise when economic wealth values appear in the problem and traditional enemies either are not involved, or they are part of a collaborative economic situation. If a subsystem is economic in function then the two belief sets (subsystem solidarity and international economic cooperation) are likely to interact. This is handled by adding all economic cooperation roles to the subsystem solidarity set.

The above describes the belief component of regime orientation as it operates in the CREON model together with arrangements for determining which core beliefs apply in a given situation. It should again be apparent from the decision rules that there are cases in which none of the decision rules apply, and therefore there is no impact on foreign policy of regime orientation. In those situations in which beliefs do come into play, the task becomes deciding which role will apply.

Role Differentiation in Core Beliefs

As evident in table 12.1, each of the six core beliefs introduced in the previous section has associated with it a number of roles. Role conceptions are the expectations a regime's leaders hold as to how government will act with respect to their beliefs. In other words, roles translate beliefs into expected behavior patterns.

A role exists for a government when, in facing a kind of problem, the regime leaders all concur that a particular pattern of action is the appropriate means for acting on the beliefs engaged by the problem. The CREON project has reviewed various patterns of action in the foreign policies of nations, identified sets of behaviors as roles, and associated them with the core beliefs that they might reasonably serve. For example, as shown in table 12.1, CREON investigators currently propose six roles for the anti-communism belief, seven roles for anti-Western capitalism, five for oppose traditional enemy, and so on. Although as researchers we may judge a role to be appropriate for a given core belief about the world, it is not assumed that a given national government will necessarily use that role even though they adhere to the belief.

Appendix 4 provides further information on some of the roles listed in table 12.1. In addition to the definition of each role, the CREON project has determined (1) the basic values present in a problem that could trigger a role, (2) assumptions about the conditions necessary for the role to exist, and (3) the situations in which an actor might use the role. The concept of situation requires further consideration.

In the classic development of role, some construct similar to situation has seemed necessary. Thus, in the theater analogy, an actor plays a role in a given play. The plot is the context or situation that determines which role in the actor's repertoire is appropriate. Similarly in foreign policy we need to establish the international situation in which particular roles might be applicable.

Because core political system beliefs about the world are necessarily broad, a number of roles are conceivable in support of any core belief —as table 12.1 makes evident. The second concern of this paper is precisely with this problem—determining which of several roles is appropriate. As has been suggested, one basic means of distinguishing any type of role is by situation. In the CREON project, we have constructed five types of situations based on the acting government's relationship to the other systemic roles described briefly in the previous section. These situations can be used to sort out roles. The five CREON situations are:

1. *Confrontation.* The acting government is also either the source or the subject of the problem. Such situations precipitate the following question for the acting government: How can we reduce the adverse effects that the other entity (or entities) in the problem has produced for us?

2. *Intervention.* The acting government is neither the source nor the subject in such situations. It faces the question: Should we intervene in this problem on one side, mediate, or remain aloof?

3. *Assistance needed.* When the acting government is both the source and the subject of the problem it may seek outside help. The question becomes: Who can give us assistance to reduce the adverse effects we are experiencing from this problem?

4. *Assistance resource.* If another entity is the source and the subject and the acting government is a potential facilitator (that is, a role with resources), then the question is: Should we provide assistance to those who are experiencing adverse effects from the problem?

5. *Collaboration.* When the actor and one or more other entities mutually recognize that they are each both source and subject,

Table 12.2   Roles applicable to situations

		Situations				
Core beliefs	Roles	Con-fron-tation	Inter-vention	Assis-tance needed	Assis-tance resource	Collab-oration
Anti-communism or anti-capitalism	Defender of the faith	X	X			X
	Donor				X	X
	Godfather/ protector		X		X	X
	Liberator		X		X	
	Mediator		X			
	Policeman		X		X	
	Recruiter/ promoter			X		X
Oppose traditional enemy	Combatant	X	X			
	Concilia-tionist			X	X	X
	Defender of the faith		X		X	
	Opponent	X	X			
	Policeman		X			

the question is: Can we reach a substantive agreement with those with whom we share this problem?

This situation classification enables some differentiation of roles associated with various core beliefs. For example, when the belief to oppose traditional enemies is engaged and the situation is a confrontation between the actor and a traditional enemy, the donor role (as defined in the appendix) is exceedingly unlikely. Table 12.2 provides a matrix indicating what roles might reasonably be associated with particular core beliefs. As is evident from the table, however, knowledge of the situation alone cannot establish one and only one role for most core beliefs. As important as situation is in determining roles, it is insufficient to achieve the second objective of this paper.

To complete the task it is necessary to introduce some additional sorting information. In addition to situation, we use selected information about (1) the problem (that is, the basic values involved), (2) the alignment of entities in the systemic roles (whether other entities are

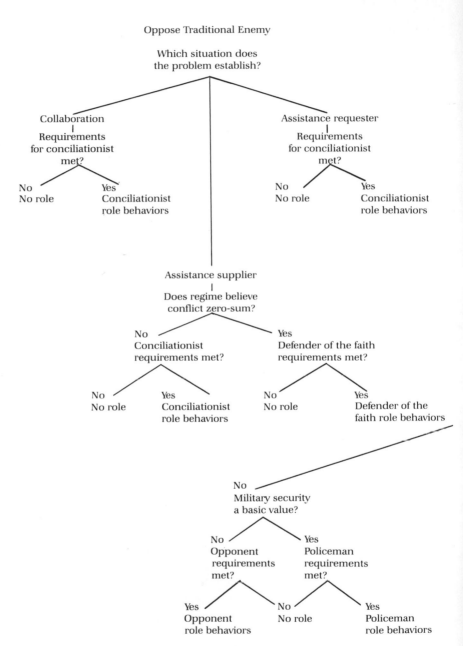

Figure 12.1 The decision tree for oppose traditional enemy belief, which determines whether any of the five associated roles apply.

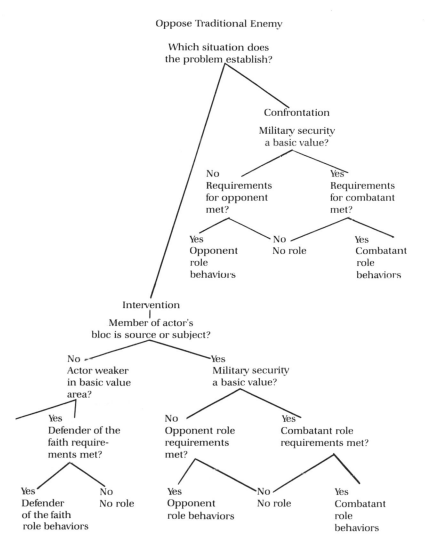

Oppose Traditional Enemy

Which situation does
the problem establish?

Confrontation

Military security
a basic value?

No
Requirements
for opponent
met?

Yes
Requirements
for combatant
met?

Yes
Opponent
role
behaviors

No
No role

Yes
Combatant
role
behaviors

Intervention

Member of actor's
bloc is source or subject?

No
Actor weaker
in basic value
area?

Yes
Military security
a basic value?

Yes
Defender of the
faith require-
ments met?

No
Opponent role
requirements
met?

Yes
Combatant role
requirements met?

Yes
Defender
of the faith
role behaviors

No
No role

Yes
Opponent
role behaviors

No
No role

Yes
Combatant
role
behaviors

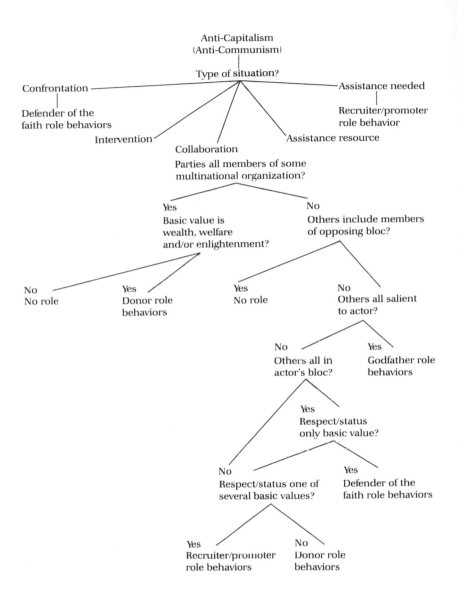

Figure 12.2   The confrontation, collaboration, and assistance needed branches of the decision tree for anti-capitalism (anti-communism) beliefs, which determine which role may apply in those types of situations. *Note*: This tree includes only information for differentiating among roles. The tree outcomes do not note the necessary check to see if all requirements for a given role are met. If they are not, no role occurs.

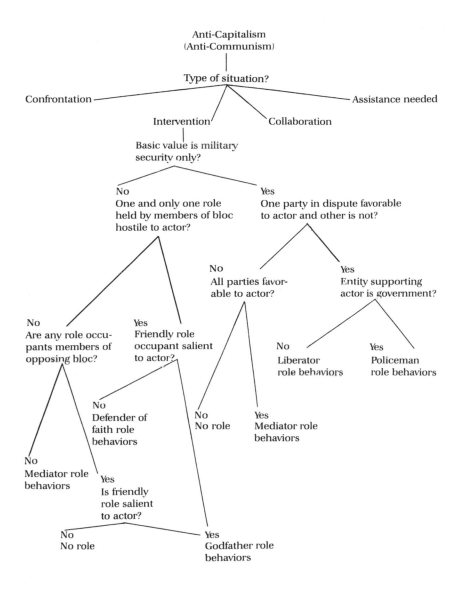

Figure 12.3 The intervention branch of the decision tree for anti-capitalism (anti-communism) beliefs, which determines which role may apply in that type of situation. *Note:* This tree includes only information for differentiating among roles. The tree outcomes do not note the necessary check to see if all requirements for a given role are met. If they are not, no role occurs.

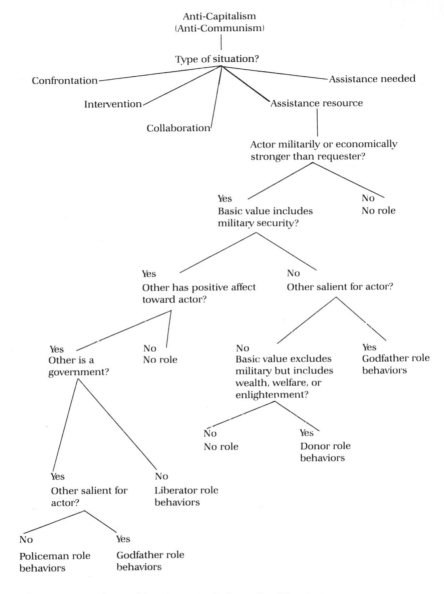

Figure 12.4 The assistance resource branch of the decision tree for anti-capitalism (anti-communism) beliefs, which determines which role may apply in that type of situation. *Note:* This tree includes only information for differentiating among roles. The tree outcomes do not note the necessary check to see if all requirements for a given role are met. If they are not, no role occurs.

members of the same bloc as the actor or an opposing one), and (3) the relationship among entities in the systemic roles (their salience for the actor; gross strength relative to the actor). With such additional information the differentiation of roles can be completed. Two further observations should be made. First, all this information is not necessary to distinguish the roles associated with each core belief. Second, the information required is quite obtainable for nations and is relatively stable.

The actual process of sorting roles is accomplished by use of decision rules that employ the role definitions, stipulated assumptions, basic values, and situations associated with each one (see appendix 4). Although not difficult, the process can be protracted. For that reason the roles associated with only two core beliefs are illustrated here: oppose traditional enemy and anti-communism. The sequential application of the decision rules using the sorting information and the role specifications is represented through a decision tree. Figure 12.1 displays the process for oppose traditional enemies and figures 12.2 through 12.4 show the comparable procedure for anti-communism. A similar type of decision tree can be used to sort the roles associated with other core beliefs.

Properties of Foreign Policy Behavior Associated With Roles

Regime orientation enables any shared beliefs of authoritative policymakers to influence foreign policy decision making through expected national roles. That is the perspective we have developed. The practical issue is what beliefs and roles come into play when a government faces a given kind of foreign policy problem. In this paper we have proposed a system of decision rules that, in response to specifiable conditions, can determine both the set of beliefs and a single associated role. Still to be addressed is the question of the effect a particular role would have on foreign policy if the government pursued the expectations it created.

To deal with this issue we must be clear about the nature of foreign policy as it is to be explained or forecasted by roles. In the CREON project we have posed the task as the explanation of the most likely response of a national government to a problem, involving external entities, that is recognized by the regime. The government's response is viewed as an action of verbal or physical communication designed as an attempt to influence others. Rather than trying to account for certain acts of foreign policy communication directly (for example, trade agreements, diplomatic visits, troop maneuvers), we have opted to explain the attributes or properties that combine to create various kinds of foreign policy behavior. The properties of an act of communication—of which we contend foreign policy is a type—frequently have been posed as who does what to whom, when and how?

For the moment we regard the actor (the "who") and the timing ("when") as a given; that is, we specify what national government or ruling political party will be the actor and assume that action follows promptly after decision. The behavior properties we want to explain are (1) the recipients—whom will the actor address? (2) the affect —what does the actor do in terms of expressed feelings? (3) the commitment—what does the actor do toward its resolution or resolve to do? (4) the instruments—what skills and resources of statecraft will the actor use in its behavior?

Recipients. Even though it may be clear whom a national government may ultimately wish to influence, its action may be addressed to any number of other parties to seek further information, mobilize support, obtain mediation, and so on.

Affect. A key to the actor's intentions is the basic dimension of expressed affect—the stated desire to assist and support or oppose and obstruct.

Commitment. The resolve with which an actor binds itself or allocates its resources to another entity conveys a great deal about the intensity with which it pursues its course.

Instruments. The tools of statecraft available to an actor comprise the skills and resources it can use in various ways to affect another.

These measurable properties are common to all foreign policy behaviors. If we are able to understand why they are likely to assume certain values under certain conditions, we have gained much of practical and theoretical worth in understanding foreign policy. By combining these properties together with the classification of situations, we can reconstruct most of the familiar acts of foreign policy behavior. The individual properties, however, provide basic and ever-present behavior features that lend themselves effectively to theory building (see Callahan et al. 1982; Dixon and Hermann 1982). It is these individual properties of foreign policy behavior that we wish to associate with various roles.

Given the previously created verbal descriptions of each role's general pattern of behavior and the assumptions established to specify when a given role occurs, it is not difficult to infer the probable behavior properties for each role. For example, the defender of the faith role has been described as an ideological commentary on world affairs that criticizes those that do not accept the actor's ideology and praises those that adhere to it. It is assumed to occur most often when the government elects to take no stronger action. When a defender of the faith role is followed in confrontation or intervention situations, we can be confident that the government is addressing a member of an opposing ideological bloc as the recipient. The affect will be negative because the acting government in this role will be condemning the nonbeliever. Because the ideological attack is being conducted in lieu of stronger action, we can assume that only diplomatic instruments of statecraft are being engaged and that no commitment of the actor's resources or future behavior will be made. Using a similar process for all roles, the most probable foreign policy behaviors have been determined for each role and are listed in appendix 4 as the fifth item in each role characterization.

Illustrations and Conclusions

The postulated effects of regime orientation on the properties of foreign policy behavior are stated so as to permit investigation through systematic empirical analysis. Data collection for that purpose is under way. In the meantime, this essay will conclude with the introduction of several illustrations drawn from Soviet and American actions in Africa. These examples in no way constitute a test of the proposed relationship. They may, however, clarify this presentation and outline the basic procedures that more formal tests will follow.

We assert that in the 1960s and 1970s the shared political beliefs of the Soviet Union's authoritative decision makers (notably the Politburo) included anti-capitalism and oppose traditional enemies. Furthermore, the United States was one of the traditional enemies of the Soviet Union. Similarly we contend that during the same period the authoritative decision makers of the United States (represented by members of the National Security Council) included among their shared political beliefs both anti-communism and oppose traditional enemy, with the Soviet Union as one of their enemies. Some might argue that the period of détente in the late 1960s and early 1970s may have reduced the consensus on these beliefs. Although empirical research can provide a better basis for assessing core beliefs, we contend that, at best, détente confirmed that conflict between the United States and USSR had become non-zero sum. The beliefs of both sides can be applied to their actions in Africa.

On the eve of the Ogaden War of 1977–78 in the Horn of Africa between Somalia and Ethiopia, the relationships of both the United States and the Soviet Union to those two African nations underwent dramatic changes (Napper 1983). Under Haile Selassie, Ethiopia and the United States had been strong allies. During the first several years after Selassie's demise, the United States tried to sustain the relationship with the military junta and even increased its already substantial military assistance. Following the internal struggles in the winter of 1976–77 and the emergence of Lt. Colonel Mengistu Haile Mariam as head of state, the United States changed its policy. In late February 1977 the United States first reduced military assistance, claiming human rights violations, and then in April suspended all weapons shipments.

Consider the situation from the Soviet perspective in the spring of 1977. One of its traditional enemies — the United States — is experiencing a serious rupture of relations with a client. For the Soviet Union it is an intervention situation and the question the Soviet leaders face is whether they should intervene. The decision tree in figure 12.1 can be consulted to reveal what we would expect the Soviet Union to do. Neither the source (United States) nor subject (Ethiopia) are Soviet bloc members. Nor is the Soviet Union clearly weaker in the pertinent area of military capabilities. Furthermore, the basic value the problem entails is military security. These conclusions lead down the decision tree to the point where one must see if the USSR meets the requirements for the policeman role. They do. According to the appendix, the probable behavior properties are positive affect, moderate commitment, and military instruments addressed to the regime the actor wants to help.

In fact, the Soviet Union invited the Ethiopian leader Mariam to Moscow in May 1977 where he met with Soviet First Secretary Brezhnev and Defense Minister Ustinov. Also in the spring of 1977, 200 Cuban troops arrived in Ethiopia to help with military training. This action undoubtedly was encouraged, if not actually arranged, by the USSR. Thus, the Soviet Union addressed the foe of its enemy (Ethiopia) as the recipient with positive affect, military instruments, and what CREON would scale as moderate commitment.

Because the Soviet Union sought to befriend Ethiopia, its relationship with Ethiopia's own traditional adversary, the Somali Democratic Republic, faltered and then ruptured. A mirror image of the American-

Ethiopian division now presented itself to the United States in the emerging split between the Soviet Union and Somali. Our decision tree in figure 12.1 would suggest that the United States too would move down the intervention branch of the tree and assume the policeman role with Somali. In the summer of 1977 the Carter administration made initial gestures toward Somali and suggested it would consider requests for military assistance. When Somali invaded the Ethiopian Ogaden, however, the United States withheld its offer. Thus, the expected role behavior was disrupted by change in the American perception of the recipient.

As a second illustration let us examine the struggle among the competing liberation movements in Angola — the National Liberation Front of Angola (FNLA), the Popular Movement of the Liberation of Angola (MPLA) and the National Union for the Total Independence of Angola (UNITA) — following the Portuguese decision to grant it independence. In their combat with each other the liberation movements sought outside military assistance. The MPLA had been receiving Soviet and Cuban military aid. The FNLA gained aid from Zaire and the People's Republic of China. In the summer of 1975 following a considerable increase in the flow of Soviet aid and Cuban advisors (and the withdrawal of Chinese support for the FNLA), the MPLA appeared to be on the verge of gaining control of much of the country.

At that juncture the anti-communist beliefs of the American decision makers may have come into play (Davis 1978). To the policymakers in Washington it appeared possible to distinguish between a communist-backed MPLA with a Marxist ideology and a non-communist FNLA-UNITA coalition. The latter faced extremely serious difficulties. In July 1975 the U.S. government's Forty Committee decided to channel substantial covert military assistance to FNLA-UNITA through Zaire. The South Africans also intervened in Angola on behalf of the new coalition. In terms of the decision tree for anti-communist beliefs diagrammed in figure 12.2, the United States should have viewed the problem as an intervention situation and should have played a liberator role. In fact it did so with policies having the behavior properties described for the liberator role in the appendix.

Again, we have a mirror image condition for the superpowers. When the FNLA-UNITA fortunes improved with assistance from the United States, South Africa, and Zaire, we would expect the Soviet's anti-capitalism beliefs to be engaged with adoption — like the United States — of a liberator role. Subsequent Soviet behaviors are congruent with the expectation.

Several concluding observations are in order about this attempt to design a system with which to model the effects of regime orientation (political beliefs plus roles) on foreign policy behavior. First, it should be recalled that we do not expect the conditions for regime orientation to be present in all occasions for foreign policy decision making. There may be no consensus in beliefs among regime leaders in many areas. Moreover, the historical experience necessary to establish role expectations for some problems may be insufficient even when core beliefs are shared.

Second, in situations where the conditions for regime orientation are met, the orientation should not be expected to determine foreign policy behavior all the time. As in the American example with Somali in the summer of 1977, role expectations may be outweighed by other considerations in the decision process. An adequate model of foreign policy decision making must integrate regime orientation with some of these other major explanatory factors.

Finally, we recognize that authorities on Third World countries and regions may be uncomfortable with a system that proposes to interpret Soviet and American behavior toward so much of the world in terms of anti-communism, anti-capitalism, and traditional enemies beliefs. As suggested in table 12.1, there are other beliefs, not developed in this paper, that the CREON project has identified and still others that are unique to single countries which we do not attempt to include. Nevertheless, it may be appropriate to ponder how much of the superpowers' behaviors toward the Third World can be understood in terms of these beliefs in which the Third World explicitly figures only marginally.

V Conclusion

13

Role Theory and Foreign Policy
Analysis: An Evaluation

Stephen G. Walker

An evaluation of role analysis for understanding foreign policy involves an assessment of its descriptive, organizational, and explanatory value. In the course of such an appraisal, it becomes necessary as well to confront the criticism that role theory is conceptually rich but lacks the methodological refinement necessary to be more than a mere conceptual framework and achieve the status of a genuine theory. These questions were raised briefly in the introduction, and it is now appropriate to address them in a more exhaustive way. Many aspects of these topics have already been covered by the three authors of the essays in part I of this volume, who make claims regarding these issues as they argue the case for a role-oriented theoretical perspective in the study of foreign policy. A review of their claims, therefore, is one way to organize an over-all evaluation into a series of manageable tasks. This approach should also lend itself readily to a review of the other contributions in this volume, in order to see how they support the claims of those scholars making the case for role theory.

Holsti: National Role Conceptions in the Study of Foreign Policy

There are four main claims advanced in the essay by Holsti, who contends that (a) foreign policymakers have national role conceptions, (b) national role conceptions are more influential than the role prescriptions emanating from the external environment in shaping foreign policy behavior, (c) the sources of national role conceptions are a complex mixture of location, capabilities, socio-economic characteristics, system structure, and the personalities of leaders, and (d) the consequences of national role conceptions include both a constraining effect upon foreign policy behavior for a particular nation as well as a type of input that affects stability and change in international systems.

The first claim is relevant for assessing the *descriptive* value of role theory. Holsti's own content analysis supports the claim that foreign policymakers have national role conceptions. He coded almost a thousand documents and generated seventeen different types of role conceptions for the seventy-one nation-states in his data set. An evaluation of this kind of evidence raises questions of reliability and validity. Holsti does not report standard measures of intercoder or intracoder reliability; he does state that when intracoder reliability was not high for a particular item, it was discarded. The validity of the typology is supported by a comparison of "activity-passivity" rankings for each country's role conceptions with its reputation for an "active" foreign policy. Holsti concludes that an overlap is present for most nations, a pattern which supports the typology's validity.

Efforts by other investigators test the validity of the Holsti typology of role conceptions more extensively and also address the explanatory value of role theory. My investigation of the link between foreign policy rhetoric and behavior is a test of the typology as well as the claim that national role conceptions are more important in shaping foreign policy behavior than role prescriptions emanating from the external environment. The analysis of the correspondence between rhetoric and behavior for forty-five nations is an attempt to examine the degree of fit between the distribution of each country's national role conceptions and the distribution of its foreign policy behavior, controlling for the effects of role prescriptions emanating from the target of the behavior.

Holsti's claim, that role conceptions are more influential than role prescriptions, is not uniformly supported in those instances where role conceptions and role prescriptions created a role-conflict situation for the nation's foreign policymakers. When the target of the foreign policy behavior was the United States, national role conceptions were more influential than the cues emitted by American actions. If the target was the USSR, then Soviet cues were more influential than national role conceptions. In the absence of role conflict, there was usually a balanced relationship between role conceptions, cues, and role enactment. On the other hand, the degree of congruence among them was not very consistent. All of these results are rather inconclusive, given the use of secondary data and the corresponding existence of incompatibilities across data sets. Further research regarding this claim is clearly in order.

Holsti also hypothesized that there is a link between national role conceptions and various domestic and external sources. Wish explores this claim, as do Sampson and Walker. Wish reports statistically significant bivariate relationships for seventeen nations between their size, modernity, political orientation, and several properties of their national role conceptions, including individualism, competitiveness, orientation toward change, scope of influence, and sensitivity toward different types of issues. Since Holsti does not identify any particular combinations of sources and role conceptions for investigation, it is appropriate for Wish to advance some ad hoc, middle-range hypotheses to guide her research. She found support for twelve of her twenty-one hypotheses, which is only slightly above the number which could be expected if her hypotheses were given an equiprobable (50-50) chance of confirmation. The need to improvise in the absence of a well-developed theoretical context may account for these inconclusive results.

Sampson and Walker address the same claim from a more mature theoretical context developed from the literature dealing with national culture. They test the proposition that the source of some differences in national role conceptions may be differences in national culture, plus they begin to explore Holsti's fourth claim regarding the relationships between these differences and foreign policy behavior. Building upon previous research by Sampson (1987), the secondary data provided by Holsti's role-conception frequencies, and the behavioral profiles available from CREON, the authors compare the patterns of cultural norms, national role conceptions, and foreign policy behavior exhibited by Japan and France. They report sharp, theoretically consistent differences that support Holsti's speculations regarding the sources of national role conceptions and the link between them and foreign policy behavior. They are also able to discount the possibility of spuriousness in the analysis of their findings. Their work is the most recent effort to test directly Holsti's application of role theory to foreign policy analysis.

Holsti has inspired other scholars, but their own research interests have led them to advocate different research strategies less obviously consistent with Holsti's approach. However, they do concern themselves indirectly with the first three claims under examination, and they focus directly upon Holsti's fourth claim regarding the consequences of differences in national role conceptions across countries and leaders. The rationale for their research strategies is the subject of the essay by Rosenau.

Rosenau: Roles and Role Scenarios in Foreign Policy

In his essay on roles and role scenarios, Rosenau articulates the claim that role theory has *organizational* value for understanding foreign policy. He argues that the concept of role answers a need for a unifying dimension across several levels of analysis — individual, governmental, societal, and systemic. By adopting role as the unit of analysis, a micro-macro synthesis becomes possible. The decision-making activities of officials are conceptualized as responses to role conflicts created by conflicting forces, practices, values, and expectations from various levels of analysis. The individual is actually defined as a complex of public and private roles, while collectivities are defined as aggregations of such individuals. The boundaries that circumscribe these collectivities may be relatively formal, as in the case of the state, or less obviously structured across individuals, groups, and nations by a common focus upon a unique value or issue area.

Rosenau's formulation, therefore, provides an emphasis upon role conflict as a key concept in analyzing foreign policy decision making. Although he does not offer specific rules for resolving role conflicts when they occur, he does make the claim that the process of role location proceeds through the use of role scenarios or action scripts by decision makers. These constructs are projections of the consequences of alternative responses to role conflicts and are based upon two key components. One is the expectations which the decision maker attributes to the other members of the collectivity and which define the existence of role conflict. The other is the decision maker's own expectations regarding how others in this role set will conduct themselves.

From these two sources an individual derives scenarios regarding how events are likely to develop, as each participant conforms to the expectations associated with each role and reacts to one another. Rosenau hypothesizes an inverse relationship between the length and the clarity of a role scenario: "the longer and more diffuse it is—that is, the greater the number of choice points through which it fans out from time 1—the more obscure will be its segments at the distant ends (time n) and the more clear-cut will be those in the near future (say times 2 and 3)." The rationale for this hypothesis rests upon the assumption that a combination of complexity and uncertainty accompanies any attempt to stretch a scenario very far into the future. Rosenau also includes in his essay a discussion of how the characteristics of individuals and variations in the institutional contexts of different societies may affect the quality of operative role scenarios and their consequences. Other scholars, including the Hermanns, Singer and Hudson, and Walker and Simon, have engaged in research which supports the claims advanced by Rosenau.

Certainly the theme in the Rosenau essay regarding variations in the quality of role scenarios is relevant in evaluating the significance of the research by M. Hermann. Her focus upon the individual characteristics of policymakers, as these interact to generate role conceptions and foreign policy decisions of different quality in different institutional contexts, is consistent with Rosenau's concerns. She shows how different institutional power structures and personality structures may dispose individual policymakers to deal with information uncertainty differently. Hermann proposes a series of linkages between ways of coping with information uncertainty and the role conceptions of individuals in a variety of small group decision-making contexts.

These propositions are specific hypotheses about how the incumbents of Rosenau's roles may go about constructing role scenarios and resolving role conflicts generated between the individual's private characteristics and the public context provided by the organization of their governments. Subsequently Hermann investigates the relationship between role conceptions, experience in foreign affairs, and sensitivity to the political environment in Sub-Saharan Africa. These research questions also dissect the concerns which Rosenau articulated regarding the relationships among experienced leadership, the relative salience of different issues, and the quality of role scenarios.

The policy analysis by Walker and Simon plus the behavioral analysis by Singer and Hudson address Rosenau's concern with the impact of societal and international sources upon the construction of role scenarios and the process of role location. The policy analysis of the Southeast Asian role set by Walker and Simon employs the role-scenario technique to identify and evaluate alternative foreign policy role sets available to Vietnam, China, Cambodia, and the ASEAN bloc. Their interpretive identification of Vietnamese expectations as they intersect with the expectations of other states regarding the ZOPFAN and Kuantan proposals is quite consistent with the intuitive examples of role-scenario construction in Rosenau's narrative. Singer and Hudson accept Rosenau's methodological challenge to program the construction of role scenarios more systematically by means of their "external predisposition model." Their identification of decision logics for various types of relationships between different characteristics of the decision-making situation take the form of branches on a series of decision trees. These decision trees represent the sets of expectations associated with role scenarios for different types of situations.

As Rosenau anticipates, these types of role scenarios are relatively clear but rather short, projecting only the next move (behavior) rather than a series of moves or a policy change. Also, the external predisposition model focuses only upon situational characteristics outside the nation and does not incorporate the cultural beliefs, personal values, and unconscious motives of the policymaker. Rosenau maintains that these variables are important in the construction of role scenarios and distinguish it from an exercise encompassed by game theory. Also omitted as well by the Singer and Hudson model is the impact of the intragovernmental institutional context upon the process of role location.

C. Hermann's exploration of superpower involvement in the horn of Africa addresses some of these omissions. He identifies the core beliefs and role conceptions that define "regime orientations" for the United States and USSR and employs them in combination with the decision trees associated with the external predisposition model. The result is the creation of a more refined decision logic for the superpowers. His effort advances the art and science of constructing role scenarios further along the path of complexity at a given point in time, but he does not attack the problem of projecting further than one move beyond the present.

Rosenau concludes his essay with the suggestion that the microelectronic revolution and the advent of a fifth generation of computers may provide the technology to overcome the methodological challenges associated with the projection of role scenarios further into the future. However, he does not address the problem of external validity associated with such an exercise. The core of this problem is the accuracy and the completeness of the data fed into the computer. As various computer scenarios for the ecological future of the planet have demonstrated, the projections are only as valid as the assumptions which they reflect (Hughes 1985). This problem is common to all simulations, but it looms particularly when the goal is to project the future rather than to reconstruct the past.

Moreover, it is desirable to resolve the accuracy and completeness dimensions of the validity problem in a parsimonious form. Feeding every variable into a computer in the name of completeness simply exacerbates the accuracy dimension in two ways. It creates more possibilities for initial errors of measurement. Also, the number of relationships among variables, which must be specified and evaluated as either accurate and significant or not, multiplies rapidly. There appear to be two paths out of this cul-de-sac which achieve parsimony without sacrificing validity. They are the respective paths associated with rationalistic and nonrationalistic world views (Steiner 1983).

These two approaches appear to be antithetical; however, a closer examination reveals that they are complementary. Steiner (1983, 378) contrasts them as follows:

At the heart of the nonrationalistic worldview is a vision of incongruity, novelty, and fluidity, rather than an orderliness that can be embraced by causal and probabilistic logics. The future is not the product of causal or probabilistic laws; it is emergent. Nor is the nonrationalistic world essentially tangible and empirical, for appearances are deceptive and explicit information is incomplete, ambiguous, and often misleading. Boundaries and distinctions are not clear-cut, but vague and elusive. The tendency of objects and events to blend into one another undermines the relevance of analytic dissection and quantitative precision. Apprehension of wholes and qualitative factors assumes primary importance. Ambiguity and paradox are not puzzles that can be solved once and for all; they are part of "the nature of things." Whereas the assumption of the rationalistic approach is that decision makers can know what to expect and can plan their actions accordingly, the watchword here is to expect the unexpected. . . .

Intuition and imagination are the dominant intellectual processes in the nonrationalistic approach, while logical and empirical analyses drive the rationalistic world view.

Steiner (1983, 395–96) accounts for the origins of these contrasting approaches to reality by reference to the uneven development of these psychological capacities across individuals. She takes the position that analysis (and good decision making) should rest upon the intellectual products generated by both approaches. The relevance of each one depends partly upon the circumstances. A rationalistic emphasis may be more appropriate for clear-cut, structured environments, whereas a nonrationalistic stance is better suited for ambiguous and fluid environments (Steiner 1983, 410).

Steiner's discussion is relevant to our concerns because she does identify two intellectual paths away from a technological version of barefoot empiricism and toward the construction of parsimonious and valid role scenarios. On the one hand, the construction of role scenarios with nonrationalist methods becomes an art in which the scenario undergoes constant adaptation during the course of its enactment. It is an existential act of creation with a dialectical dynamic very closely attuned to the ebb and flow of possibilities unfolding into the future. On the other hand, the construction of role scenarios with rationalist techniques becomes a science in which the components of the scenario and the range of possible combinations among these components are identified. While not all variations are examined, the parameters which define their range and specify conjunctions among them are sought.

Equally important, Steiner locates the origins of these different approaches in the discipline of psychology, and her discussion of their interrelationships portrays the two approaches as complementary capacities of the human psyche in understanding the political world. These latter points are relevant to our broader concern with the *explanatory* value of role theory in understanding foreign policy. Role theory qua theory is a psychological explanation laden with nonrationalistic connotations. The key concepts of "cues," "role conceptions," "role expectations," and "role location," the strategies of merger, interpenetration, alternation, and altercasting as responses to role conflict, the origins of the concept of role in the theater, all communicate different nuances of the nonrationalist processes of intuition and imagination. At the same time there has been a rationalistic conversion of these concepts for use in social science analysis within the area of social psychology (Biddle and Thomas 1966; Sarbin and Allen 1968; Walker 1979).

In the remainder of this essay the main task is to evaluate the claim that role theory is a psychological explanation capable of bridging the nonrationalist and rationalist world views and their corresponding artistic and scientific explanations of foreign policy and international politics. This claim appears first in Rosenau's discussion of the construction of role scenarios. He recognizes their complementarity in decision making by his insistence that the construction of role scenarios is more than an exercise in game theory. However, his later conclusion, that "the most stringent criteria of parsimony in the theory-building enterprise can be relaxed," diffuses the key decision-making feature that both intuitive and systematic thinking share so that they are complementary—the capacity to get parsimoniously to "the heart of the matter." A more explicit and extensive treatment of their parsimonious complementarity appears in my essay on role theory and the international system.

Walker: Role Theory and the International System

Briefly, the argument in support of role theory as a complementary bridge between rationalist and nonrationalist explanations of foreign policy decisions and actions is as follows: the dichotomy between artistic and scientific analysis is artificial. Instead, they are complementary stages in a cyclical process. No matter at which stage one begins the intellectual task of understanding foreign policy, eventually one is driven into the other stage or else progress in understanding is arrested. Put another way, there are successive stages in the intellectual process of explaining foreign policy: moments of intuition and imagination, longer periods of logical and empirical exploration of those insights, and eventually a new phase of intuitive understanding. These nonrationalist and rationalist stages may occur at various levels of abstraction, ranging from very general concerns to minutiae. The best products of these stages, respectively, are concepts and laws. My contention is that the introduction of role theory amplifies significantly both the moments of intuition and the longer periods of logical and empirical exploration in the explanation of foreign policy.

In my attempt to link role theory with structural realism, the more obvious complementary relationship is between my role theory of foreign policy and Waltz's realist theory of international politics. However, as the adoption of Waltz's definition of "theory" early in the essay reflects, complementarity appears as well between the intellectual processes in the development of a role theory of foreign policy and the presentation of a realist theory of international politics. Waltz is very explicit in his insistence that the intellectual process of theorizing contains a moment of intuition as well as a period of logical and empirical analysis: "the longest period of painful trial and error will not lead to the construction of a theory unless at some point a brilliant intuition flashes, a creative idea emerges. . . . Both induction and deduction are indispensable in the construction of a theory, but using them in combination gives rise to a theory only if a creative idea emerges" (Waltz 1979, 9–11).

Earlier, he distinguishes between statements which describe laws that are established by rigorous observation and the concepts and assumptions which explain them. Whereas laws are intimately tied to reality, a theory is invented by the intellectual processes of speculation and the exercise of the imagination (Waltz 1979, 5–9). This complementary relationship between theories and laws is one manifestation of the more general one between artistic and scientific approaches to the explanation of politics.

There are, of course, various interpretations of this relationship. Waltz's general position on the elements of theoretical thinking is not universally understood or accepted in the area of international politics. He contrasts his view with a widely held position that "theories are collections or sets of laws pertaining to a particular behavior or phenomenon" (Waltz 1979, 2). In fact, this debate over what a theory is has appeared at various points over the past two decades in roughly the same form (Young 1969, 1972; Phillips 1974; Job and Ostrom 1976).

By thinking of the process of explanation as successive, repetitive stages of intuitively and logically driven empiricism, it is possible to break out of the confines of the debate and view the contenders as either emphasizing one stage or else grasping the complementarity of the two stages in varying degrees. This vantage point allows one to anticipate and eventually dispense with the case against role theory qua theory and additionally to place critiques of political realism in sharper perspective. These tasks engage a criticism that has taken the same theme in this volume as well as others, namely, that role theory is conceptually rich but methodologically poor.

For example, Hall and Lindzey (1978, xx) state the argument against role theory relatively concisely within the context of the discipline of psychology: "Role theory, it seems to us, is less systematically developed than most of the other positions. . . . It is true that the theory contains a leading idea of considerable value and importance but this idea has not as yet been incorporated into a network of concepts which deal comprehensively with human behavior." Although these words were originally written in 1957 for the first edition of their survey of personality theories, the authors saw fit to continue the omission of role theory from its contents in successive editions. The third edition (1978, 724) contains only one citation for "roles" in its index—a reference to the statement (p. 542) that "roles and sets have so far not received extensive empirical exploration by Cattell and his associates." This omission continued in spite of the appearance of Biddle and Thomas's (1966) anthology of role analyses during this period in response to a similar indictment of role theory in the area of social psychology by Newcomb (1966, vii).

A review of role theory by Sarbin and Allen (1968) in the *Handbook of Social Psychology* yields a more active profile, but the pattern is one characterized by the adaptation of role concepts to the propositions associated with various environmental contexts, for example, small groups, large organizations, or social systems. There is no extensive set of propositions that link the psychological concepts associated with role theory across these various social contexts. However, the presumption that this absence of general laws indicates a weakness is not necessarily correct—or so I shall argue after an examination of a similar critique leveled against structural realism.

The reviews of Waltz's realist theory by several critics classify it as a theory of structural realism (Ruggie 1983; Keohane 1983; Ashley 1984). Waltz himself uses the concept of structure as the central one in his theory. The simplest statement of this theory is that international structure limits international processes and the range of international outcomes; the laws or regularities which appear in international processes and outcomes occur because of the principles which generate international structure (Ruggie 1983, 264–66). The three generative principles which define structure are: the self-help ordering principle of the anarchic environment, the functional homogeneity of the units necessary in an anarchic environment, and the varying distribution of capabilities across the units in the environment (Waltz 1979, 100–101; Ruggie 1983, 264–66). The structure defined by these principles accounts for the balance-of-power processes so prominent in international politics along with the international outcomes of war, peace, hegemony, and equilibrium.

As Keohane (1983, 513) has pointed out, Waltz's articulation of the balancing processes and their relationships with international outcomes is somewhat diffuse: "it is difficult for [Waltz] to state precisely the conditions under which coalitions will change. He only forecasts that balances of power will periodically occur. Indeed, his theory is so general that it hardly meets the difficult tests that he himself establishes for theory." In other words, Waltz's realist theory is more explicit about its good ideas and less explicit about its laws—a shortcoming also associated with role theory by its critics.

This particular pattern of uneven development is perhaps to be expected from a theorist who emphasizes the importance of good ideas and who criticizes notions of theory that emphasize laws. The implication in this criticism is that Waltz's theory of international politics has certainly experienced a moment of intuition. In order to progress, however, it should perhaps address more self-consciously some of the problems associated with the empirical aspects of the logically driven empiricist stage of theorizing.

However, Waltz anticipates this conclusion and rejects it with two arguments. First, he argues that a desirable property of theory is elegance, which "means that explanations and predictions will be general" (Waltz 1979, 69). The implication is that a trade-off exists between a theory's elegance and its specificity. "A theory of international politics will, for example, explain why war recurs, and it will indicate some of the conditions that will make war more or less likely; but it will not predict the outbreak of particular wars" (Waltz 1979, 69). Second, Waltz points out that structural theories explain continuities and not variations. "Structural concepts, although they lack detailed content, help to explain some big, important, and enduring patterns" (Waltz 1979, 70). The inference here would appear to be that significant changes occur only when structures change.

Behavior and outcomes do vary in international systems whose ordering principle of anarchy endures but whose structures differ in the distribution of capabilities among states, defined as changes in the number of great powers (poles) and not in terms of the number of power blocs (Waltz 1979, 129). With this theoretical statement and others which he borrows from the economic theory of oligopolies, Waltz specifies the following relationships between polarity and outcomes:

> a. Among the great powers in an international system, military and economic interdependence among them is lower in a bipolar system than in a multipolar system. (Waltz 1979, 143–46, 163–70)
> b. The smaller the number of great powers, and the wider the disparities between the few most powerful states and the many others, the more likely the former are to act for the sake of the system and to participate in the managerial tasks of transforming or maintaining the international system, preserving the peace,

promoting economic development and ecological stability. (Waltz 1979, 198–99)

Waltz then proceeds to discuss these propositions in an attempt to establish their plausibility as laws.

In the process of making the case for a systemic explanation, Waltz asserts that some systems theorists have not really formulated genuine systems theories. Instead, they are actually reductionist theories, which are inadequate when the following condition obtains: "If the organization of units affects their behavior and their interactions, then one cannot predict outcomes or understand them merely by knowing the characteristics, purposes, and interactions of the system's units" (Waltz 1979, 39). His examination of reductionist theories and pseudosystemic theories leads Waltz to conclude that a genuinely systemic theory is needed.

However, three friendly critics, who were not targets of Waltz's critical review, qualify this conclusion from different points of view. Ruggie (1983, 285) makes a structuralist critique of Waltz's theory: "The problem with Waltz's [anti-reductionist] posture is that, in any social system, structural change itself ultimately has no source *other than* unit-level processes." He argues that Waltz fails to realize this point because he underestimates the impact of the functional differentiation of the international system's units upon its processes and outcomes.

Keohane (1983, 526) concludes that the Waltzian theory of structural realism is also not adequate to explain important aspects of change that stops short of structural change: "Domestic politics and decision-making, . . . 'internal-external interactions,' and the workings of international institutions all play a role, along with international political structure, in affecting state behavior and outcomes." My own assessment earlier in this volume is that "Waltz does not explain the actions of states but only their consequences. Even with this limited focus he does not . . . specify particular outcomes. . . . From the perspective of a foreign policy analyst . . . this variety is significant as the primary puzzle to be understood in theoretical terms along with the variety of actions by states which contribute to these outcomes." A common theme running through the comments of these three friendly critics is that Waltz's theory is *too* parsimonious.

This theme is amplified by less friendly critics and expanded to encompass all realist theories of foreign policy and international politics. The most vehement and extensive recent critiques are by Ashley (1981, 1984), Mansbach and Vasquez (1981), Vasquez (1983), and Coate and

Murphy (1985). Ashley argues that Waltz and other "neorealists" have omitted important good ideas associated with "classical realism." He joins with the other critics in asserting that both classical realism and neorealism omit necessary dimensions of international politics in formulating what, in Waltz's (1979, 8) phrase, a good theory should provide: "a picture, mentally formed, of a bounded realm or domain of activity." In various forms Mansbach and Vasquez (1981), Vasquez (1983), and Coate and Murphy (1985) make a similar indictment, that the realists omit an important part of the picture. For them the missing component is a conceptualization of "issues," "values," or "needs." All of these critics are indicting the adequacy of the "good ideas" associated with realist theory, *self-help*, *balance of power*, *polarity*, and not merely its laws. They are questioning the very definition of international politics advanced by the realists.

Definitions of International Politics and Foreign Policy: Do They Make (All) the Difference?

It is difficult to overstate the fundamental character of this attack by the unfriendly critics of realist theory. The definition question goes to the core of any theoretical formulation. For example, Ashley's basic criticism of the neorealist "orrery of errors," stated succinctly, is that the good ideas of neorealism exclude the community aspects of politics associated with classical realism. More generally, Ashley (1984, 225) illuminates the fundamental character of this criticism by citing Bourdieu's insight, "the theory of knowledge is a dimension of political theory because the specifically symbolic power to impose the principles of the construction of reality—in particular social reality—is a major dimension of political power." Ashley contends that the most fundamental flaw in neorealist theory is epistemological—what Steiner would call an excessively rationalist worldview and its corresponding inattention to the intuitive, nonrationalist understanding of politics associated with classical realism. He grounds this argument in the "critical theory" approach of contemporary European political philosophy (Shapiro 1981) rather than the discipline of psychology.

By whatever route one arrives at this insight, it has one very immediate practical implication: how one defines politics, either implicitly or explicitly, determines how one expends effort in explaining it. Although the various critics identify different weaknesses, their diagnoses share the judgment that the realist definition of international politics in its neorealist form is too narrow in scope. Its preoccupation with the structural aspects of the balance of power results in imprecise laws and conceptual blindness regarding important aspects of foreign policy and international politics (Keohane 1983, 527–32). Even classical realism's broader definition of the balance-of-power scheme as a multifaceted struggle for power is too narrow (Ashley 1984, 273–75).

Role theory's contribution to a broader conceptualization of foreign policy within the context of the debate over neorealism can take two forms. In an artistic, nonrationalist mode of explanation the concept of role can supplement the intuitive context already provided by realism's concepts of power and interest for what Geertz (1973) calls "thick description." According to Keohane (1983, 506), power and interest perform the same function in realist foreign policy analysis that the concept of culture does in anthropological studies. That is, culture "is not a power, something to which social events, behaviors, institutions, or processes can be causally attributed; it is a context—something within which they can be intelligibly—that is, thickly—described" (Geertz 1973, 14; cited in Keohane 1983, 506). The partitioning of the concept of role into role conceptions, role expectations, and role conflict would aid in the process of "thick description," but the theoretical function of such an elaboration would be "not to codify abstract regularities but to make thick description possible, not to generalize across cases but to generalize within them" (Geertz 1973, 26; cited in Keohane 1983, 506). These distinctions would serve as nonrationalist heuristics to develop an understanding and sensitivity for "subjective contexts—to emotional climates, moods, and subjective standpoints" (Steiner 1983, 318–82).

If this type of intuitive function is all that is required, then the contribution of role theory to political realism's understanding of foreign policy would be to sensitize the realist analysis to the subjective aspects of the balancing process. Ashley (1984, 276–81) has argued that classical realism as practiced by statesmen is highly attuned already to these nuances. Its nonrationalist contribution to neorealist scholarship would be merely to restore and perhaps expand this sensitivity in an explicit manner. However, it would not do so ultimately in a parsimonious way, since thick description does not codify abstract regularities across cases.

For this reason Keohane (1983, 506) is uneasy about the theoretical implications of Geertz's position. He would like to supplement structural realism with something between it and rich interpretations of domestic structure and foreign policy: "systemic theories that retain some of the parsimony of Structural Realism, but that are able to deal better with differentiations between issue-areas, with institutions, and with change" (Keohane 1983, 531–32). Does a rationalist application of role theory to structural realism meet these goals?

Role Sets: The Rationalist Interface
Between Role Theory and Structural Realism

In chapter 4, I made the argument that role theory articulates a rationalist postscript to Waltz's theory of international politics and extends the moment of intuition associated with structural realism by supplying good ideas which systematically supplement its explanatory scope. This exercise relocated the realist tradition within a broader definition of politics beyond structuralism. At the same time, it extended the realist tradition to include an explicit focus upon foreign policy without abandoning the parsimonious level of generality associated with Waltz's theory of structural realism. This contribution primarily takes the form of concepts, assumptions, and definitions rather than laws. Consequently it is open to the same criticisms leveled at the Waltzian theory's laws. More generally, as we have seen, this criticism has also been directed at role theory independently of its application to the study of politics (Hall and Lindzey 1978; Newcomb, 1966).

In its application to the domain of foreign policy analysis, however, this criticism may no longer be relevant. It is true that "realist role theory" does not contribute lawlike statements directly to the Waltzian theory of structural realism. But its conceptual links to the decision-making and comparative foreign policy traditions offer the possibility that the lawlike statements by role theorists within these research traditions may be explained by the concepts and assumptions associated with the interface between role theory and the tradition of political realism. I will refer briefly to the contributions in this volume that focus upon role sets in order to illustrate the argument in support of this possibility.

The Walker and Simon policy analysis of the Southeast Asian role set employs a mix of the concepts, assumptions, and definitions of role theory and structural realism to engage in a thick description of foreign policy and international politics in Southeast Asia. This example uses an amalgam of role theory and realist theory to organize a description of foreign policy that is compatible with the explanation offered by *realist role theory*, the postscript to structural realism. However, the generalizations in this analysis are based upon a single case, the Southeast Asian role set defined by the issues associated with the Cambodian conflict, so it is hardly appropriate to declare that these generalizations are laws. In this instance realist role theory falls somewhere between acting as the context for thick description and serving as the source for the codification of abstract regularities. The interpretation is theoretically informed, but it is driven as much by the nonrationalist projection of role scenarios as by the rationalist specification of them by realist role theory.

A more explicitly rationalist application of role theory within the decision-making and comparative foreign policy traditions is the research by the associates of the CREON project. The most obvious linkages are between their "external predisposition model" and the concepts and assumptions of realist role theory. The lawlike statements in the decision tree associated with the various decision-making situations assume that foreign policy behavior occurs only in response to a "problem" perceived by the decision makers involving one of the following issue areas: security/physical safety, economic/wealth, respect/status, well-being/welfare, and enlightenment. As Singer and Hudson point out, the "problem" also defines the role set associated with each problem. "From the perspective of the acting regime or leader (the actor), every recognized problem will produce a role set that includes a 'source' role and a 'subject' role—and possibly 'facilitator,' 'aggravator,' or 'potential facilitator/aggravator' roles as well."

The selective introduction of prior affect, salience, and relative capabilities into the decision logic of the external predisposition model permits the CREON associates to assert lawlike covariations in the role-location process across confrontation, intervention, assistance, and collaboration situations. Realist role theory can serve as the underlying explanation for these laws by subsuming the types of situations under the exchange and conflict processes associated with realist role theory (see figure 13.1). For example, the CREON confrontation situation has decision rules which introduce prior relative capabilities as one relevant condition in selecting a role for enactment. Since a confrontation situation is defined as one in which a country either deprives another or is itself deprived by another, it is also by definition a situation in which the conflict process from realist role theory occurs (Walker 1987).

In addition to explaining why the CREON decision rules describe foreign policy behavior in different types of situations, the corresponding role conceptions associated with these situations can in principle be parsimoniously subsumed under the consumer, producer, belligerent, facilitator, and provocateur typology of roles associated with real-

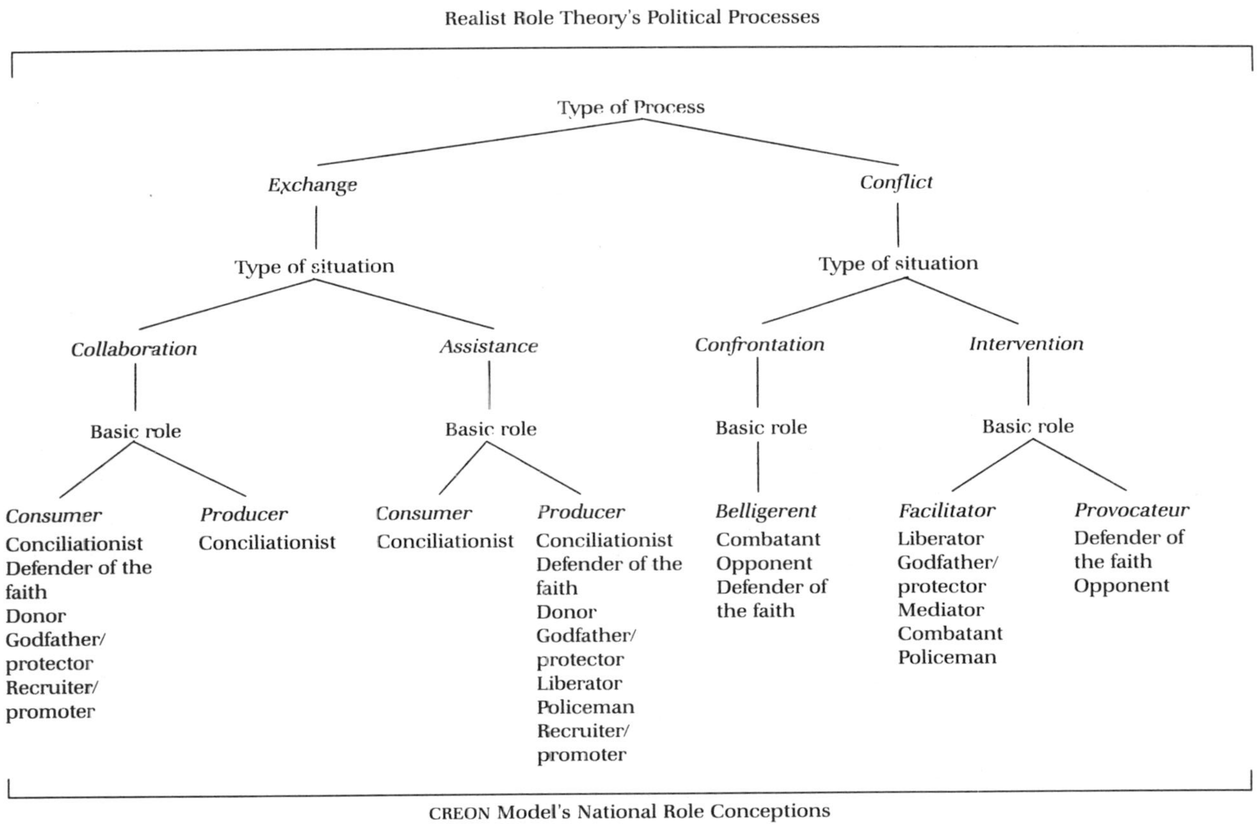

Realist Role Theory's Political Processes

Type of Process

Exchange

Conflict

Type of situation

Type of situation

Collaboration

Assistance

Confrontation

Intervention

Basic role

Basic role

Basic role

Basic role

Consumer
Conciliationist
Defender of the
faith
Donor
Godfather/
protector
Recruiter/
promoter

Producer
Conciliationist

Consumer
Conciliationist

Producer
Conciliationist
Defender of the
faith
Donor
Godfather/
protector
Liberator
Policeman
Recruiter/
promoter

Belligerent
Combatant
Opponent
Defender of
the faith

Facilitator
Liberator
Godfather/
protector
Mediator
Combatant
Policeman

Provocateur
Defender of
the faith
Opponent

CREON Model's National Role Conceptions

Figure 13.1 Linkages among national role conceptions, basic roles, types of situations, and political processes

ist role theory. CREON role conceptions for confrontation situations should be variants of the belligerent role in the conflict process, while the CREON role conceptions for the collaboration or assistance situations should be subsumable under the consumer or producer roles in the exchange process. CREON role conceptions for the intervention situation already duplicate the facilitator or provocateur alternatives defined by realist role theory.

For example, many of the CREON role conceptions from C. Hermann's analysis of American and Soviet shared political beliefs are subsumable under the basic roles associated with the processes defined by realist role theory (see figure 13.1). In order to make these classifications, each CREON role conception needs to be associated first with a type of decision-making situation. Since Hermann's exploratory research does not fully define or associate all of the U.S. and Soviet role conceptions with a type of situation, all of them cannot be classified (see tables 12.1 and 12.2; appendix 4). The placement of the ones for which there is sufficient information, however, does not appear to do violence either to their original meanings or to the meanings of the basic roles in realist role theory (Walker 1987).

Linkages among CREON's key situational variables, its national role conceptions, the basic roles, and the political processes of realist role theory reinforce the argument that the CREON model's laws of role location are explainable by the concepts, definitions, and assumptions of realist role theory. If so, then role theory provides a parsimonious extension of structural realism and also bridges the gap between its concepts and the laws associated with CREON's theoretical efforts. The testing of those propositions is only in the preliminary stages, however, so the statements in the CREON model are really hypotheses rather than laws. More empirical research needs to be done before a definitive judgment of role theory's explanatory value in foreign policy analysis is possible.

Appendixes

1

Properties of National Role Conceptions
and Their Sources

The following criteria were employed in choosing the twenty-nine leaders who are included in the sample (table A1.1):

a. Since the CREON data set was chosen for the behavior measures, the perceptual indicators had to be gathered from leaders representing nations which were included in that data set.

b. Heads of state who did not have apparent final authority in foreign policymaking, such as titular heads of state, were eliminated. Yet in some cases, leaders without the head of government designation were included if they did have this authority (M. Hermann 1976).

c. Leaders were eliminated if a varied set of English translations of their speeches was not accessible, since translating costs were beyond this researcher's ability to pay.

At the first training session, the three coders were given the coding questions and several paragraphs which contained national role statements. After the coding process was explained, coders were given

Table A1.1 Nature of Sample

Nation	Policymaker	Years in office during 1959–68
China	Zhou En Lai Lin Piao	(1959–August 1966) (August 1966–68)
Cuba	Castro	(1959–68)
East Germany	Ulbricht	(1959–68)
Egypt	Nasser	(1959–68)
France	DeGaulle	(1959–68)
Ghana	Nkrumah	(1959–February 1966)
India	Nehru Shastri Gandhi	(1959–May 1964) (May 1964–66) (1966–68)
Israel	Ben-Gurion Eshkol	(1959–June 1963) (June 1963–68)
Kenya	Kenyatta	(December 1963–68)
Mexico	Mateos Ordaz	(1959–November 1964) (December 1964–68)
Philippines	Macapagal Marcos	(December 1961–65) (December 1965–68)
Soviet Union	Khrushchev Kosygin	(1959–October 1964) (October 1964–68)
United States	Eisenhower Kennedy Johnson	(1959–January 1961) (January 1961–November 1963) (November 1963–68)
Venezuela	Betancourt Leoni	(February 1959–November 1964) (December 1964–68)
West Germany	Adenauer Erhard Kiesinger	(1959–October 1963) (October 1963–October 1966) (November 1966–68)
Yugoslavia	Tito	(1959–68)
Zambia	Kaunda	(October 1964–68)

identical additional paragraphs to code by the next training session. They were also requested to refrain from consulting each other and instead to indicate at the next session exactly which questions were ambiguous. The same procedure was followed at three more training sessions. After each session, the ambiguous questions were revised, and the intercoder agreement was calculated. By the end of the four sessions, coders had attained 82 percent pairwise intercoder agreement, and they began the actual coding.

Although a multiple-indicator strategy is used for economic development and national capability or size, the single-indicator press freedom index was used for political orientation or accountability for three reasons:

a. Moore (1974, 177) has demonstrated that "variables measuring freedom of the press, representativeness of the government, the degree of electoral competition, and the degree of legislative vs. executive power . . . all correlate very highly with each other." He also demonstrates how freedom of the press can be used quite successfully as an indicator of political accountability by itself.

b. In a preliminary analysis, the press freedom variable was more highly correlated with all of the role-conception variables than a composite indicator of political accountability used to measure the representative character of the regime in East and Hermann's research (1974).

c. The distinguishing characteristic of an open versus closed political system is the more or less continuous public debate over governmental policies and those who currently make them. Press freedom is the best indicator of this debate.

Status of Roles

International status may be measured by its domain of influence and its degree. A domain of influence may be as small as a domestic domain or as large as a global domain. Greater international status usually involves being influential in large rather than small domains. Thus every role conception was assigned a value of 1 (for domestic) through 6 (for global). The mean of the numerical values for a policymaker was used as his "level of influence domain" score.

Role status is measured also by the degree of influence a nation has relative to its partners in cooperative ventures. Roles associated with leadership or dominance involve a great degree of status or influence. In order to differentiate dominant and equal-status roles, they were classified into three categories:

a. An equal status ally or cooperative partner: the state cooperates with other actors in an equal partnership or cooperative venture.

b. An example for others to follow: the nation is an example or model for others to follow.

c. A dominant ally or cooperative partner: the state leads, defends or protects other cooperative actors or allies and thus performs a dominant role.

A score on "perception of dominance" was determined by assigning the values *1* through *3* for these categories and computing a mean for each policymaker.

Motivational Orientation of Roles

Decision makers' role conceptions may be individualistic, cooperative, competitive, or mixed (cooperative-competitive). An example of an individualistically motivated role is the isolate. The foreign policymaker who perceives his nation performing this role might recognize severe domestic problems and discern that it is better for his nation (and/or himself) to expend very little of its resources in the international arena.

However, most national roles have an international rather than an individualistic or domestic orientation. They are either competitively or cooperatively motivated. Examples of cooperative roles are the faithful ally, mediator-integrator, and regional subsystem collaborator (Holsti 1970). Roles which involve more competition are the bastion of the revolution-liberator, anti-imperialist agent, or anti-communist agent. If foreign policymakers perceive their nations cooperating with one nation or group of nations in order to compete with others, these roles are clearly both competitive and cooperative. Functions involving blocs are prime examples of this type of role, especially when some type of competition with the other bloc is clearly the purpose. Two role variables are provided by this classification — "individualistic motivations" and "competitive motivations." These were measured, respectively, by (a) the percentage of individualistic motivations, and (b) the percentage of external (nonindividualistic) motivations that are either competitive or mixed.

However, roles also vary according to their motivation for change or the amount of system change which the decision maker desires. An example of a role associated with a great deal of change is the bastion of the revolution-liberator (Holsti 1970). Mediator or developer roles suggest moderate change, while the protectee or isolate roles are associated with very little change or maintenance of the status quo. The categories for this variable were ordered, from low to high. An "amount

Table A1.2 East's factor scores and nation groupings
for the seventeen nations on size

Very large states	
United States	−7.39
Soviet Union	−5.97
China, People's Republic	−3.35
India	−1.45
Large states	
West Germany	−0.60
France	−0.54
Mexico	−0.13
Medium states	
East Germany	0.10
Yugoslavia	0.13
Egypt	0.15
Small states	
Venezuela	0.19
Israel	0.22
Philippines	0.23
Zambia	0.24
Cuba	0.26
Kenya	0.29
Ghana	0.34

Source: East 1975, appendix, 5.

of change" score was devised for each policymaker by computing the mean of his total scores on this scale.

Role Issue or Substantive Problem Area

Roles may also be categorized according to issue or substantive problem area. These categories were defined as follows:

a. *Territorial/defense*. The nation maintains, defends, or expands its own or its collaborator's territorial integrity or security, or inhibits that of his competitors.

b. *Ideological*. The nation defends, promotes, or inhibits a value system or way of life (Examples: communism, capitalism, socialism, democracy).

c. *Political/diplomatic*. The nation affects the positions or relationships between states—for example, a decision maker identifies

Table A1.3 East's factor scores and nation groupings for the seventeen nations on modernity

Very modern states	
United States	− .320
Modern states	
Soviet Union	−1.77
East Germany	−1.71
West Germany	−1.59
France	−1.55
Israel	−1.35
Modernizing states	
Venezuela	−0.60
Yugoslavia	−0.57
Mexico	−0.09
Cuba	−0.04
Unmodernized states	
Egypt	0.10
Philippines	0.11
Zambia	0.30
China	0.35
India	0.71
Ghana	0.81
Kenya	0.81

Source: East 1975, appendix, 9.

his nation's relationships with other states as nonalignment, peaceful coexistence, or a mediator between states.

d. *Universal values*. The nation promotes a situation of peace, racial harmony, justice, etc.

e. *Economic*. The nation maintains or expands its own or another's economic resources or industrial development.

The coders used a multiple-choice form to code each of the paragraphs on the variables described above. Scores for each leader were based on their responses.

Size and Modernity Indicators

The size and modernity indicators are factor scores (tables A1.2 and A1.3). These factor scores were derived by performing a principal component factor analysis on seven variables associated with size. They are: (1) population, (2) total area, (3) agricultural area, (4) energy consumption, (5) gross national product, (6) total military manpower, and (7) total defense expenditures. East's original factor analysis results in two factors. He labels these factors nonmilitary and military resources. Since they are highly correlated, he reduces these two factors to one, obtaining the factor scores in table A1.2 on a size factor.

The factor scores in table A1.3 were derived by performing a principal component factor analysis on eight variables associated with modernity. They are: (1) population in cities over 100,000, (2) literacy rate, (3) students in higher education per million population, (4) percent of GDP originating in industry, (5) newspapers per 1,000, (6) GNP per capita, (7) energy consumption per capita, and (8) proteins per capita per diem. East's original factor analysis revealed three separate factors. Since the first factor accounted for approximately 66 percent of the variation and all eight variables had high loadings on this factor, it alone was utilized to obtain the factor scores above.

2

Description of Foreign Policy
Role Orientations

Expansionist Orientation

Conceptualization. By an expansionist orientation is meant a willingness to urge one's government or like-minded parties to consider enlarging their territorial or resource claims or power over others. For the expansionist the world is divided into "we" and "them." Generally the "we" is the nation-state. It is important to improve the condition of the "we" and avoid the attempts of "them" to disrupt these efforts. There is a basic distrust of the motives of the "them" since they are perceived as intent on taking over the same resources, territories, or peoples as "we" but for their own ends. Conflict thus becomes the name of the game as others' moves are judged thwarting to "our" goals and desires. Given the expansionist's basic "we-they" interpretation of the world, all actions in the international system take on a black-white character—for us, for them/against us. There is little need to search for information or alternatives in making foreign policy decisions. "We" know why "they" acted.

Political leaders with an expansionist orientation are likely to perceive foreign policy problems as issues of power precipitated by out-side sources. They will try to rally their regimes and politically active units in the society around retaliatory activities to minimize any effects of foreign policy issues on their tenure in office. Toward these ends, leaders with expansionist orientations will work to maintain tight con-trol over the foreign policymaking process.

Way individual traits are combined. Expansionist orientations are likely in political leaders who have a strong interest in maintaining their nation's sovereignty and identity (high nationalism), are quite distrustful of others, have a need to manipulate and control others (high need for power), tend to stereotype objects and persons in their environment (low conceptual complexity), have little desire or need to maintain friendly relations with others (low need for affiliation), and believe what they do can and does have an impact on events (high belief in ability to control events). In determining this orientation nationalism, need for power, and distrust of others are weighted more heavily (given twice the impact) than the other characteristics. The formulae for combining scores on the various traits into scores for the orientations are explained in detail in Hermann (1983).

Foreign policy behavior likely to urge on government. Political lead-ers with expansionist orientations are likely to favor low commitment behaviors for their government, being unwilling to lose control over resources. Their aim is to gain not lose resources. Such leaders when they espouse change will urge immediate change in the international environment, changes over which they can have control. Moreover, much of the expansionists' behavior will be hostile in tone as they attempt to aid their governments in gaining more power and status in the international system. Indeed, most of their activity focuses on issues of power and status. The relationships with commitment, goal statements, and affect are particularly likely if the political leader has little interest in foreign affairs; the relationships with commitment and goal statements are also more likely if the political leader has had little training in foreign affairs before coming to office. (The relationships described in this section have received support in previous research examining the impact of leaders' orientations on national foreign pol-icy behavior; see M. Hermann, 1976, 1978, 1980.)

Regimes and nations where likely to gain office. Political leaders with expansionist orientations are more likely to be found in Middle Eastern and African countries. They are more likely to come to power under illegal rather than legal means. Moreover, they tend to gain leadership positions in less-developed countries and countries where there is little political competition. See M. Hermann (1979) for a discussion of these findings.

Behavior likely to display in the decision-making process. Leaders with expansionist orientations will be directive in decision-making activity, being manipulative and deceitful if this behavior will guarantee the leader his way. Such policymakers will not be highly tolerant of deviant points of view, putting a premium on loyalty. Leaders with this orientation will not be very sensitive to the needs of members of the group. In fact, leaders who are expansionists are often wary of members of their decision-making groups, suspecting power moves on the part of these members at any time. For an initial exploration of these relationships, see M. Hermann, C. Hermann, and Dixon (1979).

Active Independent Orientation

Conceptualization. The active independent orientation refers to an interest in participating in the international community but on one's own terms and without engendering a dependent relationship with any other country. K. Holsti (1970, 262) suggests that political leaders with this orientation "emphasize at once independence, self-determination, possible mediation functions, and active programs to extend diplomatic and commercial relations to diverse areas of the world." Individuals with an active independent orientation have a dogged interest in maintaining their national separateness but also realize the importance of other nations to their continued existence. These leaders attempt to resolve this dilemma by never wedding themselves to any one country, keeping close control over their interactions with other governments. Maintaining their independence requires an ability to differentiate clearly among foreign policy actors and among foreign policy actions. It is important to think through the possible outcomes or consequences of the alternatives one is considering before making a decision.

Political leaders with this orientation perceive that foreign policy problems are generally precipitated by other governments but are able to recognize that some problems pose opportunities. They seek to focus the attention of their governments and publics on such opportunities, thus reducing any negative impact of foreign policy problems to themselves. They work to create an image of providing advantages to their nation through their activities in the foreign arena. These leaders try to manage all aspects of the foreign policy process in order to minimize the appearance of foreign policy problems and to maintain their independence.

Way individual traits are combined (see M. Hermann 1983). Active independent orientations are likely in political leaders who have a strong desire to maintain national sovereignty (high nationalism), have an intense belief in their own ability to control what happens (high belief in ability to control events), tend to differentiate among objects and persons in their environment (high conceptual complexity), have a desire to establish and maintain friendly relations with others (high need for affiliation), tend to trust others (low distrust of others), and have little need to control others (low need for power). In determining this orientation, conceptual complexity, nationalism, and belief in one's own ability to control events are weighted more heavily (given twice the weight) than the other characteristics.

Foreign policy behavior likely to urge on government (see M. Hermann 1976, 1978). Political leaders with active independent orientations are likely to urge their governments to make low-level commitments, if any. One of the basic tenets of the active independent is the shunning of commitments that limit maneuverability and sense of independence. These leaders perceive the need for long-term change in the international system to enable their nations and nations like theirs, if they so desire, to remain unaligned. To remain independent, these political leaders are likely to "cultivate relations with as many states as possible" (K. Holsti 1970, 262) so as to appear impartial. Such cultivation leads to extensive use of positive affect. Political leaders who are active independents tend to focus on security and economic issues in their dealings with other governments.

Regimes and nations where likely to gain office (see M. Hermann 1979). Leaders who have an active independent orientation are more likely to come to power through legal as opposed to illegal means in countries that are in the process of modernizing and in countries with some degree of political competition. Such leaders seem to appear more often in Asian, Atlantic Community, and Latin American countries than in nations from other regions of the world.

Behavior likely to display in decision-making process (see M. Hermann, C. Hermann, and Dixon, 1979). Political leaders with an active independent orientation are likely to be quite directive in decision-making situations, encouraging presentation of conflicting viewpoints in hopes of ferreting out all possible consequences of particular options. For similar reasons they will also consult widely with experts before making a decision. They will be sensitive to information gained from the environment, often creating an extensive intelligence-gathering operation. Such leaders will maintain an active interest in overseeing what happens in their government in the foreign policy area.

Influential Orientation

Conceptualization. The influential orientation centers around an interest in having an impact on other nations' foreign policy behavior — in playing a leadership role in the international system. Political leaders with this orientation want to shape the nature of events in the foreign policy arena, to have their goals become the goals of some, if not all, of the other nations in the international system. Ideological commitments are less important to political leaders with this orientation, particularly if such ideological commitments can prevent them from having an influence on the foreign policy arena. Leaders with this orientation have an uncanny ability to be responsive and sensitive to the desires of those they are trying to influence and lead. They are attuned to the many nuances of these constituencies, subtly changing tactics to meet the situation. In effect, leaders with an influential orientation will seek out problems in the foreign policy arena so that they can exercise power over the output, gaining prestige abroad as well as at home.

Way individual traits are combined (see M. Hermann 1983). An influential orientation is likely in political leaders who have a strong need to control others (high need for power), believe they can control what happens (high belief can control events), have a need to establish and maintain friendly relations with others (high need for affiliation), can differentiate among objects and persons in their environment (high conceptual complexity), have little distrust of others, and have no overriding concern with maintaining their own national identity separate from others (low nationalism). Need for power and belief in ability to control events are weighted more heavily than the other traits (given twice the impact) in determining this orientation.

Foreign policy behavior likely to urge on government (see M. Hermann 1976, 1978). Leaders with characteristics suggestive of an influential orientation are likely to urge their governments to be very friendly (show positive affect) toward other governments. For these leaders good relationships with other nations are important to furthering their own nation's position in the foreign policy community. Leaders interested in being influential will promote a mixture of independent and interdependent activities depending on the situation and country that is the target. In order to keep their options open, however, such leaders are unlikely to want their governments to make extensive commitments to other nations. For leaders with an influential orientation, military issues—issues of power and prowess—occupy center stage. All of the relationships for leaders with this orientation are more likely if the leaders are very interested in foreign affairs and have training in foreign affairs.

Regimes and nations where likely to gain office (see M. Hermann 1979). Political leaders who have an influential orientation are as likely in regimes that come to power through legal as illegal means. These leaders are more often found in Asian countries than in countries in other regions of the world.

Behavior likely to display in decision-making process (see M. Hermann, C. Hermann, and Dixon 1979). Leaders with an influential orientation will be highly manipulative, although subtle in the use of manipulation techniques. These leaders can be interested either in solving the problem at hand or in the morale of the group, depending on the needs of the members. Given this adaptability, they may appear charismatic. Leaders with this orientation will engage in a lot of "behind the scenes" power-play activity and are not beyond pitting factions against one another so that they can appear as mediators or "great compromisers" to settle the problem.

Mediator/Integrator Orientation

Conceptualization. By mediator/integrator orientation is meant a concern with reconciling differences between other nations, an interest in playing a "go-between" role (see K. Holsti 1970, 265). Political leaders with this orientation want to gain a reputation for third-party politics as they try to resolve problems in the international system. These political leaders perceive themselves and their nations as peacemakers in the international arena. They are interested in the welfare of other nations, particularly as it relates to their own welfare, and are open to listening to both sides of a controversy. They generally are able to raise options and alternatives where none had been perceived before. In some sense, political leaders with this orientation are willing to "take a back seat" in foreign policymaking, having an impact without seeming to interfere or to control others. By playing a "good Samaritan" role in international politics, leaders with a mediator/integrator orientation make it difficult for politically active elites in their countries to criticize them effectively.

Way individual traits are combined (see M. Hermann 1983). A mediator/integrator orientation is likely in political leaders who are skilled in differentiating among the many aspects of their environments (high conceptual complexity), believe that they can influence what happens (high belief can control events), have a strong need to maintain friendly relations with others (high need for affiliation), have little distrust of others, have little overriding concern with national identity or sovereignty (low nationalism), and have little need to control or dominate others (low need for power). In determining this orientation, conceptual complexity and need for affiliation are weighted more (given twice the impact) than the other characteristics.

Foreign policy behavior likely to urge on government (see M. Hermann 1976, 1978). Political leaders with a mediator/integrator orientation are willing to commit political resources for foreign policy activities if by such commitments they build a reputation for standing behind what they say. They are interested in having their government act in conjunction with other governments and maintain friendly relations with other governments in order to foster mutual understanding and trust. Leaders with this orientation tend to focus more on economic issues than other types of concerns. These relationships are more evident the less interested the political leader with this orientation is in foreign affairs and the less training he or she has had.

Regimes and nations where likely to gain office (see M. Hermann 1979). Leaders with this orientation are more likely in nations that have sizeable resources, that are modernized, and that have a high degree of political competition. Such leaders are more likely to come to power by legal than by illegal means. Given this profile, it is not surprising that leaders with this orientation are more likely in Atlantic Community countries than in countries from other regions.

Behavior likely to display in decision-making process (see M. Hermann, C. Hermann, and Dixon 1979). Leaders who have a mediator/integrator orientation will encourage participation by others in the decision-making process but will work to prevent conflict from surfacing among those who do participate. Such leaders prefer to be part of cohesive groups. These leaders see their role in the group as providing enough structure for the group to make a decision while urging members to consider a range of alternatives.

Opportunist Orientation

Conceptualization. The opportunist orientation refers to a willingness to be expedient, to take advantage of present circumstances. Ziller et al. (1977) have proposed that this orientation is an important aspect of political man. Political leaders with this orientation are situation-sensitive — they are guided by what they perceive to be the demands and opportunities of the moment. These leaders are little tied to ideological commitments. The beliefs they do espouse are determined by what seems appropriate to the politics of the time. Should a change in position be demanded, there is little psychic disturbance in making the change. Such leaders are skillful in their ability to discriminate among objects and persons in their environment. Moreover, they continuously monitor the environment, seeking information to confirm or disconfirm the relevance of a particular action or decision. The goals of leaders with this orientation reflect the goals of the constituency they serve.

Way individual traits are combined (see M. Hermann 1983). An opportunist orientation is likely in political leaders who are able to discriminate among objects and persons in their environment (high conceptual complexity), have little distrust of others, have little belief in their own ability to control events, have little need to dominate others (low need for power), have little need to maintain friendly relations with others (low need for affiliation), and have no overriding concern with the maintenance of national identity or sovereignty (low nationalism). Conceptual complexity is weighted more heavily in determining this orientation than the other traits; it is given three times the weight of the other traits.

Foreign policy likely to urge on government (see M. Hermann 1976, 1978, 1980). Political leaders with an opportunist orientation will urge their governments to remain attuned to what is going on in the international arena, since much of their direction comes from such information. To keep contacts open, governments with opportunistic leaders will have to allocate or commit political resources. Moreover, they will engage in conjoint activities with these same countries. Such leaders will be interested in having their governments' "hands in many pies" to keep on top of what is happening in foreign policy elsewhere. These leaders will try to maintain a low positive profile. By being friendly, but not excessively so, they keep on everybody's good side. Given their intense interest in information from the environment, it comes as little surprise that these leaders tend to focus about equally on security, economic, and respect/status issues. The relationships just described are particularly evident in leaders with this orientation who have had extensive training in foreign affairs.

Regimes and nations where likely to gain office   (see M. Hermann 1979). Like the leader with a mediator/integrator orientation, leaders with opportunist orientations are more likely in governments with sizeable resources that are modernized and have a high degree of political competition. Moreover, they are more likely to come to power by legal as opposed to illegal means and in Atlantic Community nations.

Behavior likely to display in decision-making process   (see M. Hermann, C. Hermann, and Dixon 1979). Leaders with opportunist orientations are more likely to listen in group decision-making situations than to participate. They will often use trial balloons to test others' responses. These leaders are very interested in reaching consensus before a decision is made. In reaching such a consensus they will consult widely. If conflict or disagreement among members should emerge, they will urge a confrontation to iron out the differences, wanting to know what ideas and arguments will achieve a compromise.

Developmental Orientation

Conceptualization   By developmental orientation is meant an interest in building one's own nation's position in the world by developing useful and rewarding dealings with other countries. Political leaders with this orientation have a strong commitment to their nation's improvement but feel the only way to better its position is through interrelationships with others, through seeing what others have of value and what they might help one to attain. These political leaders are uncertain that they or their nations can govern events. However, they expect that with constant vigilance they can seek out those who appear able to shape events. And indeed these leaders often seem aware of the availability of rewarding relationships before most other actors in the international system. To some degree political leaders with this orientation engage in controlled dependence. They use others but do not become symbiotic with these others, nor do they try to control or dominate others.

Way individual traits are combined   (see M. Hermann 1983). A developmental orientation is likely in political leaders who have a strong concern for maintaining their nation's identity and sovereignty (high nationalism), have a definite need to establish and maintain friendly relations with others (high need for affiliation), are capable of discriminating among persons, objects, and programs in their environment (high conceptual complexity), have little belief in their own ability to control what happens, have little distrust of others, and little need to dominate others (low need for power). In determining this orientation, need for affiliation and nationalism are weighted more heavily (given twice the impact) than the other traits.

Foreign policy behavior likely to urge on government (see M. Hermann 1976, 1978). Leaders with a developmental orientation urge their governments to play what may seem to many a contradictory game. They are quite willing to have their nations act interdependently with others but do so while committing only a moderate amount of their own resources. They try to get more than they give. Although favoring friendly relations with other nations, leaders with this orientation are not above using threats to gain allies in a specific situation. Developmentally oriented leaders tend to focus their attention on security and economic issues.

Regimes and nations where likely to gain office (see M. Hermann 1979). Leaders with developmental orientations are more likely in modernizing nations and in nations where there is a high degree of political competition. They are more likely to come to power by legal than extralegal means, generally appearing in Atlantic Community nations.

Behavior likely to display in decision-making process (see M. Hermann, C. Hermann, and Dixon 1979). Leaders with developmental orientations will be sensitive to others' needs and concerns but will probably not choose to work with those who differ from them on substantive matters. These leaders are likely to be directive in their dealings with decision-making groups. They will be particularly interested in seeking out information that is supportive to their positions and will seek allies through their powers of persuasion.

3

Operationalization Procedures for
Relational and Behavior Measures

Prior Affect

Prior affect was measured using the Azar/Sloan Conflict-Cooperation Scale from the Conflict and Peace Data Bank (COPDAB) (Azar 1980). This scale was chosen because it (a) is event based, (b) has an affect score assigned to each event, (c) is dyadically structured, and (d) is categorized by issue. To render the 15-point Azar/Sloan scale more comparable to the explanatory variable of prior affect as conceptualized for this research, qualitative categories of positive, negative, neutral, no prior affect, and mixed prior affect were constructed by using such measures as the median and the range of a time series of COPDAB affect scores for each dyad of nations. (For detailed construction rules for these categories, see Hudson, 1983.) To increase the likelihood that we were focusing on the current feelings of prior affect for the entities involved in the situation under consideration, a prior affect score for a particular dyad was determined for each year by examining the COPDAB affect data for the five previous years.

Because changes in a nation's leaders through such occurrences as coups d'état and revolutions might lead to dramatic changes in affect between governments, we used *World Handbook* (Taylor and Hudson 1972) data on irregular executive transfers to determine when such changes occurred. When a change of this kind was noted, prior affect scores up to that point were discarded and affect toward these countries was assumed to be none or neutral for six months to allow for the build-up in affective experience with the new regime.

Salience

In assessing salience we were interested in the importance of other entities to the actor, judging these entities to be salient or nonsalient based on their ability to impede the actor's realization of four basic values: security/physical safety, economic/wealth, respect/status, and well-being/enlightenment. Separate indicators of salience were used for each of the four basic values.

For an event classified as involving the value of physical/military security, salience was determined by identifying entities that could be classified either as "traditional enemies" of the acting nation or entities with geographical proximity to the actor. Such entities were thought to have the greatest ability to affect the actor's physical and military security and thus were considered salient to the actor. As part of the larger data-collection effort associated with CREON, a list of traditional enemies and nations in physical proximity had been prepared for each nation.

When economic/wealth values were involved, salience was assumed to result from the actor's trade dependence on another country or another international entity (for example, multinational corporation). Trade dependence was measured by noting when an entity accounted for 3 percent or more of the imports or exports of an actor for whom trade was important (that is, the value of the imports/exports exceeded 10 percent of the actor's GNP). These data were collected from the International Monetary Fund/World Bank Direction of Trade Data.

If an event involved the value of respect/status then salience occurred if the actor had above average frequency of interactions of all kinds with another party. Such interaction served as an indicator of the diplomatic importance one nation placed on another. The COPDAB data were used to determine the amount of interaction an acting nation had with all other entities; interaction was considered above average if it was twice the mean activity for the acting nation across the decade.

Finally, in cases where an event involved the value of well-being and enlightenment, salience was defined as present if the acting nation was dependent for economic, scientific, and technical aid upon another country or other international party. Aid data were compiled by searching for such specialized transactions for each acting country in *Keesing's Contemporary Archives*.

Relative Capabilities

In determining an actor's capabilities vis à vis another entity, we were interested in finding indicators that would permit us to make a rough judgment of whether the acting nation possessed significantly more, significantly less, or about the same capabilities in a particular arena as the other relevant parties in the event. Once more we used the four basic values to define the arenas in which we sought indicators of relative strength.

For the events involving the value of security/physical safety, relative capabilities were determined by using data on national defense expenditures. Data on defense expenditures in constant dollars for the decade being examined in the present study were obtained from *World Military Expenditures and Arms Trade* (U.S. Arms Control and Disarmament Agency 1973). To determine relative strength of the acting nation vis à vis other nations, we used the concept of "step" developed by Tukey (1977). Another nation's military capabilities were considered to be significantly more or significantly less than the actor's depending on whether its defense expenditures were a step above or below the actor's when the defense expenditures for all nations were put into an ordered set. "Step" means that a data point is one and one-half times the range of the inner two quartiles of an ordered data set from a second data point. Although used by Tukey (1977) primarily to identify outliers in an ordered batch of data, the step can also be used to identify those data points "very much above" or "very much below" *any* given point in the data. This self-ordering quality was seen as superior to merely dividing the data into three parts and then declaring every pair of points within each trecile to be similar, and every pair of points in different treciles to be dissimilar. In this approximation, nations within a step of each other were considered to have roughly equivalent military capabilities. These data were collected for two points in time during the decade—1960 and 1965. The relative strengths for 1960 were applied to the prediction years of 1959, 1960, 1961, 1962, and 1963, and the relative strengths for 1965 were applied to the prediction years of 1964, 1965, 1966, 1967, and 1968.

For events involving economic/wealth values, relative capabilities were estimated by using Gross National Product data. Data on GNP (in constant dollars) were obtained from *World Military Expenditures and Arms Trade* (U.S. Arms Control and Disarmament Agency 1973). The step technique was again used to determine which nations had significantly more, significantly less, or about the same economic strength as each acting nation. As before, estimates were made for two time points, 1960 and 1965.

For those events concerning the basic value of respect/status, relative capabilities were indicated by the diplomatic importance scores devised by Small and Singer (1973). These scores reflect the number of diplomatic missions found in a given nation at a specific point in time. Small and Singer gathered their data for half-decades, and we used the data from 1960 and 1965. The step technique was used to determine the relative diplomatic importance of the actor vis à vis the other parties in the situation.

Finally, for events involving well-being/enlightenment values, relative capabilities were derived from indicators of data on the percent of a nation's population aged fifteen or older that were literate as reported in the *United Nations Statistical Yearbook* (1960–70). As these data were presented in percentage form, the standard deviation, rather than the step, was used to determine the cutoff points for the relative strength of a nation vis à vis all others. To maintain consistency, the two data years of 1960 and 1965 were again chosen.

Behavior

Recall that the model proposes to characterize all foreign policy behaviors in terms of four properties—affect, commitment, instrumentality, and recipient. It is the varying values of these output variables that mark the end of each branch of the decision tree and form the predictions. Measures for these four behavior variables were part of the original coding of each event and were performed according to procedures described in Callahan et al. (1982) and in Hudson (1983).

4

Descriptions for Roles Associated with Selected Core Political System Beliefs in the CREON Regime Orientations

Role: Combatant

1. Description. An expectation that the government will use military force to contain, thwart, and eventually defeat the enemy. The government should take such military steps as may be necessary in terms of organizing, maintaining, and conducting military activities in order to defend the country and to contain the enemy. Should oppose enemy by force at every advantageous opportunity.

2. Basic values involved in problems triggering role. Military security/physical safety.

3. Assumptions. A traditional enemy exists which will be opposed by force in all military confrontations and in situations where any member of the actor's bloc or subsystem faces a military challenge from the enemy.

4. Situations. This role applies in all confrontation situations involving the enemy which have military security as a basic value. It also applies in *intervention* situations involving the enemy and the military security basic value and in which one role is assumed by a member of the actor's bloc or subsystem.

5. Probable behaviors.   The enemy will be the recipient of the behavior which will be characterized by negative affect, use of the military instrument, and moderate to high commitment.

Role: Conciliationist

1. Description.   An expectation exists that the government, while doing everything necessary to protect the security, welfare, and international interests of the country against the enemy, also will pursue opportunities to resolve or limit the disagreements with it. It is believed that although the conflict with the enemy is real, there may be means of resolving or containing the disagreement. The government should pursue activities that explore these possibilities including direct and third-party mediated communication with the enemy. Where worthwhile agreements seem feasible there should be negotiations. Unilateral initiatives to that end may be appropriate.

2. Basic values involved in problem triggering role.   Any basic values can be involved.

3. Assumptions.   There is a traditional enemy involved in the situation, but the conflict is not viewed as zero sum.

4. Situations.   The context for this role can be either collaboration or assistance needed (where the actor asks enemy for assistance in containing conflict or makes a unilateral gesture in that direction); also assistance resource situations can occur (responding to comparable acts by enemy) if the actor does not believe the conflict is zero sum.

5. Probable behavior.   Recipient is enemy and the action involves the diplomatic instrument (perhaps in conjunction with other instruments if appropriate for problem), affect will be neutral, and commitment will be none or low.

Role: Defender of the Faith

1. Description.   An expectation exists that the government will interpret and comment upon world affairs in terms of an ideology to which the regime adheres. In the ideological commentary the world will tend to be dichotomized into followers of the ideology and those who reject or misinterpret it for their own ends. The actions—and possibly the existence—of those in opposition will be condemned. The behavior and existence of those who follow the ideology will be praised and the necessity for maintaining the correct interpretation of the ideology will be stressed.

2. Basic values involved in problem triggering role. If the situation is confrontation or intervention, then any basic value may occur. When the situation is collaboration, the respect/status value must be involved.

3. Assumption. The actor adheres to a world view that is opposed or resisted by other governments. The actions associated with the role will be verbal only and will occur when the actor does not wish to take physical action—usually because the actor is not stronger than the target or the target is a former bloc member whom the actor hopes to reintegrate into the bloc.

4. Situations. The situation can be confrontation if the actor faces a challenging (deviating) bloc member or a former member of its bloc as either the source or subject. Intervention applies when (1) the source and subject are both members of an opposing bloc, (2) either the source or the subject is an opposing bloc member and the other role is occupied by a neutral or nonbloc member, or (3) when one role is assumed by a traditional enemy and the other by nonbloc members and the actor is weaker than the enemy. Collaboration applies when the actor and the members of its own bloc are involved. Assistance resource occurs when the enemy makes a request and the actor regards the conflict between them as zero sum.

5. Probable behaviors. If the situation is confrontation, assistance resource, or intervention, then the recipient will be the opponents of the actor's ideological view, affect will be strongly negative, the instrument will be diplomatic, and there will be no commitment. If the situation is collaboration, then the recipient will be its own bloc members, the affect will be positive, the instrument diplomatic, and there will be no commitment.

Role: Donor

1. Description. An expectation exists that the government will invest its own resources to promote the economic development and social welfare (for example, relief of poverty, hunger, etc.) of friendly but needy countries. The government also will use multilateral assistance organizations to aid other countries lacking a history of friendship, providing that the regime in the acting country believes it can influence the aid organization. The pattern of assistance actions rests on the belief that the actor's own interest will be enhanced by the further development of the countries assisted.

2. Basic values involved in problem triggering role.   Economics/wealth; well-being/welfare; education/enlightenment.

3. Assumptions.   The actor's economic status (for example, GNP per capita) must be greater than that of the country(ies) to be assisted. None of those to be assisted must be traditional enemies of the actor, unless the assistance is through a multilateral source whose policies the actor helps determine. Even then, the actor must see the conflict with the enemy needing aid as non-zero sum.

4. Situations.   Assistance resource occurs when country(ies) requesting assistance are the source and subject or collaboration can occur when the actor together with other members of a multilateral organization are source and subject.

5. Probable behaviors.   The actor will address, as recipient, the entity requesting aid (if bilateral) or the organization to which it belongs (if multilateral); the instrument will be diplomatic plus any other instruments associated with the basic values found in the problem, affect will be moderately positive, and the commitment will be moderate. Essentially the actor will act to supply assistance when requesting country has been friendly.

Role: Godfather/Protector

1. Description.   An expectation exists that the government has a special responsibility to help salient but weaker countries for which the acting government has a strong affinity. A supportive bilateral relationship should be preserved with the nation that is weaker militarily and economically than the actor who serves as the protector. Actions taken should protect and sustain the weaker country. The protector's affinity with the target country results from the saliency it has for the actor —politically, ideologically, or in terms of the target's supplying the actor with some needed commodity. To sustain the relationship the protected country should seek to maintain positive relations with the godfather.

2. Basic values involved in problems triggering role.   Any or all of the five basic values may be involved.

3. Assumptions.   There must be a nation involved in the situation which (a) is weaker than the actor economically and militarily, (b) is salient to the actor, (c) has a history of positive affect with the actor, and

(d) is not a member of any major bloc opposing the actor.

4. Situation. It may be an intervention situation in which the protectee is the source or subject of the problem, assistance resource situation in which the protectee makes a request of the actor or collaboration in which the protectee and the actor negotiate.

5. Probable behaviors. A. If protectee is recipient, then affect will be positive, commitment will be moderate to high, and diplomatic instruments will be used in combination with instruments relevant to what is needed by protectee. Actor's behavior is designed to support the protectee consistent with its role expectations. B. If enemy or potential enemy of the protectee is recipient, then the affect will be negative, the commitment low, and the instrument will be diplomatic. The actor will want to discourage the protectee's adversary by making clear the actor's continuing support.

Role: Liberator

1. Description. An expectation exists that the government will provide military and promotional (propaganda) support for an organized revolutionary or guerrilla force providing it meets certain conditions. The conditions are that the guerrillas must be attempting to overthrow the government of their own country by military force and that the revolutionaries must give verbal allegiance to the acting government and its ideology while the ruling government does not. The pattern of behavior associated with the role includes providing military assistance (mostly small arms) and training for the guerrillas. This may be accompanied by diplomatic gestures of support such as having guerrilla leaders visit the acting country and issuing statements in support of guerrillas.

2. Basic value involved in problem triggering role. The situation must involve military security/physical safety.

3. Assumptions. Those being assisted must not be the internationally recognized government of a country. Military conflict must be occurring between these forces and the government of a country. The guerrilla or revolutionary forces must express support for the acting government and its world view, whereas the existing government which they seek to overthrow does not.

4. Situations. The role can arise in intervention situations in which the guerrilla/revolutionary movement is either the source or the subject or in assistance resource situations where the guerrillas are the source and subject and have requested that the acting government assist them as a potential facilitator.

5. Probable behaviors. The guerrillas will be addressed as the recipients to whom positive affect will be expressed using both military and diplomatic instruments. A moderate level of commitment will be involved.

Role: Mediator

1. Description. An expectation exists that the government will use its good offices to attempt to settle disputes when it is not a direct party to the disagreement and none of the conflicting parties is a traditional enemy of the actor. The mediation actions stem from a belief that the actor benefits from the absence of conflict between the parties in the dispute either because of its direct interest in the parties or because of its concern for avoiding conflict in the international system.

2. Basic values involved in problem triggering role. Military security/ physical safety, economic/wealth, or respect/status.

3. Assumptions. A dispute exists between two or more international entities, none of whom is the actor and none of whom are currently hostile to the actor. (Note: The latter is usually indicated by a history of positive prior affect, but in some cases even negative affect can be overcome if the regime in question declares a change in its alignment, for example, Egypt after the 1973 war.) It is further assumed that the actor's commitment is higher if all parties are members of its bloc or subsystem.

4. Situation. Intervention situations trigger the role when the parties to the dispute are source and subject.

5. Probable behaviors. The actor will address its behavior to the parties to the dispute, using a diplomatic instrument, neutral affect, and low commitment—unless all parties are members of actor's bloc or subsystem, in which case commitment will be moderate.

Role: Opponent

1. Description. An expectation exists that the government will oppose—by all means short of war—the expansionist and corrupt activities of the adversary. Except to throw the opponent off guard, or acquire time to develop one's own strength, nothing will be done that enhances the enemy's ability to continue to rule. On the contrary, the government will act to undermine the adversary whenever possible in all non-military fields of endeavor—economic, social, and technological/scientific. The government also must take actions domestically and internationally to maintain itself against non-military initiatives of the enemy.

2. Basic values involved in problem triggering role. All basic values except military security may be involved.

3. Assumptions. (1) A traditional enemy exists whose containment, alteration, or elimination is a primary purpose of the actor.

4. Situations. This role applies in confrontation or intervention situations in which the source or subject includes the enemy.

5. Probable behaviors. The enemy will be addressed as the recipient of the behavior; the instrument will be appropriate to the basic values triggered by problem. The behavior will have negative affect and carry low or moderate commitment.

Role: Policeman

1. Description. An expectation exists that the government will provide military assistance to a smaller but friendly or neutral regime when the latter is faced with an overt and active military threat from (1) within its own society (guerrillas, civil war) by forces that appear to be supported by enemies of the actor or (2) by external forces which the actor regards as its enemies. The expectation is that the acting government will preserve the status quo by protecting regimes usually described by the actor as "freedom-loving" or "democratic," but whose actual required characteristic is the positive or benign attitude toward the actor and their preparedness to fight the actor's enemies.

2. Basic values involved in problem triggering role. Military security/ physical safety must be the basic value involved.

3. Assumptions. The government to be supported by the actor must (a) be militarily weaker than the actor; and (b) be facing an actual threat of overthrow by forces that are enemies of the actor or—in a civil war—the opponents must be openly supported or allied with enemies of the actor. The threatened regime must be (a) at least strictly neutral toward the actor in the past or preferably friendly (certainly not from an opposing bloc), and (b) using its own forces to resist the threat.

4. Situation. The situations can be either intervention, where the regime to be aided is the source or the subject, or assistance resource, where the regime to be aided has requested assistance.

5. Probable behaviors. The actor will address as recipient the regime it seeks to help with positive affect, moderate commitment, and military instruments. (The actor will seek to strengthen the regime's ability to retain control of its country by sending military equipment and possibly military training missions.)

Role: Recruiter/Promoter

1. Description. An expectation exists that the government will seek occasions to recruit additional qualified states into the actor's bloc, organization, or subsystem. In an attempt to make the advantages of participation most attractive, those pursuing this role will accept some degree of diversity among members and will expect to minimize differences that may exist between present and potential members. The behavior will stress the merits of participation and the liabilities of not belonging.

2. Basic values involved in problem triggering role. The values involved depend to a degree upon the nature of the bloc involved (that is, ideological bloc, military alliance, economic community, etc.), but respect/status will always be in combination with any other values involved.

3. Assumptions. The actor is a member of a bloc, organization, or subsystem and there exist one or more other states which (1) are not members of the bloc, organization, or subsystem, (2) are not members of a rival bloc or subsystem—or have independently moved (or been forced) to separate themselves to a substantial degree from that rival bloc of which they formerly were members, and (3) are not traditional enemies of the actor.

4. Situations. Assistance requested situations trigger the role when the actor (perhaps with other members of its bloc) is the source and subject of the problem (possibly the bloc is inadequate to deal fully with challenges it faces or to reap all the benefits) and asks another entity who is a potential facilitator to join it (or them). Alternatively, the actor and other entity may be in a collaboration situation. In such a case the actor's preferred outcome would be to have the other entity agree to join the bloc.

5. Probable behaviors. Actor will address nonbloc, non-enemy, other entity as the recipient with positive affect, diplomatic instrument, and no commitment.

References

Abelson, R. P. 1973. The structure of belief systems. In *Computer models of thought and language*, edited by R. C. Shanck and K. M. Colby. San Francisco: W. H. Freeman and Company.

Africa biographies. 1967. Bonn: Research Institute of the Friedrich-Ebert-Stiftung.

Allison, G. 1971. *Essence of decision*. Boston: Little, Brown.

Anglin, D. G., and T. M. Shaw. 1979. *Zambia's foreign policy: Studies in diplomacy and dependence*. Boulder: Westview Press.

Apple, R. W., Jr. 1984. Mrs. Thatcher said to see no way to keep Hong Kong. *New York Times*, January 23, 1984.

Ashley, R. 1981. Political realism and human interests. *International Studies Quarterly* 25:204–36.

———. 1984. The poverty of neorealism. *International Organization* 38:225–86.

Atkinson, J., ed. 1958. *Motivations in fantasy, action, and society*. Princeton, N.J.: Van Nostrand.

Axelrod, R. 1973. Schema theory: An information processing model of perception and cognition. *American Political Science Review* 47:1248–67.

———. 1976. *Structure of decision: The cognitive maps of political elites*. Princeton: Princeton University Press.

———. 1981. The emergence of cooperation among egoists. *American Political Science Review* 25:306–18.

Azar, E. E. 1980. The codebook of the conflict and peace data bank (COPDAB). Mimeo.

Backman, C. 1970. Role theory and international relations. *International Studies Quarterly* 14:310–19.

Baldwin, D. 1978. Power and social exchange. *American Political Science Review* 72:1229–42.

Bales, R. F. 1951. *Interaction process analysis*. Cambridge: Addison-Wesley.

Bandura, A. 1969. *Principles of behavior modification*. New York: Holt, Rinehart, and Winston.

Banks, A. S., and R. B. Textor. 1968. *A cross-polity survey*. Cambridge: MIT Press.

Banton, M. 1965. *Roles: An introduction to the study of social relations.* London: Tavistock Publications, Ltd.

Barber, J. D. 1965. *The lawmakers.* New Haven: Yale University Press.

Barnlund, B., and S. Araki. 1985. Intercultural encounters: The management of compliments by Japanese and Americans. *Journal of Cross-Cultural Psychology* 16(1):9–26.

Barnlund, D. 1975. Communication styles in two cultures: Japan and the U.S. In *Socialization and communication in primary groups,* edited by T. Williams. The Hague: Mouton.

Berkowitz, B. 1986. Levels of analysis problems in international studies. *International Interactions* 12:199–227.

Biddle, B., and E. Thomas. 1966. *Role theory: Concepts and research.* New York: John Wiley and Sons.

Blalock, H. 1972. *Social statistics.* 2d ed. New York: McGraw-Hill.

Blau, P. 1964. *Exchange and power in social life.* New York: John Wiley and Sons.

Borrows, R. 1974. Mirror, mirror on the wall . . . : A comparison of event data sources. In *Comparing foreign policies,* edited by J. Rosenau. New York: John Wiley.

Brecher, M., et al. 1968. A framework for research on foreign policy behavior. *Journal of Conflict Resolution* 13:74–101.

Burgess, P., and R. Lawton. 1972. *Indicators of international behavior: An assessment of events data research.* Beverly Hills, Cal.: Sage Publications.

Burns, J. M. 1978. *Leadership.* New York: Harper and Row.

Burton, J. W. 1983. The individual as the unit of explanation in international relations. *International Studies Newsletter* 10(2):1, 14–17.

Byars, R. S. 1972. The task/affect quotient. *Comparative Political Studies* 5:109–20.

———. 1973. Small group theory and shifting styles of political leadership. *Comparative Political Studies* 5:443–69.

Callahan, P., L. Brady, and M. G. Hermann, eds. 1982. *Describing foreign policy behavior.* Beverly Hills, Cal.: Sage Publications.

Cathcart, D., and R. Cathcart. 1976. The Japanese social experience and concept of groups. In *Intercultural communication,* edited by L. A. Smovar and R. E. Porter. Belmont, Calif.: Wadsworth Publishing Company.

Clark, P. 1979. Cultural context as a determinant of organizational rationality: A comparison of the tobacco industries in Britain and France. In *Organizations alike and unalike,* edited by C. J. Lammers and D. S. Hickson. London: Routledge and Kegan Paul.

Coate, R., and C. Murphy. 1985. A critical science of global relations. *International Interactions* 12:109–32.

Crabb, C. V., Jr. 1972. *American foreign policy in the nuclear age.* New York: Harper and Row.

Crockett, W. H. 1965. Cognitive complexity and impression formation. *Progress in Experimental Personality Research* 2:47–90.

Crow, W. J., and R. C. Noel. 1977. An experiment in simulated historical decision making. In *A psychological examination of political leaders,* edited by M. G. Hermann. New York: Free Press.

Crozier, M. 1964. *The bureaucratic phenomenon.* Chicago: University of Chicago Press.

———, and E. Friedberg. 1980. *Actors and systems: The politics of collective action.* Chicago: University of Chicago Press.

Cushman, D., and S. King. 1985. National and organizational culture in conflict resolution. In *Communication, culture, and organizational process,* edited by W. Gudykunst, L.

Stewart, and S. Ting-Toomey. Beverly Hills, Calif.: Sage Publications.

Davis, N. 1978. The Angola decision of 1975. *Foreign Affairs* 57(Fall):109–24.

DeRivera, J. H. 1968. *The psychological dimension of foreign policy.* Columbus, Oh.: Merrill.

Dickie, J., and A. Rake. 1973. *Who's who in Africa.* London: Africa Buyer and Trader.

Dixon, W. J., and C. F. Hermann. 1982. Reconstructing foreign policy from behavior attributes. Paper presented at the annual meeting of the International Studies Association, Cincinnati, March 24–27.

Doi, L. 1976. The Japanese patterns of communication and the concept of *amae.* In *Intercultural communication,* edited by L. Samovar and R. Porter. Belmont, Calif.: Wadsworth Publishing Company.

Driver, M. J. 1977. Individual differences as determinants of aggression in the inter-nation simulation. In *A psychological examination of political leaders,* edited by M. G. Hermann. New York: Free Press.

East, M. A. 1975. Explaining foreign policy behavior using national attributes. CREON Publication, No. 52. Prepared for delivery at the annual meeting of the American Political Science Association, San Francisco, September 2–5.

———. 1973. Size and foreign policy behavior: A test of two models. *World Politics* 25:566–76.

———., S. A. Salmore, and C. F. Hermann, eds. 1978. *Why nations act: Theoretical perspectives for comparative foreign policy studies.* Beverly Hills, Cal.: Sage Publications.

———., and C. F. Hermann. 1974. Do nation types account for foreign policy behavior? In *Comparing foreign policies,* edited by J. N. Rosenau. New York: John Wiley & Sons.

Easton, D. 1953. *The political system.* New York: Alfred A. Knopf.

———. 1965. *A framework for political analysis.* Englewood Cliffs, N.J.: Prentice-Hall.

Emerson, R. 1972a. Exchange theory, part I: A psychological basis for social exchange. In *Sociological theories in progress,* edited by J. Berger, M. Zelditch, Jr., and B. Anderson. Boston: Houghton Mifflin.

———. 1972b. Exchange theory, part II: Exchange relations and network structures. In *Sociological theories in progress,* edited by J. Berger, M. Zelditch, and B. Anderson. Boston: Houghton Mifflin.

Falkowski, L. S. 1978. *Presidents, secretaries of state, and crises in U.S. foreign relations: A model and predictive analysis.* Boulder: Westview Press.

Farrell, R. B., ed. 1966. *Approaches to comparative and international politics.* Evanston: Northwestern University Press.

FBIS. 1985. Indochinese foreign ministers conference ends—text of communiqué. In *Daily Report Asia Pacific.* Washington, D.C.: Foreign Broadcast Information Service (August 16).

Frank, J. D. 1968. *Sanity and survival.* New York: Random House.

Gardner, L. 1970. The origins of the cold war. In *The origins of the cold war,* edited by L. Gardner. Waltham, Mass.: Ginn and Company.

Geertz, C. 1973. *The interpretation of cultures.* New York: Basic Books.

George, A. L. 1972. The case for multiple advocacy in making foreign policy. *American Political Science Review* 66(3):751–85.

———. 1974. Adaptation to stress in political decision making: The individual, small group, and organizational contexts. In *Coping and adaptation,* edited by G. V. Coehlo, D. A. Hamburg, and J. E. Adams. New York: Basic Books.

———. 1975. The use of information. In *Report of the commission on the organization of the government for the conduct of foreign policy,* appendix D. Washington, D.C.: U.S.

Government Printing Office.

————. 1980. *Presidential decision making in foreign policy*. Boulder: Westview Press.

Gilpin, R. 1984. The richness of the tradition of political realism. *International Organization* 38:287–304.

Goffman, E. 1961. *Encounters*. Indianapolis: Bobbs-Merrill.

Goodenough, W. 1965. Rethinking status and role. In *The relevance of models for social anthropology*, edited by M. Banton. New York: Praeger.

Granick, D. 1978. International differences in executive reward systems: Extent, explanation, and significance. *Columbia Journal of World Business* 13:45–55.

————. 1979. Managerial incentive systems and organizational theory. In *Organizations alike and unalike*, edited by C. Lammers and D. Hickso. London: Routledge and Kegan Paul.

Gross, N., W. Mason, and A. McEachern. 1958. *Explorations in role analysis*. New York: John Wiley and Sons.

Gwyn, D. 1977. *Idi Amin: Death light of Africa*. Boston: Little, Brown.

Hagan, J., M. G. Hermann, and C. F. Hermann. 1982. How decision units shape foreign policy behavior. Paper presented at the annual meeting of the International Studies Association, Cincinnati, March 24–27.

Hall, C., and G. Lindzey. 1978. *Theories of personality*. 3rd ed. New York: John Wiley and Sons.

Hall, R. 1969. *The high price of principles: Kaunda and the white south*. London: Hodder and Stoughton.

Hanrieder, W. 1967. West German foreign policy, 1949–1963. Stanford: Stanford University Press.

Hartmann, F. 1965. Germany between east and West. Englewood Cliffs, N.J.: Prentice-Hall.

Hermann, C. F. 1978. Decision structure and process influences on foreign policy. In *Why nations act*, edited by M. East, C. F. Hermann, and S. Salmore. Beverly Hills: Sage.

————. 1979. The effects of decision structures and processes on foreign policy behavior. Paper presented at the annual meeting of the International Society of Political Psychology, Washington, D.C., May 24–26.

Hermann, C. F., M. East, M. Hermann, B. Salmore, and S. Salmore. 1973. *CREON: A foreign events data set*. Beverly Hills: Sage.

Hermann, C. F., and M. G. Hermann. 1979. Summary of the external component in the CREON project's conceptual framework for explaining foreign policy. Paper presented at the annual meeting of the Northeastern Political Science Association, Newark, November 8–10.

Hermann, C. F., M. G. Hermann, and W. J. Dixon. 1979. Working memorandum on the interaction of personal characteristics and decision unit properties on foreign policy behavior. Paper presented at the International Studies Association meeting, Toronto.

Hermann, C. F., with V. Hudson. 1983. A new round of foreign policy theory building. Presented at the annual meeting of the International Studies Association, Mexico City, April 5–9.

Hermann, M. 1974. Leader personality and foreign policy behavior. In *Comparing foreign policies*, edited by J. Rosenau. New York: John Wiley.

————. 1976. The effects of political leaders' orientations to foreign affairs on foreign policy behavior. Paper presented at the Peace Science Society (International) meeting, Chicago, April 29–May 1.

————. 1977. *A psychological examination of political leaders*. New York: Free Press.

————. 1978. Ascertaining foreign policy orientations of political leaders. Paper presented at the International Studies Association meeting, Washington, February 22–25.

————. 1979. Who becomes a political leader? Some societal and regime influences on selection of a head of government. In *Psychological models in international politics*, edited by L. S. Falkowski. Boulder: Westview Press.

————. 1980. Explaining foreign policy behavior using the personal characteristics of political leaders. *International Studies Quarterly* 24:7–46.

————. 1982a. Independence/interdependence of action. In *Describing foreign policy behavior*, edited by P. Callahan, L. Brady, and M. Hermann. Beverly Hills: Sage.

————. 1982b. Feedback: Acceptance and rejection. In *Describing foreign policy behavior*, edited by P. Callahan, L. Brady, and M. Hermann. Beverly Hills: Sage.

————. 1983. *Handbook for assessing personal characteristics and foreign policy orientations of political leaders*. Columbus, Oh.: Mershion Occasional Papers.

————. 1984. Personality and foreign policy: A study of 53 heads of government. In *Foreign policy decision making: Perceptions, cognition, and artificial intelligence*, edited by D. A. Sylvan and S. Chan. New York: St. Martin's Press.

————, C. F. Hermann, and W. J. Dixon. 1979. Decision structures and personal characteristics in comparative foreign policy. Paper presented at the Midwest Political Science Association meeting, Chicago, April 19–21.

————, and C. F. Hermann. 1982. A look inside the "black box": Building on a decade of research. In *Biopolitics, political psychology, and international politics*, edited by G. Hopple. London: Frances Pintner, Ltd.

————, C. F. Hermann, and J. D. Hagan. 1982. The relationship between beliefs and roles in shaping governments' foreign policy behavior. Paper presented at the annual meeting of the International Society of Political Psychology, Washington, D.C., June 24–27.

————, C. F. Hermann, and J. D. Hagan. 1987. How decision units shape foreign policy behavior. In *New directions in the study of foreign policy*, edited by J. N. Rosenau, C. W. Kegley, Jr., and C. F. Hermann. London: Allen and Unwin.

Hoffmann, S. 1978. *Primacy or world order*. New York: McGraw-Hill.

Hofstede, G. 1980. *Culture's consequences*. Beverly Hills: Sage.

Hoggard, G. 1974. Differential source coverage and the analysis of international interaction data. In *Comparing foreign policies*, edited by J. N. Rosenau. Beverly Hills: Sage.

Holsti, K. 1970. National role conceptions in the study of foreign policy. *International Studies Quarterly* 14:233–309.

Holsti, O. 1966. External conflict and internal consensus: The Sino-Soviet case. In *The general inquirer*, edited by P. Stone, D. Dunphy, M. Smith, and D. Ogilvie. Cambridge: M.I.T. Press.

————. 1977. The operational code as an approach to the analysis of belief systems. *Final Report to the National Science Foundation*, Grant No. SOC75-15368. Durham, N.C.: Duke University.

Homans, G. 1961. *Social behavior: Its elementary forms*. New York: Harcourt, Brace, and World.

————. 1974. *Social behavior: Its elementary forms*. Revised ed. New York: Harcourt, Brace, and Jovanovich.

Hopple, G. W. 1979. Elite values and foreign policy analysis: Preliminary findings. In *Psychological models in international politics*, edited by L. S. Falkowski. Boulder: Westview Press.

Horovitz, J. 1978. Management control in France, Great Britain, and Germany. *Columbia*

Journal of World Business, 13:16–20.

———. 1980. *Top management control in Europe*. New York: St. Martin's Press.

Hudson, V. M. 1983. The external predisposition component of a model of foreign policy behavior. Ph.D. diss., Ohio State University.

———, E. Singer, and C. Hermann. 1982. Explaining the foreign policy behaviors of Ghana, Kenya and Zambia: A test of the predictive power of the external predisposition component. Paper presented at the annual meeting of the International Studies Association, Cincinnati, March 24–27.

Hughes, B. 1985. World models: The bases of difference. *International Studies Quarterly* 29:77–101.

Indochina Report. 1984. The Vietnamization of Kampuchea. Singapore (October), No. 1:1–9.

International Monetary Fund. 1958–68. Direction of Trade Data.

Iriye, A. 1979. Culture and power: International relations as intercultural relations. *Diplomatic History* 3(2):115–28.

Jackson, R. H., and C. G. Rosberg. 1982. *Personal rule in black Africa*. Berkeley: University of California Press.

Janis, I. L. 1972. *Victims of groupthink*. Boston: Houghton Mifflin.

Jervis, R. 1976. *Perception and misperception in international politics*. Princeton: Princeton University Press.

Job, B., and C. Ostrom. 1976. An appraisal of the research design and philosophy of science of the correlates of war project. In *Quantitative international politics: An appraisal*, edited by F. Hoole and D. Zinnes. New York: Praeger.

Johnson, L. 1977. The operational code of Senator Frank Church. In *A psychological examination of political leaders*, edited by M. G. Hermann. New York: Free Press.

Kaplan, M. 1979. The genteel art of criticism, or how to boggle minds and confooz a discipline. In *Towards professionalism in international theory*, edited by M. Kaplan. New York: Free Press.

Keesing's Contemporary Archives. 1958–68. Bristol: Keesing's Publications.

Kennedy, M. M. 1983. Working knowledge. *Knowledge* 5(2):193–212.

Keohane, R. 1982. The demand for international regimes. *International Organization* 36:325–56.

———. 1983. Structural realism and beyond. In *Political science: The state of the discipline*, edited by A. Finifter. Washington, D.C.: American Political Science Association.

———. 1984. *After hegemony: Cooperation and discord in the world political economy*. Princeton, N.J.: Princeton University Press.

———. 1986. *Neorealism and its critics*. New York: Columbia University Press.

Keohane, R., and J. Nye. 1977. *Power and interdependence*. Boston: Little, Brown.

Kim, C. I., and L. Ziring. 1977. *An introduction to Asian politics*. Englewood Cliffs, N.J.: Prentice-Hall.

Kochen, M. 1981. Can the global system learn to control conflict? *From national development to global community: Essays in honor of Karl W. Deutsch*, edited by R. L. Merritt and B. M. Russet. London: George Allen and Unwin.

Krasner, S. D. 1982. Structural causes and regime consequences: Regimes as intervening variables. *International Organization* 36(2):185–206.

Kratochwil, F. 1984. Errors have their advantage. *International Organization* 38:305–20.

Kume, T. 1985. Managerial attitudes toward decision making. In *Communication, culture, and organizational process*, edited by W. Gudykunst, L. Stewart, and S. Ting-Toomey. Beverly Hills, Cal.: Sage Publications.

Kunkel, J. 1977. The behavioral perspective of social dynamics. In *Behavioral theory in sociology: Essays in honor of George Homans*, edited by R. Hamblin and J. Kunkel. New Brunswick, N.J.: Transaction Books.

Kunkel, J., and R. Nagasawa. 1973. A behavioral model of man: Some propositions and implications. *American Social Review* 38:530–43.

Kurian, G., ed. 1978. *The encyclopedia of the Third World*. New York: Facts on File.

Lasswell, H. D. 1971. *A preview of the policy sciences*. New York: Elsevier.

Laurent, A. 1980. Once a Frenchman always a Frenchman. . . . *International management* 35:45–46.

Legum, C., ed. 1969–81. *African contemporary record*, vols. 1–13. New York: Africana Publishing.

LeVine, R. A. 1966. *Dreams and deeds: Achievement motivation in Nigeria*. Chicago: University of Chicago Press.

Linton, R. 1945. *The study of man*. New York: Appleton-Century-Crofts, Inc.

Lowi, T. 1964. American business, public policy, case-studies, and political theory. *World Politics* 16:677–715.

Mansbach, R., and J. Vasquez. 1981. *In search of theory: A new paradigm for global politics*. New York: Columbia University Press.

Maurice, M. 1979. For a study of 'societal effect': Universality and specificity in organization research. In *Organizations alike and unalike*, edited by C. Lammers and D. Hickson. London: Routledge and Kegan Paul.

McClelland, D. 1975. *Power: The inner experience*. New York: Irvington Publishers.

McGowan, P., and S. Walker. 1981. Radical and conventional models of U.S. foreign economic policymaking. *World Politics* 33:347–82.

McGowan, P., and M. O'Leary. 1975. Methods and data for the comparative analysis of foreign policy. In *International events and comparative analysis of foreign policy*, edited by C. Kegley, Jr., G. Raymond, R. Rood, and K. Skinner. Columbia: University of South Carolina Press.

McWilliams, E. F. 1984. Hanoi's course in Southeast Asia. *Asian Survey* 24:878–85.

Miller, J. G. 1978. *Living systems*. New York: McGraw-Hill.

Moore, David W. 1974. National attributes and nation typologies: A look at the Rosenau genotypes. In *Comparing foreign policy*, edited by James N. Rosenau. New York: John Wiley and Sons.

Morgenthau, H. 1970a. Origins of the cold war. In *Origins of the cold war*, edited by L. Gardner. Waltham, Mass.: Ginn and Company.

———. 1970b. The intellectual and political functions of theory. In *Truth and power*, edited by H. Morgenthau. New York: Praeger.

———. 1978. *Politics among nations: The struggle for power and peace*. 5th ed., rev. New York: Alfred A. Knopf.

Morse, E. L. 1970. The transformation of foreign policies: Modernization, interdependence, and eternalization. *World Politics* 22:371–92.

Murphy Commission. 1975. *Report on the organization of the government for the conduct of foreign policy*. Washington: U.S. Government Printing Office.

Nadel, S. 1957. *The theory of social structure*. Glencoe, Ill.: Free Press.

Nadler, L., M. Nadler, and B. Broome. 1958. Culture and the management of conflict situations. In *Communication, culture, and organization process*, edited by W. Gudykunst, L. Stewart, and S. Ting-Toomey. Beverly Hills, Cal.: Sage Publications.

Napper, L. C. 1983. The Ogaden war: Some implications for crisis prevention. In *Managing U.S.-Soviet rivalry*, edited by A. L. George. Boulder: Westview Press.

Newcomb, T. 1966. Foreword. In *Role theory: Concepts and research*. New York: John Wiley and Sons.

North, R. C., and N. Choucri. 1983. Economic and political factors in international conflict and integration. *International Studies Quarterly* 27(4):443–62.

North, R., O. Holsti, M. Zaninovich, and D. Zinnes. 1963. *Content analysis*. Evanston: Northwestern University Press.

Osgood, C., and L. Anderson. 1957. Certain relations among experienced contingencies, associative structure, and contingencies in encoded messages. *American Journal of Psychology* 70:411–20.

Paige, G. D. 1977. *The scientific study of political leadership*. New York: Free Press.

Phillips, W. 1974. Where have all the theories gone? *World Politics* 26:155–88.

Przeworski, A., and H. Teune. 1970. *The logic of comparative social inquiry*. New York: John Wiley Interscience.

Puchala, D. 1971. *International politics today*. New York: Harper and Row.

Quinn-Judge, P. 1985. Vietnam keen to leave Kampuchea—on its own terms. *The Christian Science Monitor* (August 20):12.

Richardson, N. 1978. *Foreign policy and economic dependence*. Austin: University of Texas Press.

Riker, T. 1962. *The theory of political coalitions*. New Haven: Yale University Press.

Rosecrance, R. 1981. International theory revisited. *International Organization* 35:691–713.

Rosenau, J. N. 1966. Pre-theories and theories of foreign policy. In *Approaches to comparative and international politics*, edited by R. B. Farrell. Evanston, Ill.: Northwestern University Press.

———. 1968. Private preferences and political responsibilities: the relative potency of individual and role variables in the behavior of U.S. senators. In *Quantitative international politics: Insight and evidence*, edited by J. D. Singer. New York: Free Press.

———, and G. Hoggard. 1974. Foreign policy behavior in dyadic relationships: Testing a pre-theoretical extension. In *Comparing foreign policies*, edited by J. Rosenau. New York: John Wiley.

Ruggie, J. 1983. Continuity and transformation in the world polity. *World Politics* 35:261–85.

Sampson, M. 1987. Cultural influences on foreign policy. In *New directions in the comparative study of foreign policy*, edited by C. Hermann, C. Kegley, Jr., and J. Rosenau. London and New York: George Allen and Unwin.

Sarbin, T., and V. Allen. 1968. Role theory. In *The handbook of social psychology*, 2d ed., vol. 1, edited by G. Lindzey and E. Aronson. Reading, Mass.: Addison-Wesley.

Schlesinger, A. 1970. Origins of the cold war. In *Origins of the cold war*, edited by L. Gardner. Waltham, Mass.: Ginn and Co.

Schofield, W. 1976. *Obedience and revolt*. Beverly Hills: Sage Publications.

Scott, W. A. 1955. Reliability of content analysis: The case of nominal scale coding. *Public Opinion Quarterly* 19:321–25.

———. 1963. Cognitive complexity and cognitive behavior. *Sociometry* 26:66–74.

Sennett, R. 1976. *The fall of public man*. New York: Alfred A. Knopf.

Shapiro, M. 1981. *Language and political understanding: The politics of discursive practices*. New Haven: Yale University Press.

Silverman, J. 1974. Historic national rivalries and interstate conflict in mainland Southeast Asia. In *Conflict and stability in Southeast Asia*, edited by M. Zacher and R. Milne. New York: Doubleday-Anchor.

Simon, S. 1982. Vietnam. In *Security policies of developing countries*, edited by E. Kolodziej and R. Harkavy. Lexington, Mass.: Lexington Books.

————. 1983. Davids and Goliaths: Great power-small power security relations in Southeast Asia. *Asian Survey* 23(1):302–15.

————., and S. Walker. 1983. Role analysis and Asian security conceptions. Paper presented at the annual meeting of the American Political Science Association, Chicago, September 1–4.

Singer, E., and V. M. Hudson. 1983. Role theory and African foreign policy. Paper prepared for the annual meeting of the American Political Science Association, Chicago, September 1–4.

Singer, J. 1961. The level of analysis problem in international relations. *World Politics* 14:77–92.

————. 1968. Man and world politics: The psycho-cultural interface. *Journal of Social Issues* 24:127–56.

Singer, M. 1972. *Weak states in a world of powers*. New York: Free Press.

Small, M., and J. D. Singer. 1973. The diplomatic importance of states, 1816–1970: An extension and refinement of the indicator. *World Politics* 25:577–99.

Snyder, R., H. Bruck, and B. Sapin. 1962. *Foreign policy decision-making*. New York: Free Press.

Stassen, G. H. 1972. Individual preferences versus role-constraint in policy making: Senatorial responses to secretaries Acheson and Dulles. *World Politics* 25(1):96–119.

Steiner, M. 1983. The search for order in a disorderly world: World views and prescriptive decision paradigms. *International Organization* 37(3):373–414.

Stewart, E. 1985. Cultures and decision making. In *Communication, culture, and organizational process*, edited by W. Gudykunst, L. Steward, and S. Ting-Toomey. Beverly Hills, Cal.: Sage Publications.

Stewart, P. D. 1977. Attitudes of regional Soviet political leaders: Toward understanding the potential for change. In *A psychological examination of political leaders*, edited by Margaret G. Hermann. New York: Free Press.

Stuart, D., and H. Starr. 1981–82. The inherent bad faith model reconsidered: Dulles, Kennedy and Kissinger. *Political Psychology* 3:1–33.

Swanson, D. 1982. Specificity. In *Describing foreign policy behavior*, edited by P. Callahan, L. Brady, and M. Hermann. Beverly Hills: Sage.

Taylor, C., and M. Hudson. 1972. *World handbook of political and social indicators*. New Haven: Yale University Press.

Ting-Toomey, S. 1985. Toward a theory of culture. In *Communication, culture, and organizational process*, edited by W. Gudykunst, L. Stewart, and S. Ting-Toomey. Beverly Hills, Cal.: Sage Publications.

Tsuji, K. 1968. Decision making in the Japanese government. In *Political development in modern Japan*, edited by R. Ward. Princeton: Princeton University Press.

Tucker, R. 1965. The dictator and totalitarianism. *World Politics* 17:55–83.

Tukey, J. W. 1977. *Exploratory data analysis*. New York: Addison-Wesley.

U.S. Arms Control and Disarmament Agency. 1973. *World military expenditures*. Washington, D.C.: U.S. Government Printing Office.

United Nations Statistical Yearbook. 1960–70. New York: United Nations Printing.

Vasquez, J. 1983. *The power of power politics: A critique*. New Brunswick, N.J.: Rutgers University Press.

Verba, S. 1969. Assumptions of rationality and non-rationality in models of the international system. In *International politics and foreign policy*, edited by James N. Rosenau. New York: Free Press.

Wahlke, J., H. Eulau, W. Buchanan, and L. Ferguson. 1962. *The legislative system*. New York: John Wiley.

Walker, S. G. 1977. The interface between beliefs and behavior: Henry Kissinger's operational code and the Vietnam war. *Journal of Conflict Resolution* 21:129–68.

———. 1978. National role conceptions and systemic outcomes. Prepared for the annual meeting of the International Studies Association, Washington, D.C., February 22–25.

———. 1979. National role conceptions and systematic outcomes. In *Psychological models in international politics*, edited by L. Falkowski. Boulder: Westview Press.

———. 1981. The correspondence between foreign policy rhetoric and behavior: Insights from role theory and exchange theory. *Behavioral Science* 26:272–81.

———. 1982a. Psychological explanations of international politics: Problems of aggregation, measurement, and theory construction. In *Biopolitics, psychology, and international politics*, edited by G. Hopple. London: Frances Pintner, Ltd.

———. 1982b. Role theory and foreign policy analysis. Paper presented at the annual meeting of the International Studies Meeting, Cincinnati, March 24–27.

———. 1983a. The motivational foundations of political belief systems: A re-analysis of the operational code construct. *International Studies Quarterly* 27(2):179–202.

———. 1983b. The origins of foreign policy in a self-help system: A postscript to Waltz's theory of international politics. Paper presented at the annual meeting of the International Studies Association, Mexico City, April 5–9.

———. 1987. Role theory and the origins of foreign policy. In *New directions in the comparative study of foreign policy*, edited by C. Hermann, C. Kegley, Jr., and J. Rosenau. London and New York: George Allen and Unwin.

Wallerstein, I. 1974. Dependence in an interdependent world: The limited possibilities of transformation in the world capitalist economy. *African Studies Review* 1:1–26.

Waltz, K. 1959. *Man, the state, and war*. New York: Columbia University Press.

———. 1979. *Theory of international politics*. Reading, Mass.: Addison-Wesley.

Watson, G., and D. McGaw. 1980. *Statistical inquiry*. New York: John Wiley and Sons.

Wight, M. 1967. Why is there no international theory? In *Diplomatic investigations*, edited by H. Butterfield and M. Wight. London: George Allen and Unwin.

Wilkenfeld, J. 1968. Domestic and foreign conflict behavior of nations. *Journal of Peace Research* 1:57–68.

———. 1980. *Foreign policy behavior*. Beverly Hills: Sage Publications.

Wilkinson, D. 1969. *Comparative foreign relations: Framework and methods*. Belmont, Cal.: Dickenson Publishing Company.

Winter, D. G. 1973. *The power motive*. New York: Free Press.

———., and A. J. Stewart. 1977. Content analysis as a technique for assessing political leaders. In *A psychological examination of political leaders*, edited by M. G. Hermann. New York: Free Press.

———. 1980. An exploratory study of the motives of Southern African political leaders measured at a distance. *Political Psychology* 2:75–85.

Wish, N. B. 1977. Relationships between national role conceptions, national attributes, and foreign policy behavior. Ph.D. diss., Rutgers University.

———. 1980. Foreign policy makers and their national role conceptions. *International Studies Quarterly* 24:532–54.

Woronoff, J. 1972. *West African wager: Houphouet versus Nkrumah*. Metuchen, N.J.: The Scarecrow Press.

Young, O. 1969. Professor Russett: Industrious tailor to a naked emperior. *World Politics* 21:486–511.

———. 1972. The perils of Odysseus: On constructing theories of international relations. In *Theory and policy in international relations*, edited by R. Tanter and R. Ullman. Princeton: Princeton University Press.

Zagoria, D. 1962. *The Sino-Soviet conflict, 1956–1961*. Princeton, N.J.: Princeton University Press.

Zajonc, R. 1968. Cognitive theories in social psychology. In *The handbook of social psychology*, edited by G. Lindzey and E. Aronson, vol. 1. 2d ed. Reading, Mass.: Addison-Wesley.

Zartman, I. W. 1982. The future of Europe and Africa: Decolonization or dependency? In *Alternative futures for Africa*, edited by T. M. Shaw. Boulder: Westview Press.

Ziller, R. C., W. F. Stone, R. M. Jacobson, and N. J. Terbovic. 1977. Self-other orientations and political behavior. In *A psychological examination of political leaders*, edited by M. G. Hermann. New York: Free Press.

Zimmerman, W. 1973. Issue area and foreign policy process. *American Political Science Review* 67:1204–12.

Index

Contributors

Stephen G. Walker is Professor of Political Science at Arizona State University

Charles F. Hermann is Professor of Political Science and the Director of the Mershon Center at Ohio State University.

Margaret G. Hermann is Senior Research Associate at the Mershon Center at Ohio State University.

K. J. Holsti is Professor of Political Science at the University of British Columbia.

Valerie M. Hudson is Assistant Professor of Political Science at Rutgers University.

James N. Rosenau is Professor of International Relations and the Director of the Institute for Transnational Studies at the University of Southern California.

Martin W. Sampson III is Associate Professor of Political Science at the University of Minnesota.

Sheldon W. Simon is Professor of Political Science and the Director of the Center for Asian Studies at Arizona State University.

Eric G. Singer is Visiting Assistant Professor at Goucher College.

Richard C. Snyder is cofounder of the decision-making approach to foreign policy analysis. He has served as Chair of the Political Science Department at Northwestern University, Dean of the Graduate School of Administration at the University of California (Irvine), Director of the Mershon Center at Ohio State University, and Adjunct Professor of Political Science at Arizona State University.

Naomi Bailin Wish is Professor of Political Science at Seton Hall University.